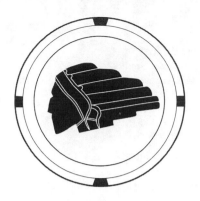

REVENGE OF THE PEQUOTS

How a Small Native American Tribe
Created the World's Most
Profitable Casino

KIM ISAAC EISLER

University of Nebraska Press
Lincoln

Library of Congress Cataloging-in-Publication Data
Eisler, Kim Isaac.
Revenge of the Pequots: how a small Native American tribe created the world's most profitable casino / Kim Isaac Eisler.
p.   cm.
Originally published: New York: Simon & Schuster, c2001.
Includes bibliographical references and index.
ISBN 0-8032-6745-2 (pa.: alk. paper)
1. Pequot Indians—Gambling.   2. Pequot Indians—History.   3. Pequot Indians—Government relations.   4. Gambling on Indian reservations—Connecticut—Ledyard.   5. Casinos—Government policy—Connecticut—Ledyard.   6. Ledyard (Conn.)—Economic conditions.   7. Ledyard (Conn.)—Social conditions.   I. Title.
E99.P53 E57   2002
974.6'5—dc21
2001057481

For Judy, Sara,
and in memory of Uncle Peter

Contents

REVENGE OF
THE PEQUOTS

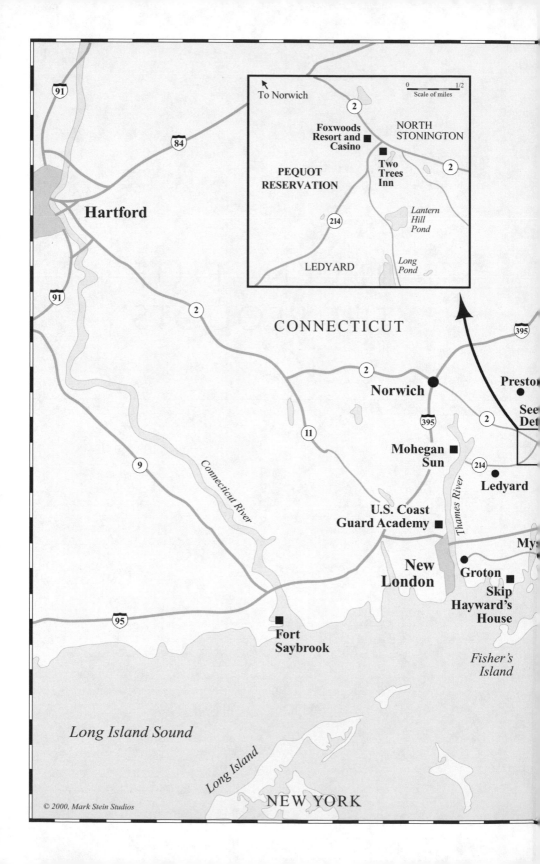

To Norwich

2

Foxwoods
Resort and
Casino

NORTH
STONINGTON

Two
Trees
Inn

2

PEQUOT
RESERVATION

214

Lantern
Hill
Pond

LEDYARD

Long
Pond

0   1/2
Scale of miles

91

84

91

Hartford

2

CONNECTICUT

395

2

Norwich

Presto

See
Det

9

11

395

2

Mohegan
Sun

214

Ledyard

Connecticut River

U.S. Coast
Guard Academy

Thames River

Mys

New
London

Groton

95

Fort
Saybrook

Skip
Hayward's
House

Fisher's
Island

Long Island Sound

Long Island

NEW YORK

© 2000, Mark Stein Studios

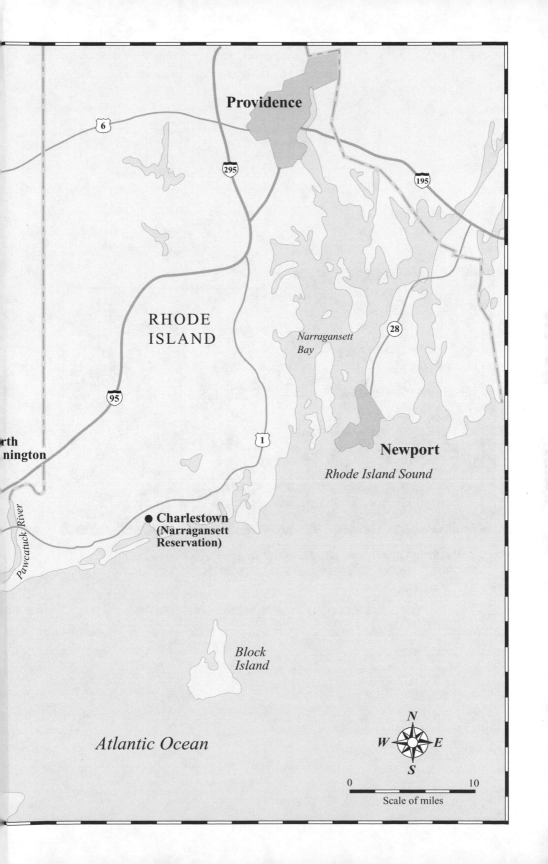

Providence

6

295

195

RHODE
ISLAND

*Narragansett
Bay*

28

95

rth
nington

1

Newport

Rhode Island Sound

Pawcatuck River

● **Charlestown
(Narragansett
Reservation)**

*Block
Island*

Atlantic Ocean

N

W ✦ E

S

0   10
Scale of miles

President Clinton and Skip Hayward (left) at the White House, 1994

Introduction

THE CALL FROM THE PRESIDENT

ON OCTOBER 18, 1994, in the small town of Ledyard, Connecticut, the chief of the richest and most powerful Native American tribe in the United States strode purposefully into the white construction trailer that served as his temporary office and waited while an operator connected him to the White House. At 10:00 A.M., the call went through and an official-sounding voice told Mashantucket Pequot tribal chairman Richard "Skip" Hayward to "stand by, for the president." A moment of American history as significant as this, Hayward figured, was certainly worth waiting for.

At 10:18 A.M., the familiar sound of Bill Clinton's voice came over the line. Their conversation lasted just about thirteen minutes. Clinton began by thanking Hayward for his past generosity, for the chief had recently contributed nearly $500,000 to the Democratic Party to support candidates in the 1994 congressional elections. Hayward told the president how much he had supported his and his wife Hillary's health-care initiatives, and volunteered a little bit of information about the federally designed tribal health-insurance plan. He expressed his hope that the president would support the tribe's request to the Department of the Interior and the Bureau of Indian Affairs for help in building a health clinic for members of his fast-growing Pequot tribe. "We're going to do everything we can to help you," Clinton promised, emphasizing the word "you," in his distinctive Arkansas accent. Hayward also expressed his concern that the president be sensitive about issues of Indian sovereignty and not support any efforts to tax the giant gambling casino that his tribe had recently begun operating. The conversation ended amiably with Clinton's assurances on that score, and the president took the next in his line of calls. Hayward leaned back in exultation.

It was a singular moment for Hayward and his tribe, a moment ripe with historical significance. Direct contacts between American presidents and Indian leaders had been rare and controversial going back to the momentous first visit of Oglala Sioux chief Red Cloud and Brulé chief Spotted Tail to Washington during the administration of Ulysses S. Grant on June 6, 1870. Seven years later, Red Cloud came to Washington again, this time to negotiate with President Rutherford B. Hayes over the establishment of the Pine Ridge and Rosebud Reservations in South Dakota.

In the hundred years since their brutal forced relocation to reservations, American Indians had come to live in abject poverty. Forced into a fenced existence that as historically free-roaming people they did not understand, they watched settlers take more and more of their ancestral lands while they signed treaties they could not read and sold thousands of acres of property for bottles of whiskey that they could not tolerate. Alcoholism, discrimination, and woefully inadequate education steadily stripped American Indians of their dignity, pride, and economic status. The land they were left with was no good for farming, mineral rights were taken away from them, and federal agencies that were supposed to be managing their accounts were stealing from them. The businesses they had tried to start over the years—smoke shops, museum stores, basket-making companies—had largely failed, and over time they had become what the government considered impoverished wards of the state. No wonder that since that meeting in 1870, Indian leaders and American presidents had met on various occasions, almost always to discuss what aid the U.S. government could give the tribes.

But in 1994, for the first time in the history of Native American relations, it was not a tribe that was seeking federal help, but the president of the United States asking to be the beneficiary of Indian wealth. In the preceding year, Hayward had already sent, on behalf of his tribe, some $215,000 in legal but unregulated so-called soft money to help president Clinton's party repay the campaign debts incurred in the 1992 election. In a January 5, 1993, confidential memo from an official of the Democratic National Committee, Hayward was listed as one of the party's "top ten supporters," with an accompanying memo that he should be the recipient of what would become one of those controversial overnight stays in the White House Lincoln Bedroom. The memo, written by Democratic national finance chairman Terry McAuliffe, listed Hayward third on a list of ten of the country's best-known industrialists. "If there are any opportunities to include some of our key supporters in some of the President's activities, such as golf games, morning jog, e.g., it would be greatly appreciated," McAuliffe wrote. After the memo was written, Hayward and his Chippewa wife, Carol, a former Interior Department employee, became frequent guests at private breakfasts and dinners with the president and key administration officials. On the day before his call to Clinton, Hayward had signed a check for $50,000 to the Democratic National Committee. A short time after the call, on November 4 and November 21, he wrote two more checks for the same amount and over the next year contributed another $100,000. Hayward no doubt wrote these checks with the hope that the Clinton administration would respond favorably to his tribe's request to annex 165 acres of rural farmland that it had bought adjacent to its reservation in Ledyard. The property included a lake and an old Boy Scout camp that the tribe hoped to turn into a golf course, spa, and boating area. And in late 1994, Interior Secretary Bruce Babbitt approved the annexation despite vocal opposition from three neighboring towns concerned about crass development and worried that adding the land to the rest of the reservation—which was held in a tax-free trust by the federal government— would take the property off the local tax rolls.

After the 1994 phone conversation with the president, Hayward's then 175-member Mashantucket Pequot tribe would send nearly $800,000 in cash to the Democratic Party. They hedged their bets after Republican congressional victories of 1994 by giving $190,000 to the Republican Party, a decision that only infuriated House Speaker Newt Gingrich, who told colleagues that as long as the disparity between what they gave to the parties was so large, the Pequots would not have much clout with him.

In that crucial year of 1994, Hayward's largess would have immediate and tangible results. He would have a meeting with Democratic National Committee chairman David Wilhelm, one of Clinton's closest confidantes. A few months after the contributions, as President Clinton's reelection effort neared, Chief Hayward met with Clinton strategist Harold Ickes, then the White House deputy chief of staff. "There is a lot of money in Indian Country," a White House lawyer wrote in a note about the meeting. This was not a message lost on the president.

In the months before his first election, Clinton had been extremely skeptical about the beneficial effects of allowing Indian tribes to own and operate gambling casinos. As the leader of the National Governor's Association, the Arkansas governor had led his organization's opposition to expansion of Indian gambling. His views were reflected in a speech he made at a town meeting in San Diego in May of 1992. Candidate Clinton expressed disdain for Native American casinos, saying that while "reservations have been kept dependent too long, gambling is a lousy basis for an economy." But after consultation with political advisers and fund-raisers, Clinton began to see the error of his position. Seven months after his election, on August 4, 1993, Clinton gave a rare interview to a small paper called *Indian Country Today,* in which he extolled the benefits of Indian gaming as if the speech in San Diego had never happened. "Gaming is a positive economic development tool for Indian tribes," Clinton asserted. This interview was one of the first signals of the president's increased effort to raise campaign funds from the tribes. And he had clearly been advised that the operative word was not "gambling" but "gaming."

So BEGAN A TREND, with the government catering to Native American needs for its own financial and political gain. And the Mashantucket Pequots, owners of the world's most profitable casino—just north of Hayward's office in the woods of southeastern Connecticut—were at the center of it all.

In one of the greatest about-faces in American history, this obscure Indian tribe, which in 1994 had been federally recognized for only ten years and numbered fewer than 200 people, had nothing if not plenty of cash.

The Pequots' Foxwoods High Stakes Bingo and Casino, one of the most successful cash-producing enterprises in the world, rose incongruously and unexpectedly from the forest that surrounded most of Ledyard, a village some 12 miles southeast of Norwich, Connecticut, and about an equal distance west of the Rhode Island border. Nestled a dozen miles off any main road, Foxwoods, which opened in 1992, had become an entertainment complex with four hotels, two giant casinos, a nest of restaurants and buffets, a state-of-the-art museum, and extensive shopping areas. Its distinctive white and teal color scheme rose high over the forest line and could be seen for miles, not a mirage in the desert but a visage in the woodlands. Virtually every day, some 25,000 visitors would elbow each other onto the grounds, anxious to pour dollars into the tribe's slot machines, and blackjack, craps, and poker tables. On some days, such as New England's Patriot's Day, the casino seemed to reach the point of implosion. Its parking lot, longer than three football fields, would be overwhelmed with vehicles from Boston, New York, and Canada. Spots were so prized that drivers would hover near the casino exits, then give people a ride to their car in exchange for their parking place. Noise and exhaust from buses were now the norm in what was once one of the most rural and quiet corners in America. Some twenty years earlier, hippies from New York had drifted to this area to find privacy and solace, making their homes in small towns like Ledyard, North Stonington, and Preston. Previously, there had been nothing to attract adventure-seeking tourists to stop here. Thousands of New Yorkers, Philadelphians, and Washingtonians making the journey to and from Cape Cod via I-95 in the summer could travel the same highway for decades and never find a reason to wander any farther off the road than the popular Mystic Aquarium on the coast. If one ventured north of the big fish tank, the roads became winding, leafy ways, mysterious and often unmarked. There were few gas stations and no chain or convenience stores. The thought of a McDonald's, Burger King, or Wal-Mart was ludicrous.

But by 1995, Route 2, which roughly paralleled a section of I-95 about 20 miles to the north, was a constant rumble of buses and cars crammed with boisterous out-of-towners heading to or from the casino looking to buy a quick snack with $100 bills, currency that most local merchants had rarely seen, much less made change for. Refrigerated supply trucks from New York and Boston joined the procession in the early morning as uniformed guards and tribal policemen waved vehicles through a maze of hotels, casinos, and restaurants. By late 1998, some 33.6 million rolls of the craps dice later, the casino had been teeming nonstop for seven full years. Gamblers were pouring an estimated $700 million a year into the tribe's slot machines, averaging $80,000 per hour. George Washington's shiny silver face was being swallowed up by the Indians' slot machines at a rate of 7.6 million coins per day. The slots had even pushed Hayward out of his office in the tribe's main building, which was why he had called the president from a trailer. Eventually, a new $30-million city hall and community center would replace the trailers.

But with the popularity of Foxwoods came problems—both for the casino and the town. The lines at the casino's understaffed buffet extended for hours during lunch and dinner. The casino had long ago sopped up all the available labor in the New England market, with dealers and pit bosses driving in each day from Providence, Boston, and even towns as far away as New Hampshire. There was such a shortage of workers that the Pequots had to create their own "academy" to train potential employees, since the local high schools did not offer vocational training in dealing craps and blackjack. Not that the tribe didn't try to encourage them. Every year, the Pequots would make a massive donation of used cards and dice to the public school system. "To help kids in math," the school board insisted, accepting the gifts.

Services offered by casinos in Las Vegas or Atlantic City, like keno runners who took bets from customers for the ubiquitous bingolike numbers game, were often hard to find at Hayward's casino. All the pretty, long-legged local girls they could find to dress up in skimpy Indian costumes were already cocktail waitresses, dealers, or cashiers. In a region where unemployment had been unacceptably high for nearly two decades, there simply weren't enough bodies to fill the casino's voracious appetite for personnel. If you wanted to make a keno bet, it was do-it-yourself. Poker dealers were kept at their stations until their eyes were red and bleary and their fingers raw from scraping the edges of the cards. Roulette spinners whirled wheels until they were dizzy. The reservation didn't have to worry about violating labor laws, since it claimed exemption from most of them. The labor crisis was even worse outside the casino. Some shopkeepers, who had wondered hopefully what all those rumbling buses might mean for them, watched in horror as their hourly workers deserted in droves. Small business owners were left without cooks or counter workers, without salespersons or gas station attendants, without hairstylists or bookkeepers.

Suddenly, in what had once been one of the quietest patches of America, crimes were being committed that had been unheard of in the past. In their frenzied rush to the slot machines and blackjack tables, parents left their children and dogs locked in their cars, sometimes for hours. One New York City man left a five-year-old girl and a nine-year-old boy in his car for over two hours, with the motor running. A twenty-eight-year-old Massachusetts woman left four children ranging in age from two to seventeen alone for seventeen hours, while she lost the family grocery and rent money pulling slot handles. The police report indicated that she "occasionally" brought food and drink to the car for the children, who were locked inside from 9 A.M. on a Sunday until 2 A.M. Monday. Like many, their mother simply ignored the signs put up by the tribe in the parking lot stating that people leaving children in cars would be prosecuted. The towns' jails filled on account of drug and cocaine possession arrests, not merely of the tourists but also of nouveau riche tribe members suddenly swimming in cocaine and marijuana. In a three-month period in 1998, Connecticut State Police counted 340 crimes in tiny Ledyard, most of them drug or disorderly conduct crimes. Between 1990 and 1996, traffic counts on I-395 in Norwich increased from 37,000 to nearly 50,000 vehicles a day. On I-95, traffic doubled, swamping state police with at least two serious accidents to handle every day. On tree-lined Route 2, the busiest and closest road to the casino, many of the splendid oaks now showed fender-level gashes where cars had plowed into the forest.

By 1997, just five years after the opening of the casino, personal bankruptcy filings in New London County, where the casino was located, quadrupled, mostly for abusing plastic. Explained one busy bankruptcy attorney: "The casino has a credit card swipe machine every five feet." When the machines would no longer dispense cash, gamblers were given to desperation. In March 1996, when thirty-eight-year-old Laura Grauer of Stamford, Connecticut, had gone through all her credit cards and all her cash, the married mother of a teenage daughter walked into the nearby Thames River and drowned herself.

WHO WAS this nouveau riche Indian tribe that was turning a sleepy part of New England upside down? The legacy that Richard Hayward now clung to, the mantle of Pequot history, was crucial to his multimillion-dollar endeavor. As the result of a long line of controversial Supreme Court decisions, only genuine Indian tribes could legally operate casinos in Connecticut. There had once been Indians called the Pequots. Of that, there could be no doubt. But were Hayward and his family really their descendants? Some suggested that they were closer to being "Casino-Americans," opportunists who had manipulated American laws to create their own nation and then their own casino. It was this suspicion that nagged at the residents of Ledyard and Preston. Many of them had known Hayward and his family for many years. His father had been a Navy seaman; his paternal grandmother and great-grandmother had been active in the Daughters of the American Revolution. Hayward, his two brothers, and his six sisters had attended public schools both in Ledyard and in nearby Rhode Island, where his father was stationed. People had known them all their lives, and they had never identified themselves as "Indians" before. Why were they Indians now? And how, by 1998, had the Haywards become the most powerful family in the state, earning more than $1.5 million a year in salary, enjoying dinners with the president, negotiating to buy National Football League franchises, receiving honorary degrees from the most prestigious universities, and swallowing up farms, houses, historic inns, and landmarks that had been in private Yankee hands for three centuries?

The small reservation where the casino now stood had been around for as long as local residents could remember. But no one was exactly sure if the people who lived on it were truly related to the proud Pequots of four centuries ago. Suddenly, this question was at the forefront of everyone's conversations. Something had happened in Connecticut that changed the lives of those who lived here. As remarkable as these transformations were, the story behind them was even more incredible.

I

BEGINNINGS

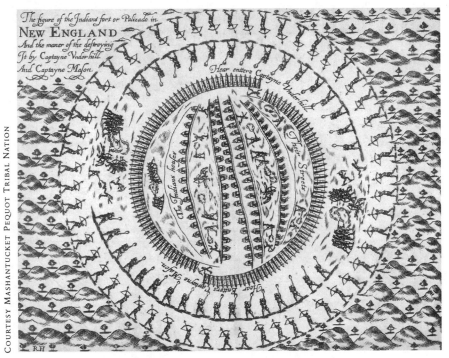

English attack on a Pequot fort, 1637

1

THE PEQUOTS MEET THE ENGLISH

THE PEQUOT LEGACY around which Skip Hayward had built an empire had its origins directly linked to the discovery and settlement of America. The Pequots were among the first Indian tribes to be encountered by English and Dutch traders, and the very first to be exterminated.

Christopher Columbus accidentally stumbled onto the New World in 1492, and in an amazingly short time—by the early 1500s—European explorers were already combing the coastline of the Hudson River Valley and Long Island Sound. Although we tend to think of American Indians in terms of the Great Plains and the West, the East Coast was densely populated with indigenous residents when the pushy newcomers from Europe arrived. The Mohegans, the Narragansetts, the Wampanoags, the Nipmucs, the Niantics, the Shinnecocks, and the Pequots ruled from what is now Long Island all the way to Cape Cod. But all the contemporary literature of the time points to the fact that in the early 1500s, the Pequot Indians were seen by Dutch and British traders as "the most numerous, the most warlike, the fiercest and the bravest of all the aboriginal clans of Connecticut." The translation of their name itself, Pequot, means "destroyers."

Both the Pequots and the neighboring Mohegans occupied the coastline of southeastern Connecticut on the north side of Long Island Sound. They were a people who lived mostly along the seacoast, harvesting crabs and other edible sea creatures, as well as collecting beads and shells for use in wampum, the currency of the Indian tribes. Some historians believe they were two factions of the same tribe. Both tribes were said to be closely related to the Mohawks and other Algonquin tribes who lived along the banks of the Hudson River. In fact, the Pequots arrived at the Connecticut coast only a few decades before the Europeans. Before that, they lived alongside the Mohicans in the Hudson River Valley. For reasons that were never recorded or permanently passed down, they were either expelled from the Hudson Valley or voluntarily migrated down to the coastline, first traveling east from the Hudson River along what would become the southern border of Massachusetts. After crossing the Connecticut River, they turned south and settled along the coast of Long Island Sound at the sites of the present-day cities of Groton, Mystic, and Noank. This immediately put them at odds with their tribal neighbors, the Narragansetts and Niantics, who were related to each other and viewed the Pequots with suspicion and even hatred. There is little doubt among anthropologists that the Pequots clashed with these tribes during their eastward migration and that at least some clans of Niantics were killed in violent confrontations, while others joined the Narragansetts.

By the time of the European arrival in New England in the early sixteenth century, the Pequots found themselves in control of a large area of land along the coast of Connecticut, but at the same time they were completely surrounded by enemies. Still, as historian John W. De Forest described it in *History of the Indians of Connecticut from the Earliest Known Period to 1850,* his definitive history of the local tribes, written in 1852, "They maintained their hold on the conquered territory with a tenacity equal to the boldness with which they had seized it." Pequot war parties created terror and frequent panic among the numerous Narragansetts to the east in what is now Rhode Island and swept smaller tribes to the west. Slowly but surely, during the late 1400s and early 1500s, the Pequots conquered and solidified their hold on southern New England with territory extending from the present border of Rhode Island all the way to New Haven. From their bases in present-day Groton, the Pequots set off in canoes to attack rival bands on Long Island as well as on Block Island. For roughly one hundred years, the Pequots' military successes were virtually unchecked, at least until they met a bolder and fiercer foe coming at them from the west.

At the beginning of the seventeenth century, the fierce Iroquois were driven out of Canada by the Adirondacks. Loose and on the warpath in the colonies, Iroquois warriors blazed wildly over eastern North America. De Forest writes that every Indian nation from the Mississippi to the Connecticut River, from Tennessee to Hudson's Bay, trembled at their mere mention.

The natives of what would become Connecticut were exposed every year to the ravages of the Iroquois. In New England, the Iroquois faction was known as the Mohawks. And up until the early 1600s, the Mohawks from the west and the Pequots from the east terrorized everyone who lived in between. But these two fierce peoples made a point of avoiding each other, and the Pequots advanced no farther west than where the Mohawks lived. Until 1614, they had only to worry about each other. But in that year, some six years before the Pilgrims landed at Plymouth Rock, a Dutch navigator named Adriaen Block maneuvered through Long Island Sound, and explored numerous rivers including the Connecticut River. In his little 44-foot sailboat called the *Restless,* Block sailed up the Connecticut River to the present site of Hartford. He was stopped by the presence of an Indian fort, and he turned around and sailed back to the Sound. Thus it was that Connecticut was officially "discovered."

Within several years, Dutch traders were buying as many as 10,000 beaver skins a year from the Indians in Connecticut. In 1632, a representative of the West India Company, Hans Eencluys, began negotiations with the Pequots to built a fort and trading post on land within the tribe's hunting range. The land in question was distant from the main inhabited section of the Pequots' 500-square-mile range and so on June 18, 1633, Pequot chief (known as a "sachem") Wopigwooit, entered into a treaty that gave a chunk of the river valley to the Dutch in exchange for cloth, household goods, and toys. But almost immediately, relations between the Pequots and the settlers fell apart. Pequot warriors attacked traders and the Dutch responded by having Wopigwooit executed. The new chief, Sassacus, vowed revenge against the Dutch for killing the tribal leader and began dealing with English settlers who were also interested in driving out the rival Dutch. An Englishman from

Plymouth Colony named William Holmes established a trading post north of Hartford at the present site of Windsor. It did not take long for the English to run into the same types of problems the Dutch were having. In the summer of 1633, a "Captain John Stone" sailed up the Connecticut River and began trading with friendly local tribes. But a Pequot war party came upon his boat and killed a landing party that was searching for turkeys, then went aboard the boat and murdered Stone with a large rock.

This incident alarmed Sassacus as much as it did the English. Ever since the attack on the Dutch trading post, the Pequots had been losing ground in constant skirmishes over a wide front. The Niantics had pushed them off Block Island, the Narragansetts had grown stronger to their east, and other rival tribes, seeking closer ties to the Dutch for their own protection, were better armed and trained for battle then they had been before the arrival of the newcomers. Sassacus, who hated the Dutch, was not yet ready to provoke a battle with the English. In October 1634, he sent an ambassador to the English seeking an alliance against the Dutch. The English replied that they would welcome peace but they had to insist that the murderers of Stone and his men be turned over for punishment. The Pequots disputed the English understanding of the episode. They claimed that Stone had provoked the attack by "violent and alarming" conduct, and all but two of the attackers had since died from a smallpox epidemic that was then sweeping through the tribes. In order to achieve peace, the Pequots promised to turn over the remaining two members of the party to the English for trial. In addition, the English would have the protection of the Pequots as they made their way up the Connecticut River Valley. In return, the English promised not to aid the Dutch in attacking the Pequots. The treaty was signed at Massachusetts Bay Colony in November 1634.

The success of the Treaty of 1634 encouraged a steady stream of settlers from the Massachusetts Bay Colony to the Connecticut River Valley. In one settlement at Wethersfield, the colonists nearly perished in a fierce winter storm, only to be saved by the intervention of friendly Pequots, who took them into their wigwams.

By 1635, the Colony of Connecticut was truly established. Larger parties of women and children made the trek southward to join their husbands on the frontier. They were welcomed "joyfully," as their own accounts put it, but in the spring of 1636 an incident occurred that broke the spirit of the treaty. An English sailor named John Oldham of Dorchester set sail with a crew of two young boys and two Narragansett Indians to trade with the Pequots. He was on his way home when his entire party was murdered and his possessions plundered. Not long afterward, a delegation of Narragansetts journeyed to Boston to express their grief at the killing of Oldham and to assure authorities that the two remaining assailants had been found and punished. Although the Pequots had not participated in the Oldham murder, the English were still angry because tribe members were reported to have harbored some of Oldham's attackers who had escaped onto Block Island. In the opinion of the English, the Pequots were coconspirators in the crime, which only served as a reminder that the tribe had never turned over the killers of Captain Stone as they had promised. As a show of force, the English instructed John Endicott to sail to Block Island and to "put every man to death." From Block Island, Endicott was ordered to go "to the country of the Pequots" and to capture the murderers of Captain Stone.

As the fleet approached Block Island, only a single Indian could be seen walking along the shore. As one of Endicott's men, John Underhill, approached the shore, 60 warriors rose and unleashed a volley of arrows. Unable to fire from their craft, the landing party abandoned their boat in waist-deep water and, firing muskets, stormed the beach. Armed only with arrows, the Pequots fled into the bushes. Underhill set fire to an abandoned Pequot village and then killed 14 Pequots he found hiding in a swamp. Having accomplished what he could, he then sailed back across the sound to the mainland, landing at a fort at the coastal site of modern-day Saybrook, Connecticut. The local commander, Lion Gardiner, was horrified at Endicott's armament and complained that it would "raise a nest of wasps." Despite his misgivings, Gardiner augmented Endicott's force with two small ships and an additional 20 soldiers. They sailed into the harbor at what is now New London and approached Pequot representatives. Endicott demanded that the Pequots turn over Stone's killer to him as well as pay 1,000 fathoms of wampum for their destruction of English property. If they could not pay a sum so large, Endicott said, they must part with 20 of their children to be held as hostages until the payment was made.

The Pequots argued that Stone had been killed in retaliation for the Dutch killing of one of their sachems. The Pequot ambassador explained that his people sometimes had trouble distinguishing between the English and the Dutch. "You know well enough the difference between the English and the Dutch," Endicott replied angrily. "You have had sufficient relations with both and therefore seeing that you have slain the King of England's subjects, we demand an account for their blood." Endicott prepared his men for battle. He lined up his soldiers on the east side of the river near the site of present-day New London and marched them to a hill where he would have a sweeping view of the countryside. Around them swirled some 300 Pequots, most of them unarmed. Frustrated, Endicott took a few young Indians as hostages, burned several wigwams, and set sail for Boston. Just as Lion Gardiner had predicted, the Endicott attack had the Pequots buzzing, and it was the Connecticut settlers who paid the price. Almost immediately after Endicott's departure, two sailors from one of the smaller ships from Gardiner's regiment at Saybrook were attacked by a band of Pequots while they were foraging a cornfield. If the Pequots had been determined to get revenge for the earlier conduct of the English and the Dutch, the actions of Endicott had strengthened their hostility. There was nothing as sacred in Pequot culture as the belief in swift reprisal for slain warriors.

The English would have to be destroyed. But to accomplish this, Sassacus concluded, he needed an alliance with his longtime foe, the Narragansetts. Sassacus thus sent two tribal leaders to the Narragansetts to make peace and to induce the tribe to "take up tomahawk" against the English.

Sassacus proposed a strategy of guerrilla warfare against the invaders, suggesting that the Pequot-Narragansett alliance not meet the English in open battle. Instead, he asked that the English be harassed secretly and unceasingly. Eventually, their lives would be made so difficult that they would "fly back across the sea" to their own country. If we are destroyed, he told the Narragansetts, "you will not be long safe from attack and overthrow."

The Narragansetts listened to the appeals of Sassacus and then re-treated to their own tribal council. The tribe was torn. Much of what Sassacus said about the English was true. But at the same time, they hated and feared the Pequots only a little less than the colonists did. This being the case, instead of dealing with Sassacus, they decided to form an alliance with the English colonists. The Narragansett chief traveled triumphantly to Boston to sign the new agreement. When word of the new alliance came to Pequot country, Sassacus began to prepare his warriors for battle, and skirmishes became common. At one town up-river, Pequots grabbed three women who were working in the fields. Two of them went along peacefully, but the third resisted and was killed with a hatchet. The Pequots then went into the town and murdered 2 more women, 6 men, and 20 cows.

Two days after the attack, the residents at Fort Saybrook saw the Pequot victors coming down the river in their canoes with the two captive girls, daughters of a man named Abraham Swain. Gardiner ordered that cannons be fired at their canoes, but none were hit and the Pequots slipped back to their homes at the base of the river.

On May 11, 1637, a committee of men from the towns of Hartford, Windsor, and Wethersfield met in Hartford to discuss what action to take. By now, 30 of their friends had been slain by Pequot arrows. It was resolved that an offensive war would have to be conducted and an army of 90 men was authorized—42 from Hartford, 30 from Windsor, and 18 from Wethersfield. Commander John Mason was named commander-in-chief. And Mason quickly discovered a very useful ally.

For years, Sassacus had experienced troubles with a part-Mohegan, part-Pequot chieftain named Uncas, who on numerous occasions had challenged Sassacus. His plotting was found out and Uncas was exiled to live with the Narragansetts. Uncas and Sassacus were such bitter ene-mies that Uncas resolved to put himself at the disposal of the English against his blood rival. Joined by a number of Indians who lived along the river and badly wanted the old days of easy trading to come back, Uncas drafted 70 warriors to fight the Pequots.

With the news that the men of Connecticut were arming, Massachu-setts supplied nearly 300 more soldiers. On May 20, 1637, Mason and

Uncas took off after the Pequot villages. To prove his loyalty along the way, Uncas personally killed four Pequots and demonstrably tortured several others. Mason sailed to Rhode Island to join his new Narragansett allies to attack the Pequots from the rear through what would be the current towns of Mystic and Groton.

On Friday, May 29, Mason and his men arrived on the shores of southern Rhode Island and Narragansett territory. At sunset the following Tuesday, Mason landed and marched up to the residence of the Narragansett chief, Canonicus. He informed Canonicus that all he wanted was safe passage through Narragansett lands. Mason was given permission and an admonition. The Narragansetts had seen many white men before try to attack the Pequots without success. They were "great captains and skillful in war," the Narragansetts warned.

Mason's men took this warning as an affront. It was clear that the Narragansetts, as well as the Pequots, did not view the English as great fighting men. The following morning, a sea army of 13 Englishmen and a few Indians set sail for the harbor nearest the camp at New London. At the same time, Mason amassed an army of 77 Englishmen and 60 of Uncas's troops and began to march westward along the path of modern-day U.S. 1.

As they marched, Narragansetts along the way joined the invasion army and induced members of another tribe, the Niantics, to come along as well. The ever-increasing army marched an additional three miles in the direction of Mystic before Mason stopped to interrogate some of the Indians in his party. He was told that the Pequots lived in two forts, one fairly close to present-day Groton, the other farther down the coast at New London. It was at the farther one that Sassacus resided.

At night, Mason encamped at a place called Porters' Rocks, from which he could hear the sounds of Pequot revelry. Mason's men were stone silent. On the morning of June 5, 1637, the English awoke silently before daybreak and murmured their prayers. Mason led them along a two-mile path but was frustrated that he couldn't see the fort that had seemed so close during the night. "Where is the fort?" Mason asked of Uncas.

"On the top of the hill," Uncas replied.

Mason asked where his Indian warriors were.

"They are in the rear, very much afraid," Uncas replied. "Tell them not to fly," said Mason. "But let them stand behind at what distance they please and see now whether the Englishmen will fight."

Mason sent Underhill to the southern slope of the fort, while Mason prepared for a frontal assault. Nearly everyone inside the fort was asleep. Mason's men crept undetected until they were right on top of the fort when a dog barked and a Pequot sentry called out, "Englishmen, Englishmen!" Firing muskets as they went, Mason and his men burst into the village, many of the Pequots staring up in astonishment from their beddings. Hand-to-hand combat was fierce, and both Mason and his men were soon weak from exhaustion. To end it, Mason seized a torch and set fire to a wigwam. The village went up in an instant and screams of those burned alive seared the spring night. Forty of the bravest Pequot warriors ran outside into the morning, but almost all were struck down by English swords or the arrows of the Narragansetts.

According to Mason's account, the fire blazed for the better part of an hour, killing 400 Pequots. Mason calculated that seven were taken prisoner and seven were judged to have escaped. The brutality of burning people alive did not faze the English. One commander wrote after the slaughter: "Sometimes the scripture declareth women and children must perish with their parents. Sometimes the case alters but we will not dispute it now. We had sufficient light from the word of God for our proceedings."

But the battle was not over. Scouts reported a cadre of some 300 Pequot warriors marching toward them from the other fort. But armed only with arrows, they were no match for 14 soldiers who sent them into retreat with musket fire. Mason then directed his own men to retreat and regroup. As they moved back, the Pequots gazed upon the destruction of their village. They were so wrought with anger and grief over what they saw that many stood and began pulling out their hair and crying. Crazed with rage, more Pequots rushed down the hill of their town only to be mowed down by more musket fire. Those who made it back to the main fort quickly exacted their revenge on the family of Uncas, immediately killing anyone whose blood could be linked to the traitor's. Sassacus called a council at his remaining fort to discuss his three options: to leave southeastern Connecticut and head northwest; to attack the English; or to wage war on the traitorous Narragansetts.

The decision was made to torch their town and divide up into smaller parties to try to escape. The main body of several hundred survivors moved westward under the command of Sassacus. Finding three colonists working in a field along his retreat route, Sassacus ordered their bodies slit open from back to breast and hung up on trees by the bank to show the English that he was unbroken and unbowed. During their retreat, the Pequots foraged for food in the forest and used their great skill at clamming to survive. One group finally halted their march at the present site of Fairfield, a good portion of the way to their ancestral homelands along the Hudson River. The English were now determined to eradicate the remnants of the Pequots while they were split and weakened. The first band, that had camped near a swamp, were captured without resistance, and 40 of them were murdered by the English in cold blood. Two lesser chiefs were spared upon the promise that they would lead the English to the main group of fleeing Pequots under Sassacus.

Some 80 of the women were handed over to the Narragansetts to become part of their tribe. The remainder were bound up and sent to the Massachusetts Bay Colony to be sold as slaves, destined for the cane fields of the Caribbean.

With Uncas as his guide, Mason tracked the Pequots, following their diggings for clams, roots, and other shellfish. In addition, the party occasionally came upon strays and stragglers who were forced under torture to provide information on the direction Sassacus had taken. Meanwhile, Mason's fleet had sailed on to New Haven. Again, a Pequot was captured and promised his life if he would simply point the English in the direction of Sassacus. He departed, obtained the exact location and number of Pequots in the main band, then stole away and reported back to the English. The stage was set for the end of the reign of Sassacus. Mason marched toward Fairfield.

Sassacus's men, whose intelligence was almost as accurate as that of Mason's, had set up camp around an area known as Fairfield Swamp. At least 100 Pequot warriors had taken defensive positions around the low-lying quicksand, and when a battalion of Mason's men came, the Pequots sprang forward and pushed back the English, inflicting casualties. The English surrounded the area and poured musket balls indiscriminately toward the campfires. Uneasy at the prospect of killing even more women and children, it was decided to enlist the services of an interpreter, to see if some sort of surrender could be arranged. The translator ventured into the Indian lines and announced that all Pequots who had not been guilty of killing Englishmen would be freed. The Pequots agreed and for a long time, women, children, and elderly Pequots passed silently out of the swamp and safely through the English lines. After 200 had come out, the English were satisfied that only warriors remained inside the perimeter. Throughout the night, the two opposing forces fought in close quarters. Nine Pequots fell to English musketry. Indian arrows proved much less effective. Shortly before dawn, a heavy seaside fog enveloped the swamp. The Pequots took this as their best chance to escape and rushed what they hoped was a weak point in the British barricade. A vicious last battle began and from 50 to 60 Pequots succeeded in getting outside the English lines and fled into the woods. Mason captured the rest, but Sassacus was not among them.

Sassacus had already slipped out of Fairfield Swamp, and accompanied by a companion named Mononotto, and with up to 40 of his most elite fighting men, he had moved even farther west into Mohawk territory. But the tribe from which his people had split many years before proved no more loyal to Indian blood than had Uncas or the Narragansetts. Knowing that the head of Sassacus had value in their dealings with the English, the Mohawks killed every Pequot but Mononotto, who escaped. The scalp of Sassacus and five of his bravest men were ignominiously sent to Fort Saybrook as proof that Sassacus and the Pequots were finally done for.

Ultimately, according to Mason, some 700 additional Pequots were killed or captured in various groups. Those that had escaped were marked men. Hardly a week passed at Saybrook that Narragansetts or Mohegans didn't appear with yet another horrible trophy. It brought joy to colonial leaders, who proclaimed gratefulness "that on this day we have sent 600 heathen to heaven."

According to the history compiled by De Forest, the remaining Pequots tired of life on the run. An emissary was sent to Hartford to propose the total and unconditional surrender of the remaining members of the tribe, if their lives would be spared. An investigation was ordered by the colonial government into exactly how many Indians of Pequot blood remained in New England and also on Long Island. On October 1, 1638, in a document styled the "Treaty of Hartford," the colonial government of Connecticut, along with its Indian allies, passed final judgment on the Pequots. Under the terms of the treaty, the remaining living Pequots were to be divided among the Narragansetts and the Mohegans. The Pequots were never again to live in their homeland and could never again use the name Pequot. All Pequot lands east of the Connecticut River would revert to the English colony of Connecticut.

As De Forest wrote, "Such was the peace that closed the famous Pequot War; and thus, for all time, was the national existence of that brave though savage people extinguished."

THAT THE PEQUOTS were "extinguished" has significant references in history. The French traveler and historian Alexis de Tocqueville recorded their extermination for the world after traveling to New England in 1833. "All the Indian tribes who once inhabited the territory of New England—the Narragansetts, the Mohicans, the Pequots—now live only in men's memories," he wrote in *Democracy in America* after returning home. Even Herman Melville made note of their disappearance in *Moby-Dick,* written in 1851. It was no accident that Melville named Captain Ahab's doomed ship the *Pequod* (using a variation of the tribe's correct spelling), explaining: "Pequod, you will no doubt remember, was the name of a celebrated tribe of Massachusetts Indians, now extinct as the ancient Medes."

If Melville, de Tocqueville, De Forest, and others are correct, how could it be that something like 600 Pequots are now living in $300,000 four-bedroom, three-car-garage wigwams that encircle the tribe's modern-day sacred hearth—the billion-dollar-a-year Foxwoods Resort and Casino. If nothing else, this seems like an egregious violation of the Treaty of Hartford, the three-party agreement that made it un-lawful for the Pequots to even exist. And according to the treaty, now locked in a vault at the Massachusetts Historical Society, it is unlawful for anyone to use the name "Pequot." Apparently, the U.S. Patent and Trademark Office isn't enforcing all the old colonial laws.

Could such illustrious observers as Melville, the count de Toc-queville, and De Forest have been mistaken? Though de Tocqueville was a tourist, he is still regarded some 150 years after his death as one of the most astute observers of early America. And if anybody had known what was happening in those Connecticut woods, it would have been Melville or De Forest, who were so personally familiar with the re-gion. How could they have been so far off? If we want to believe Melville, then who are these people who call themselves the Pequots to-day? If the experts are correct, they must be a band of opportunists who have stolen the mantle of Pequot history to take advantage of current laws and Supreme Court rulings that make it possible for Native Ameri-can Indian tribes to own and operate casinos when it would otherwise be unlawful for them to do so. In short, Foxwoods could be the grand-est, richest, and most successful scam of all time.

Aside from the issues of sovereignty, which enable them to operate virtually tax-free, immune from personal injury suits and state labor laws, the Pequots' "Indianness" itself is one of the keys to the casino's enor-mous success. Thousands of Foxwoods customers admit to alleviating their guilt by choosing to gamble in an Indian casino. Believing that their slot quarters and $5 craps and blackjack chips are helping to rectify four hundred years of American injustice makes it easier to justify the other-wise silly act of taking all the money they have worked hard for during the week and giving it away with one spin of the roulette wheel. Full of rationalizations and self-justifications, Indian-sponsored gambling has one built-in advantage that Donald Trump's casinos in Atlantic City could never match: it is freer from guilt. Every day, thousands talk them-selves into the idea that they aren't losing money but making a contribu-tion to charity. The IRS, unfortunately, does not allow gambling losses to be placed on the charitable-deduction side of Form 1040.

When it came to the status of the Pequot tribe, the historians were part right and part wrong. They were right that the tribe, as a Native American community with its own language, customs, and practices, was gone. They were wrong, however, that the Pequot people themselves had all been extinguished or had abandoned their identity.

Not much time had passed after the signing of the Treaty of Hartford in 1637 when it became apparent at the headquarters of the Massachusetts Bay Colony that the conquered Pequots were not cooperating with its provisions. The surviving remnants of the Pequot War were supposed to have been divided up between the Narragansetts and the Mohegans. But both tribes were bitter historical enemies of the Pequots and the aid that each of them had given to the English forces of Captain Mason was hardly something that could be easily overlooked or forgiven.

In late 1638, it was brought to the attention of Captain Mason that a village of Pequots had escaped from Mohegan bondage and reestablished themselves on the banks of the Pawcatuck River near the border of modern-day Connecticut and Rhode Island. English officials were quick to rule that this constituted a severe breach of the Treaty of Hartford. The settlement, they decreed, must be closed. Captain Mason was dispatched to handle the matter with a force of 40 soldiers. He sailed to the mouth of the Pawcatuck, where he became engaged in a battle with a tribe of Niantics. As Mason himself remembered the incident, the Niantic chief defended the Pequots, telling Mason, "the Pequots who live here are good men and we will certainly fight for them and protect them." The English commanders, rather than become involved in a wider campaign than they had originally anticipated, withdrew. The Connecticut colonial government was wary of doing anything that might lead to a restoration of Pequot power but did come to perceive that small Pequot pockets, like the one on the Pawcatuck, were going to persist in Connecticut. That perception was implicit in the very first law ever passed by the colonial General Assembly in 1638. That statute banned the trading of weapons to the Pequots. At the same time, English soldiers continued to hunt down individual Pequots suspected of committing "war crimes" against settlers, and bounties were posted for certain nefarious characters who had participated in pre-1638 atrocities.

With the exception of a few episodes, the English went nearly a decade without encountering any serious problems with Pequot survivors. English colonization of Connecticut continued at a rapid rate. Much of the 500 square miles of land that had once been under the domain of the Pequots was awarded to the winning commanders in the Pequot War. John Mason and Lion Gardiner were given huge plantations in what is now southeastern Connecticut. Captain Daniel Patrick, who had played a key role in the attack on the Pequot fort, was deeded much of the land around present-day Norwich. With the fear of physical violence from the Pequots removed, settlers drifted northward along the Thames River to the peripheral towns of Preston, North Stonington, Gales Ferry, Lebanon, Griswold, and Montville. Thousands of settlers from the Massachusetts and Plymouth Colonies streamed into what is today the metropolitan area of Hartford. Over the next few decades, the entire southern Connecticut coastline all the way to present-day Norwalk and Bridgeport opened up, much of it first surveyed by soldiers who had come to those regions in their pursuit of the fleeing Pequot warriors. One of the first men from Massachusetts to lead families into the former Pequot territory was John Winthrop, Jr. He had named the whole area Groton after the manor in England from which he had come. When Connecticut divided off from the Massachusetts Bay Colony to become a separate colony, Winthrop would become one of Connecticut's early colonial governors.

New London became the hub of coastal Connecticut, what with its wonderful location at the mouth of a broad river and a natural harbor so perfect that it would one day be selected as the site for the U.S. Coast Guard Academy. Before the war, the body of water that flowed to Norwich was known as the Pequot River. The nostalgic English, after the war, renamed the waterway the Thames River. Just east of New London were the towns of Groton, Mystic, and Nawayunk—now spelled "Noank." North of Groton, forming a near-perfect square some 36 square miles in area, was a region of Connecticut thick with viperous snakes, dismal swamps, and forests so dense and rocks so prevalent that one could hardly imagine trying to clear the land for farming. Bounded on the west by the Thames River and on the east by a giant granite projection known as Lantern Hill, this desolate inland area hardly even needed a name. It was among the last places in Connecticut any white European settler would think about moving. The section was referred to in official state documents as the Society of North Groton.

It was obvious to the few intrepid settlers in North Groton, as well as in Preston and North Stonington, that the rocky soil was more suitable for grazing goats or raising pigs than for plowing and growing useful crops. Compact deposits of oak, chestnut, ash, walnut, white birch, maple, poplar, and cedar posed huge challenges to farmers seeking to clear away land on which they could grow strawberries, buckwheat, corn, and oats. But before the land had been cleared for farming, the region would become known for its lumber. Sawmills quickly went up along two major brooks that intersected at the center of North Groton—Williams Brook and Lee's Brook. In the months when the many ponds and streams weren't covered with ice or flooded, they bubbled with fresh ever-rolling logs. About two miles to the east of those first sawmills were three large ponds, Lantern Hill Pond, Long Pond, and Whitford Pond. Over the first of these ponds loomed Lantern Hill, a striking rock formation that reminded some settlers of a man in a round crowned hat. Lantern Hill was a rich and handy source of granite, and it also contained small amounts of iron ore and deposits of silica from which glass could be made. In the middle of the Society of North Groton was the fearsome Cedar Swamp. As forbidding a location as there could be in New England, it harbored venomous copperheads and rattlers, poison frogs and lizards. Wolves and other predators were abundant. Agriculturally, historians of the town recount, the Society of North Groton was "like a pumpkin," with the best parts near the outside. Cedar Swamp was the worthless pulp at its center.

The inhabitants of North Groton quickly became aware that many Pequots had survived both the war and their exile by hiding out in those very thick woods and rocky outcrops. Pequots who hadn't been so lucky and had been sold or given as prizes of war to Mohegans and Narragansetts escaped and joined family members and surviving sachems in those same woods. But some forty years after their battle with the English, they were hardly the Pequot warriors of old. They were simply a broken, disorganized native people who caused little trouble, trying to stay out of the Englishman's path. They made their living, as had their ancestors, by shelling and fishing along the coasts as far south as present-day Noank and Mystic. Occasionally, the Pequots deliberately made themselves useful to the colonists, such as when an old tribe member cleared out a rattlesnake den under Lantern Hill, where some settlers were collecting minerals. He grabbed a rattler by the tail, then by the head. Then holding it carefully, he made a slit in the skin and tied the snake to a packet of gunpowder. Then to the amusement and delight of the colonists, the snake slid into the den and exploded. Hundreds of dazed rattlesnakes poured out of the canyon and made easy pickings for the crowds that stood ready with sticks, knives, and even muskets.

But while it is correct to describe the remaining Pequots as a vanquished tribe that had lost its power, by no means had they lost their pride. Over the years from 1636 to 1655, the records of the Connecticut General Assembly are marked with constant complaining from Pequot tribal members about abuses over their hunting and shelling rights along the beach. For the most part, the English, particularly Governor Winthrop, were happy with the cooperation they were getting from the Pequots. In 1651, Winthrop persuaded the Connecticut Colony to give the Pequots 500 acres at Noank, near their most popular crabbing grounds. But over time, continued encroachment from new settlements would give the Pequots less and less space.

So despite the mandate of the Treaty of Hartford, Connecticut relented on their early vow to terminate the very existence of the Pequot people and name. But it was inevitable that the natural rights of the Indians and the desires of the settlers would continue to clash. Settlement along Long Island Sound was increasing at a rapid pace, and the Indians, once a danger, were now regarded as a nuisance.

In 1667, the General Assembly finally decided to remove the Pequots, which by now had separated into two separate rival bands, and to place them in state-owned reservations. The split had come about from internal jealousies, power struggles, and religious differences. One side was led by a sachem named Robin Cassacinamon; the other followed a leader named Wequash, who had converted to Christianity. For years, Cassacinamon had asked that his faction be given land that would be free from encroachment. He requested that it be near their clamming area at Noank, next to the confluence of the Mystic River and Long Island Sound. But the colonial authorities had a different location in mind. The "western" Pequots, those who had escaped from the Mohegans' clutches, were resettled on 2,000 acres of the worst, most snake-infested, rock-ledged, swamp-filled, uninhabitable land in the whole Society of North Groton. It was called Mushantuxet, which was the Indian expression for "much-wooded land." Wequash's group, because they were not considered "heathens," were given 280 acres of tillable land just to the east of Lantern Hill near the present village of North Stonington.

Although just a few miles northwest of Lantern Hill, Mushantuxet was a stark contrast to the Eastern reservation on the hill's other side, which was much more suitable for cultivation. Cassacinamon was furious over the arrangement. He and his immediate family members refused to go to Mushantuxet, and he continued live at Noank until his death in 1692. Although the majority of Pequots were almost literally out of sight, hidden now in the woods and swamps, their constant complaining about living conditions never stopped annoying the colonial government. But on several occasions, they proved themselves to be extremely useful to the colonial government as well. In 1675, surviving western Pequots actually joined forces with the English government in a dispute with the Narragansetts called King Philip's War. Regarded as one of the bloodiest and most significant Indian wars of colonial times, King Philip's War was the second large-scale effort of the British to eradicate native peoples in order to make New England safe for European settlement, the Pequot War being the first. The turnabout was that this time the Narragansetts became the main targets and the Pequots were the ally.

"King Philip" was the chief of a New England tribe called the Wampanoags, who were closely related to the Narragansetts. His Indian name was Metacomet. Metacomet's father had been a friendly Indian chief named Massasoit, who was well known to the settlers at Plymouth Colony. Massasoit's two sons had been named Philip and Alexander by the British, who intended to honor them with the names of the two great conquerors Philip of Macedon and Alexander the Great. Although their father had tried to deal peacefully with the European invaders, the two increasingly rebellious young sons had no illusions about what the future of colonization would bring. Alexander, the older son, hated the English and dreamed of driving them out of Massachusetts. He died from natural causes in 1657. Philip, who was even more bitter and resentful of the colonists, then took over the leadership of the tribe from his brother.

From 1657 until 1675, Philip taunted and attacked English settlements. A twenty-year period of peace and settlement had come to an abrupt close, even though the numbers by now were on the side of the colonists. At the heart of the conflict was the increasingly successful effort to convert Native Americans to Christianity. Thousands had already converted and were working in English homes as servants and farmworkers. Converts were not held in high regard by Philip or his warriors. A tribe member named John Sassamon, who did convert, was stabbed to death on a frozen pond. His body was then slipped under the ice, and his hat and coat were left to mark the spot.

In early 1675, the Narragansetts became principals in a vicious war against the rapidly expanding English. In April of that year, English troops based in Connecticut captured and executed the Narragansett chief Canonchet for refusing to turn over warriors suspected of being collaborators in King Philip's attacks on colonial villages. A month later, the inhabitants of a Narragansett fishing village were slaughtered at point-blank range as they tried to flee colonial soldiers. British authorities at Boston assigned Captain Benjamin Church to subdue Philip and his band.

Church had been born in 1639 near Plymouth Plantation. His father had been an immigrant from England fleeing religious oppression. Benjamin Church himself was a physically large man of gentle piety who read and expounded upon the scriptures on a daily basis, and he was an easy choice as the leader of the local militia in the town of Bristol in Rhode Island. He had participated in numerous actions against Indians and was totally familiar with their swamps and hiding places from Rhode Island to Cape Cod. In 1674, Church surveyed land for a farm along the present border of Rhode Island and Massachusetts. But the warlike actions of Metacomet forced him to delay his building. Church decided to deal with Philip first.

Church successfully persuaded numerous members of the Pequot tribe to join him as scouts and advisors, and studied Indian tactics to fight his foe. One contemporary historian noted that Pequots from Mushantuxet "performed prodigies of valor" under Church's leadership. Among Church's first acts was to employ his Pequot scouts to locate and kidnap Metacomet's wife and nine-year-old son. They were eventually sent to the West Indies to work as slaves in the brutal sugar fields. After a wide-ranging and bloody two-year battle, Church finally cornered Philip in a swamp near the site of modern Mount Hope, Rhode Island. The date was August 12, 1676. "I have so placed my men," Church declared, "that it is scarce possible Philip should escape them."

Church sent some of his Pequot scouts to slip into Philip's camp with the purpose of scaring him out. They succeeded, and moments later a bullet whistled into the swamp. The first shot at King Philip himself was fired by one of Church's Pequot scouts. As described in *The History of the Great Indian War of 1675 and 1676,* by the commander's son Thomas Church, Philip "threw his petunk and powder horn over his head, catched up his gun and ran as fast as he could scamper without any more clothes than his small breeches and stockings; and ran directly into Captain Church's ambush."

Philip was hit first in the heart. Then another musket ball landed two inches beneath it. Philip fell on his face in the mud and water with his gun underneath him. The English then demonstrated the superiority of European "civilization" by quartering Philip's body and hanging each quarter from a different tree.

As Thomas Church was to write about the end of the war: "Thus fell the celebrated King Philip, the implacable enemy of civilization. Never perhaps did the fall of any prince or warrior afford so much space for solid reflection. Had the resources of this hero been equal to those of his enemies, what would have been their fate?" The significance of this event did not escape even those who lived through it, nor the historians who would analyze it later. Benjamin Church himself wrote: "Before the fall of Philip, the Indians for some time had been losing ground and were considered as nearly subdued but this event clearly decided their fate, doubts were no longer entertained of their appearing formidable." In retrospect, there is little debate among historians that the campaign of 1676 virtually eliminated the Native American Indian culture in Massachusetts, Connecticut, and Rhode Island. Many of those Narragansetts and Wampanoags who survived ventured north by foot, joining tribes in more remote areas like Maine, Vermont, New Hampshire, and Quebec. With the power of the colonialists now supreme and unquestioned, King Philip's War would mark the last military battle involving the Pequots. Their age as warriors was over.

2

THE RISE AND FALL OF MASHANTUCKET

IF KING PHILIP'S WAR of 1675 marked the watershed event in the history of the New England Indians, it also marked a turning point in the Pequots' relationship with their English conquerors. From this point on, the main tribe that had organized in North Groton under its lead sachem, Robin Cassacinamon, would be friendly wards of the government, with the overseers of their reservation appointed by the Connecticut General Assembly. In 1692, Cassacinamon's son Daniel, along with a sachem named Mamoho, took over the leadership of the western tribe. But two years later, Daniel died and an English court in New London picked the tribe's new chief, Scattup. Also known as Scadoab, he was not universally followed by all the Pequots. Smaller bands broke off under other rulers. Robin Cassacinamon, the son of Daniel, had his own small following, and he and Scattup repeatedly clashed over who was the authentic leader of the whole tribe. Cassacinamon, who was prone to violent extremes and had a bad drinking problem, considered Scattup to be too compliant with colonial authorities.

Because the reservation land was so desolate, the Pequots continued to venture south toward the familiar coast to make their livelihood along the shores of Long Island Sound, much to the continued annoyance of the settlers now filling up the new coastal towns of Mystic, Groton, and New London. In 1712, the English residents of Noank declared that the Pequots had no right to the shelling and crabbing lands on their peninsula. Robin Cassacinamon complained to colonial authorities that the Groton and Noank residents were attempting to displace his tribesmen from their ancestral lands. Samuel Sewall, an agent of the colonial government, sent a message to the governor of Connecticut asking him to look into the complaints of the Pequots and "not suffer wrongs to be done to a people who for more than 70 years have been submissive to the English and dependent on their protection." The sympathetic agent recognized that depriving the Pequots of Noank was contrary to promises that had been made to protect their fishing and shelling rights. He added that the Connecticut General Assembly should not only protect the Pequot property but expand upon it. "Though the natives are at present so thinned as to become like two or three berries in the top of an uppermost bough, yet God will hasten their reformation and increase," he asserted in a letter to the colonial governor.

In October 1714, a committee was appointed by the General Assembly to examine the Pequots' complaints. In the meantime, it was forbidden for colonists to prevent them from fishing, hunting, or planting on the disputed lands. This investigation ultimately concluded, however, that the Pequots had plenty of land to live on in the area that was now spelled "Mashantucket." Though they couldn't reside on the highly prized coastline, they were given permission to hunt and fish at Noank.

By 1731, nearly a century after the historic massacre, the Pequots numbered some 131 persons, of which about 66 were male. Nineteen residents of the tribe lived in Groton and New London with English families, while most of the rest lived in thirteen large wigwams on the reservation. According to colonial authorities, only 14 acres out of the 1,732 that comprised the reservation were suitable for planting, though apple trees were scattered about the reservation. As colonists continued to buy grazing land and the better planting land on the edges of the reservation, cattle and horses belonging to white settlers began to run loose over the land. The colonial overseers of Mashantucket, James Avery and John Morgan, were ordered by the General Assembly to prosecute all "trespassers and encroachers."

Complaints continued from the Pequots that their trees were being cut down and their corn destroyed. The Pequots couldn't raise pigs and cows because the English had taken all the good grassland. Encroachment from settlers had cut the reservation to just 1,037 acres by 1730 and the rest was divided up into 50-acre tracts and leased to prominent colonial families in the town. The colonists apparently felt no guilt about violating past promises and seizing arable reservation land from the Pequots. As a committee of three colonial overseers observed on October 12, 1732, "We are of the opinion that one half of the said lands is fully sufficient for the Indians to dwell, plant, and cut firewood."

Starting with a missionary movement that picked up steam in 1733, conversion of the Pequots to Christianity became an increasingly important goal of the colonists. The turning point for the tribe came on June 28, 1741, when the four surviving children of "the heathen Robin Cassacinamon," who had been executed in 1722 after drunkenly killing a woman with scalding succotash, were baptized and converted to Christianity. In 1743, a massive revival was held during which 70 Pequots sat in a circle with missionaries sent by a London gospel society and accepted Christianity as their faith.

By 1776, the year of the American Revolution, a count of Indians on the reservation totaled 151, of whom about half were under sixteen years old. Virtually all the healthy older men had shipped off with the colonial armies to fight the British in Canada or had gone to sea. Nine Pequots are recorded as having given their lives for American independence in the early battles of the Revolutionary War at Concord and Lexington, and Pequot service lasted until the last battles of the war. Several months before the British finally surrendered at Yorktown, a British fleet of thirty-two ships landed at nearby New London with orders to destroy all stores, privateers, and forts. The British commander was Benedict Arnold, who had grown up in nearby Norwich. In a vicious battle of brutal hand-to-hand combat, the British forces overwhelmed patriot cannons under Lieutenant Colonel William Ledyard, who was killed in the battle. Among the heroes of Fort Groton was a young Pequot soldier named Tom Wansuc, whose name and race is commemorated on a permanent plaque at the site. Following the end of the war, the name of the town in which the reservation resided was changed from North Groton to Ledyard.

The Western Mashantucket Reservation would from that time on be known as the Ledyard reservation, while the Eastern Reservation at Lantern Hill would be associated with the neighboring town of North Stonington. The two reservations were only a few miles apart and residents frequently moved back and forth between them.

In the years following the Revolutionary War, the condition of those who lived on the Ledyard and North Stonington reservations grew increasingly dismal. State records note that the descendants of the Pequots lived in "poverty, misery and degradation." Many of the descendants of the original New England tribes went to sea, taking jobs in the New England whaling and fishing industries. With no men around, the women and children who remained were consigned to menial jobs or basket-making and earned little income. Many of them intermarried with runaway slaves, who had found this remote corner of New England to be a good hiding place.

Unlike the American Indian tribes of the West, the Pequots had no relationship with the federal government and were wholly dependent on a state government that seemed to grow more and more oblivious to their existence as the years went on. State dependence was a result of the fact that the Mashantucket Reservation, like most eastern reservations, had been established before the creation of the federal government. As pioneers moved across the Great Plains, treaties were being made with numerous large tribes that inhabited the great western lands of the United States, and it was these tribes, with leaders like Red Cloud, Sitting Bull, Crazy Horse, and Geronimo, that captured national interest and consumed the public imagination. No one gave a thought to the existence of the Pequots. As far as the public was concerned, they were indeed, as Melville was justified in observing, quite "extinct" as Indians.

Starting with the end of the Revolutionary War and continuing into the nineteenth century, the tribe members through necessity became integrated into Connecticut's black society. Southeastern Connecticut had been the largest slaveholding section of New England, and it seemed inevitable that freed slaves and the surviving Indians, both Pequots and the neighboring Narragansetts, would intermingle. White New England society did not accept intermarriage with either Indians or blacks, and the supply of available Indian men was constantly being undermined by wars and the disappearance of men to a long life at sea, from which many never returned. When Native American women moved into the cities to work, notably Boston, Worcester, Providence, or New Bedford, they moved into black neighborhoods. They were not welcome in white society and many simple services such as haircuts or lunch-counter service would not be provided to Indians by white merchants.

In the mid nineteenth century, Ledyard town officials took a dim view of society at the Mashantucket Reservation. One overseer observed with disapproval that there was no such thing as marriage on the reservation. "The two sexes cohabited without ceremony or covenant, deserting each other at pleasure." He noted that frequently children born on the reservation were handed over to be raised by English families. By 1820, the reservation Pequots had dwindled to just 50 people. A census twelve years later reduced that number to 40, many of whom worked as servants and sometimes slaves in white households. Historian John W. De Forest observed in 1852 that "one hundred and sixty years of contact with a Christian race had not brightened the condition of the Pequots morally or intellectually, and physically had darkened it." Shortly before he finished writing his landmark work on the Connecticut Indians, De Forest received a letter from a tribal overseer, updating him on their condition. According to the letter, the band by 1852 numbered just 28, of whom 20 still lived on the reservation at Ledyard. De Forest wrote, "Those who remain in Ledyard show no disposition to attend on schooling or preaching and some are particularly given in their conversation to scolding and vulgarity. They work not above one or two days at a time, either laboring for some neighboring farmer or making baskets for sale at home. Having thus obtained a little money, they drink and idle about until it is all gone, when they set to work as in the same fashion as before."

One of those basket-makers was a tribe member named Ann Wampey. As one local resident recollected, "one Ann Wampey used to make an annual trip in the early spring past my home up through Preston City, Griswold and Jewett City selling the baskets she had made the previous winter. When she started from her home she carried upon her shoulders a bundle of baskets so large as almost to hide her from view. And after traveling a dozen or twenty miles her load would be gone. Then she would start on her homeward journey and, sad to relate, before she had reached her home a large part of what she had received for her baskets would have been expended on strong drink."

Wrote De Forest, "Some or other of [the tribe's] members are continually on the stroll around Ledyard and the neighboring townships. They are extremely hospitable to all vagabonds receiving without hesitation all that come to them whether white, mulatto, Indian or Negro." Concluded De Forest, "Such is the present situation and character of the Mushantuxet band of the once free, warlike and high-spirited tribe of the Pequots. Thus too, for the time does the sad history of this unfortunate people come to a close. Nothing is left but a little and miserable remnant, hanging around the seats where their ancestors once reigned supreme, as a few half withered leaves may sometimes be seen clinging to the upper branches of a blighted and dying tree."

With so few Pequots around, and their financial situation so destitute, the State of Connecticut in 1855 decided once again to prune the acreage of the Mashantucket Reservation. Three years after the publication of De Forest's history in 1852, Connecticut authorized the auctioning off of 800 acres of the reservation. Even the $10-per-acre price was considered high by those familiar with the miserable terrain. Still, the sale raised $8,000 for the tribe's state-administered trust account, which was put into the reservation fund to provide basic necessities for the surviving reservation residents. With the reservation nearly abandoned, for all practical purposes, the 1855 sale seemed insignificant at the time. Although a strong argument could be made that the reservation land was not Connecticut's to sell, the land that was auctioned off wasn't particularly productive and the state's motives were hardly malevolent. To the state-appointed overseers, it seemed that the money raised from the sale might help a people who were struggling along making baskets and harvesting berries.

Little did anyone realize that this sale, 120 years later, would become the most monumental event in Pequot history.

•

EVEN AS DE FOREST wrote his bleak descriptions of reservation life, there was a pair of young Pequot brothers, both identified by birth records as black, who followed the seafaring tradition of the New England Native Americans and joined the Navy. The older brother was named Austin George and the younger, Amos George. Their grandparents had been direct descendants of the Pequot sachem Scattup, Cassacinamon's rival, who had died in 1740. Austin George had signed on during the Civil War with a unit called the Connecticut Colored Volunteers and was among those standing outside the steps of the McLean House in Appomattox, Virginia, when Lee surrendered the Army of Northern Virginia to General Grant. Austin then returned to Mashantucket to help raise his son, Cyrus George, who rose to manhood living around and sometimes on the reservation. After Austin's death, he was buried in the Mashantucket burial ground. On November 2, 1879, Cyrus married a seventeen-year-old girl named Martha Hoxie. The official county record listed both as "colored," although Martha Hoxie was half-white. Together they would have seven children from 1879 to 1896, including a daughter named Elizabeth George.

The place where Martha Hoxie and Cyrus George lived had long ago ceased to be anything akin to a functioning reservation. It was a home only for the most desperate and impoverished. Virtually anyone who could escape the cold wooden houses and barren terrain had already fled to a better place. A contemporary North Stonington historian, Richard Wheeler, claimed, "The Pequot reservations at Ledyard and North Stonington do not at the present time contain a single wigwam house nor a resident of any Pequot descendent. . . ." This observation was probably inaccurate, since Cyrus George and his children did claim a remote genetic thread to the Pequot past. After Cyrus was murdered on October 1, 1898, Martha Hoxie began living with a Canadian lumberman named Napoleon Langevin. They had a daughter, Martha Langevin, in 1901, and two years later they were married. But by 1910, none of those children from her first marriage were living on the reservation, and the population had dwindled to a mere 13, divided among just three families, the Langevins and two other elderly couples, neither of which was Pequot.

In 1936, a Connecticut state official, John Williams, paid a visit to the two reservations. By then, state land sales had whittled them down to just 179 acres of the original 2,000. He noted that the nine resident "Indians" had $4,701 in their bank account and that one of the daughters of Martha Hoxie, Elizabeth George Plouffe, and the daughter from the second marriage, Martha Langevin, were the only two adults left on the reservation.

Williams described his visit to the Ledyard reservation:

Way back from the road, miserable land, rocky scrubby, high and dry.

Knocked on door, Mrs. Plouffe almost chased me off at first, very irate, shouted about being sick and tired of talking to people from the state. Had to resort to a little flattery—mentioned that I understood she was the head of this tribe. She cooled down a bit, said yes (still trying to appear angry). She could trace her ancestry back six generations on her mother's side, she said.

Finally let me in. Mrs. Plouffe is a handsome, well-built woman of about 40. No Negro blood. Exceedingly high cheek bones, large slightly slanting eyes, long slightly curved nose. Husband a French Canadian. She has two children by him and two by a former husband. The two Plouffe girls (Theresa and Loretta) are brown, have Indian faces, and color. Mrs. Plouffe almost looks Indian too.

Mrs. Plouffe has many grievances. First against all other whites who have gypped their people from time immemorial. Then against the state and overseers who made them live in such a rotten house and on such rotten ground. Then against the "niggers" at Lantern Hill. Claims that none of them belong there—squatters, etc. Envies them the comparatively good land they have. Wishes the state would run them out.

Husband and children came from huckleberrying. Plouffe, the Canuk, also would like to get away from this reservation. Asked me to find out how they could exchange this land and house for a good farm somewhere. Kids don't want to go though. House is over 200 years old and has been covered with tar shingles. Inside is about worn out though. Floors sag, no wall finishing over laths on which to plaster properly.

By the time World War II rolled around, Plouffe had gotten his wish and moved from the reservation, leaving only Elizabeth and Martha behind. Until her death on June 6, 1973, Elizabeth George Plouffe remained an active leader of what had become a two-woman tribe.

In 1949, Elizabeth's sister Flora, who was married and lived in Mystic, wrote a letter to Connecticut governor Chester Bowles asking if she could build a house on the reservation with another sister, Mabel George Colebutt. The letter highlighted the deplorable conditions at the Ledyard reservation and raised the question of whether squatters were taking the better land on the Lantern Hill reservation that she and her sisters should be entitled to. Wrote Flora:

> I am representing the Pequot Indians of Ledyard which we are the last remaining ones. I wanted to talk to you about Lantern Hill which is called the Eastern Reservation. It was bought for the Pequots in 1683 for old chief Manohoe whom we descended from. There was a large tribe at that time who couldn't get along together so a small group was given the "Western Reservation" in Ledyard where our family was born and raised.
>
> On this Lantern Hill reservation there is not one living there of Pequot Blood but who claim to be Pequots. All of them are of Negro blood and are squatters. The old Pequots who lived there are now dead but these people are getting the benefits from the reservation that should be for the Pequots.
>
> The Lantern Hill reservation has a good road, a nice lake, phone and lights and can get in and out and a living could be made there. What I want to know is why we Pequots can't go there and claim our land. It was our land in the beginning. Not one there can prove they are of Pequot blood. More and more are going there every year and taking land. There isn't much land left. Why couldn't we have the land sold at Ledyard Reservation? And the few left go to Lantern Hill. At Ledyard there is no decent

road, mountains, rocks and scrub oaks. In the wintertime you can't get in or out. No doctor will go there during the winter. One can't make a living there.

We want to go back and live there if we could have our land at Lantern Hill where we could be comfortable and make a living.

Unfortunately, the state did little to help the residents of Ledyard and they continued to live in poverty. It would be several years before a savior arrived who would finally change life for the Pequots for the better.

BORN ON THE DAY after Thanksgiving in 1947, Richard "Skip" Hayward was one of nine children of Theresa Plouffe Hayward, Elizabeth George Plouffe's oldest daughter from her second marriage. Theresa Plouffe had married a local Navy man named Richard Hayward, Sr., and together they had nine children, Skip being the third, and the oldest boy. For many of the years that Richard Sr. was in the Navy, the family lived at Quonset Point, Rhode Island. Frequently, Theresa would bring the young children to visit their grandmother at the reservation. Skip remembered the austere conditions, the cold floors, the wind-ripped walls, and especially the lack of hot running water or electricity. His grandmother's house had been built in 1856 and looked it.

Richard Sr.'s dream was for Skip to get an appointment to attend the U.S. Naval Academy, and as a naval officer, he hoped that he could work out getting the appointment through his congressman in Rhode Island. But at the last minute, Skip decided that entering the Navy would make a tour in Vietnam almost inevitable. After graduating from high school in North Kingston, Rhode Island, he rebelled and chose instead to stay near home and go directly to work for $229 a week as a pipe fitter and welder at submarine manufacturer Electric Boat in Groton. As an employee of a key defense contractor, Skip was able to get reclassified as 2B, which kept him exempt from military service. It was closer for him to spend nights and weekends at Ledyard than drive all the way back to Rhode Island, and he began spending much more time with his grandmother, Elizabeth George. All her grandchildren grew up outside the reservation. But only Skip continued to pay frequent visits to his grand-mother's home, even though he would complain that the floors were so cold, his feet would stick to them. Of all of the grandchildren, Skip was the one who seemed most rapt by stories she would tell about the old days of living on the reservation, hunting snakes and picking berries. He marveled at the way his grandmother hated things bought in stores and how she lived from the land, got her water from a well, and cooked on a woodstove.

Before Elizabeth George died at the reservation on June 6, 1973, Skip came to the house to say his final goodbyes. On his mother's side, Skip was about one-sixteenth Indian, at most. On his father's side, he was as American as pumpkin pie. Skip Hayward could actually do a better job tracing his New England ancestry back to the *Mayflower*—whose passenger manifest had included several Haywards—than he could do proving that he somehow descended from the Pequots, though there definitely was a link. When Flora George Stenhouse died, at a time when there was absolutely no advantage to mentioning it, her surviving husband supplied the obituary writer with the fact that she, like her sisters, was a direct descendant of Chief Scattup.

Elizabeth had an uncanny sense that Skip somehow represented the Pequot line's last hope for survival. Officials of the Connecticut Department of Parks and Recreation had already gotten approval from the governor that when the last Pequot was dead, the Ledyard reservation would be considered defunct and turned into a state park. Skip knew how much this would hurt his grandmother, who was so fanatically antistate that she had once killed a dog rather than put a state dog tag on it. "By 1972, they were waiting like turkey vultures for my grandmother to die," Skip would later recall. "They were waiting for her to die so the state could assume the last remnant of our whittled down tribal land and turn it into a park. There was a law that said the state could do this." He added bitterly, "They always had handy laws like that."

Hayward was skeptical of his ability to save the reservation. He had been brought up to be a seaman, not an Indian chief. "Nanny, there is no way I can do it," Hayward told his grandmother sorrowfully one afternoon.

When Hayward had taken the job at Groton's Electric Boat after high school graduation, his dreams of a good living were tied for a time to federal support of the controversial Sea Wolf submarine project, one of many new weapons systems that Congress had authorized. The submarine was to have been built at Electric Boat. But cutbacks in federal contracts made it difficult to get many hours at the plant. He took a second job at the Connecticut Yankee Power Company, working as many hours as he could fixing power lines. When boat industry layoffs came in 1975, after the end of the Vietnam War, Hayward briefly opened a clam shack in Mystic, but it did not get many customers in a town that was reeling with unemployment, and it quickly closed. The post-Vietnam-era defense cutbacks were taking a terrible economic toll on the entire region. Skip felt he had become just another statistic, just another depressed unemployed boat worker in what was formerly one of the wealthiest states in the union. His optimism about his future had all but disappeared.

Connecticut had been a hotbed of technology and innovation for two centuries as the home of manufacturing geniuses like Samuel Colt and Eli Whitney. After World War II, it had been a defense industry hub and a low-tax haven for high-income commuters from New York. As its neighbors imposed state income taxes, Connecticut's legislature, dominated by politicians like the colorful conservative J. Henry Roraback of Litchfield County, rejected the measure as a matter of faith and policy. Fugitive New Yorkers moved their homes and their millions into Connecticut to avoid state taxes, and Connecticut towns adjacent to New York had the highest per capita income in the nation. But that was hardly the case in southeastern Connecticut, where the economy verged on collapse by early 1974. President Richard Nixon had destroyed his presidency in the dual minefields of Vietnam and Watergate. In the twenty years that followed, defense appropriations would be cut over and over again. Southeastern Connecticut, with its heavy reliance on General Dynamics, United Technologies, and Electric Boat, would suffer in a way that it hadn't since the onset of World War II. Skip had no assurances that his job would be around tomorrow or the day after that. For his two brothers, Rodney and Robert, the situation was just as bleak.

The 200 acres of the reservation wasn't much, but it was property tax–free. It was also the only substantial property his family had, swamp and all, even if they didn't technically own it. After Elizabeth's death, on a Sunday afternoon in mid-1973, Skip and his younger brothers, Rodney and Robert, talked about the future of the tribe with their ninety-one-year-old uncle, Amos George of Simsbury, Connecticut. They were joined by his great aunt, Alice Langevin, and her grandson Bruce Kirchner, Skip's cousin. Bruce, who was a year younger than Skip, had been working at a state mental hospital just south of Norwich. Perhaps as an indication of just how far this family was from a "tribe," Bruce and Skip had never even met before being introduced that day by Alice.

But on that day in August, Bruce was moved by Skip's passion about keeping the reservation in the family. Skip, in many respects, was what people in those days would have referred to as a hippie. Kirchner felt that Hayward was something of a dreamer, but he was at least willing to hear his cousin out.

In Skip's opinion, the family had no choice but to move onto the reservation grounds and maintain a presence. This was the only way the Haywards could keep their family "farm" and prevent the state of Connecticut Department of Parks and Recreation from declaring the tribe "extinct" and the reservation "abandoned." Skip's arguments were convincing, and the family agreed to put the plan into action. Elizabeth's older brother, Amos, was elected their chief. To establish financial self-reliance, Skip wanted to open a hydroponic greenhouse and a logging business on the reservation as well as a small store that would sell Indian artifacts on Route 2. The store would be near a restaurant he hoped to buy, a roadside shack where one of his sisters had worked as a waitress, called Mr. Pizza. But to do all this, Skip would need some help. He and Bruce counted up fifty-five cousins and siblings that might be willing to participate. Amos gave each of them a homemade document certifying them as one-sixteenth Pequot. He signed it as "tribal chairman."

Two years later, Amos George gladly passed the title of tribal chairman to Skip. In one of his first acts as tribal chairman, Skip decided to allot each one of his cousins two acres of reservation land, and he applied for a Housing and Urban Development grant that would provide house trailers for them to live in. After the mobile homes arrived, his eight siblings and forty cousins began filtering onto the reservation. The rebirth of the Pequot tribe had begun. This renaissance was hardly a democratic process, and no attempt was made to locate Pequot descendants outside of Hayward's extended family. This new version of the Pequot tribe would at first consist solely of the descendants of Martha Hoxie George Langevin, descendants of those listed on the official U.S. census forms from either 1900 or 1910. Although there were smaller tribes in the United States, like the six-member Me-Wuk tribe of the Chicken Ranch Rancheria in California, the resurrected Pequots would clearly be one of the most exclusive.

Though a debate would later arise about who was or wasn't qualified to be a member of the tribe, or if the reborn Pequots were even a tribe at all, this issue was of little concern at the revitalized reservation in its early days. The counties around Ledyard were loaded with people who could claim to be of Indian descent, many of them with as much Indian blood as Skip, or more. But outside of the descendants of Elizabeth George, none of these people cared to claim their Pequot heritage. It was the last thing in the world people like Joan Simonds, a Ledyard resident of indisputable Pequot ancestry wanted to do. Her whole family history had been one of trying to disassociate itself from its Indian heritage. Like many families of Indian background, the Simondses, who descended directly from Robin Cassacinamon—the bitter rival of the George's ancestor Scattup—had become 100 percent Americanized, and proud of it. In 1953, Congress had ushered in a period of so-called termination, in which the stated goal of the United States was "to end the Indians' status as wards of the United States and to grant them all the rights and prerogatives pertaining to American citizenship." The Simondses were proud products of the termination policy. There was nothing about the reservation that appealed to them, especially since many of these families had achieved a degree of financial security and they had absolutely no desire to give up their homes and move to a trailer on a reservation. But for the down-on-their-luck descendants of Elizabeth George and her sisters and brothers, the story was different.

Moving to the reservation for Skip, his brothers and sisters, and his newfound cousins was a calculated gamble, but they weren't risking all that much. The decade of the 1970s was a time of increasing sympathy for Indian causes, largely because of increased militancy and the development of the American Indian Movement, which was successfully bringing the issues of Indian poverty into the public consciousness. With a Democratic president, Jimmy Carter, and a liberal congress working together in 1976, possibilities abounded for new antipoverty grants from the Bureau of Indian Affairs and the federal Department of Housing and Urban Development. In 1976, the Pequots' only revenue came from the sale of wood, crafts, and maple syrup and a $127 federal revenue-sharing check. But Skip was full of ideas. First, he wanted to try to clear away all the rock, stumps, and worthless trees from the reservation to make room for planting. He also envisioned selling firewood and establishing a swine farm where hogs could be raised. He sketched out a plan for a greenhouse where he could begin commercial production of lettuce, which he planned to sell to fancy restaurants for tourists in Mystic and Stonington Village.

In addition to all of this, though the clam shack in Mystic had not worked out, Skip still dreamed that one day he and his brothers would own the pizza restaurant on lightly traveled Route 2. Mr. Pizza, Skip believed, would be the steady financial engine that would sustain his family and allow them to keep the 214-acre reservation. Skip's goal for a long time was simply to hold on to the reservation and somehow find a way to make it self-sufficient—no more than that. But this was before he met an intensely energetic lawyer from Missouri by the name of Tom Tureen.

II

BATTLING THE ODDS

Tom Tureen

3

TOM TERRIFIC

IN THE EARLY 1960S, a frenetic teenager from Missouri was working in one of his father's four St. Louis hotels. One of them was the Fairgrounds Hotel, frequently favored by tourists from as far away as
Greenville, Mississippi, who would make the 400-mile drive north to
see their beloved Cardinals play baseball. The Fairgrounds was located
close enough to the ballpark to attract a mix of economically minded
baseball fans, along with the usual degenerate types sometimes found in
aging urban hotels.

One hot summer day, while St. Louis Cardinal legends like Stan "The
Man" Musial and prematurely bald shortstop Dick Groat were showing
their talents at old Busch Stadium in North St. Louis, Tom Tureen was
spending the afternoon delivering ice to his father's customers at one
of his hotels, running up and down the stairs with the remarkable energy
and enthusiasm that characterized the way he approached life. When
he knocked on the door of one room, he was greeted by a woman whom
he quickly realized with wide eyes "was wearing nothing but nature's
equipment."

"Oh," she said, "I was expecting the other bellman."

Though his parents had made a good-sized fortune through their
midwestern real estate investments, as well as through businesses that included drugstores, hotels, and restaurants, Tom decided he wasn't interested in the family business.

After he graduated from a St. Louis high school in 1962, Tom enrolled at Princeton. Between his sophomore and junior years, instead of

going home to work in the family hotels during the summer, he found a job as a physical education instructor at a government-run Indian high school in Pierre, South Dakota. It was a life-defining experience for a young man who had spent all of his life in upper-class suburbs.

Tom was appalled by what he witnessed in Pierre, not just by the poverty that gripped the Lakota Sioux, but also the extent to which the federal government had control over their lives. "I was fascinated out there, and I wanted to do something useful," he later told *American Lawyer* magazine. Tureen was particularly offended by the draconian rules and regulations inflicted upon Lakota Sioux teenagers and the cavalier manner with which Bureau of Indian Affairs employees denigrated Native American families. Students who wanted to go home and stay with their parents during the summer were frequently denied that "privilege" by the school's principal because of what BIA policy-makers considered "adverse family situations." Hearkening back to the federal policy of "termination," the concept that over time Native American identity should fade into history as individual Indians became Americanized, the Lakota boys were not allowed to speak their native language. If they were overheard by teachers or school authorities, they were put on detention or school work details. As an instructor, Tureen was supposed to report any conversations he overheard that were not in English, something he couldn't bring himself to do.

But many of Tureen's fellow instructors at the school had no such objections. One physical education instructor even went so far as to carry a club to ensure that the dictatorial rules were followed. As the one sympathetic member of the staff, it was Tom to whom the Lakota boys would complain when they received what they called "cracks." The beatings kept reminding Tureen of the terrible abuse of power by police in Alabama, Mississippi, and other areas in the Deep South and of the television footage of young black children being hosed and bludgeoned by Alabama state troopers. There was something about the sight of those clubs that radicalized him. He occasionally went to bed at night feeling physically ill over the conditions.

When he graduated from Princeton in 1966, Tureen focused his energy on learning more about the interrelationship between the BIA and the Indians, a relationship that was experiencing increasing tension by the late 1960s and culminated in 1972 in a weeklong Indian takeover of the Bureau of Indian Affairs Building on Constitution Avenue in Washington. After enrolling in law school at prestigious George Washington University in the fall of 1966, Tureen began working with the Citizens' Advocate Center, founded by Edgar Cahn, which taught the kind of legal activism later made more famous by attorney Ralph Nader. Nader and Cahn believed that law practice could be used to achieve broad social reforms. At the time, this was a revolutionary concept. With Cahn's organization, Tureen was director of field research for a book that was highly critical of the Bureau of Indian Affairs, entitled *Our Brother's Keeper: The Indian in White America.*

By the spring of 1967, Tureen was thirsting to return west to start exploring ways he could use his legal training to improve the conditions he had seen during his undergraduate summers. Because his girlfriend Susan Albright was in the East, Tureen decided to take a summer job that year working as a legal aid for an attorney in Eastport, Maine, named Don Gellers. His main assignment was to help Gellers work on a land claim made by the Passamaquoddies, a relatively obscure tribe of Indians who lived in northeastern Maine. Tureen enjoyed working on the case and got along well with the Passamaquoddy leaders. In 1969, after graduating from law school, he decided to accept a year-round paying legal aid job. With Susan, who was now his wife, he moved to the northeastern Maine town of Calais to work full-time for Gellers.

Gellers's theory concerning the Passamaquoddy land claim was that over the past 150 years the tribe had lost 6,000 acres of its land in apparent violation of a 1794 treaty between the Passamaquoddies and what later became the State of Maine. Like many eastern tribes whose relationships with colonists predated American independence, the Passamaquoddies historically had official relations only with the state government, not with the federal government. The 1794 treaty had somehow persuaded the ancestors of the Passamaquoddies to give up all but 23,000 acres of their vast and beautiful woodland, to say nothing of wide-ranging fishing rights along the coast. The remnants of the Passamaquoddies lived in a town in northeastern Maine called Pleasant Point until an 1851 controversy split the tribe in half between Catholics and Protestants. The Protestant Passamaquoddy stayed at Pleasant Point; the Catholics moved about 60 miles upriver to the community that became known as Indian Township. Though life for the Passamaquoddy was relatively quiet, the Catholic residents of Indian Township constantly complained about encroachment on what they believed to be their land by the big paper and lumber companies that operated in the state.

In 1957, John Stevens, the tribal leader at Indian Township, discovered the original copy of the 1794 treaty in the home of a great-aunt who had squirreled it away in a shoe box. Stevens had never seen the document before, and the item that caught his interest was a provision that the Passamaquoddy would keep title "in perpetuity" to fifteen islands in the St. Croix River and two in Big Lake, west of the reservation. The reality was that now none of those islands was in Indian hands. And while the shoe box treaty reserved 23,000 acres for the tribe, tribal members communally now had control of only 17,000 at best. Stevens began to wonder how and when his people had lost the other 6,000 acres. It wasn't hard to see who had it, though. Most of the land described in the document was clearly being controlled by the large paper companies that dominated the economy of rural Maine. Stevens felt a sense of outrage as he perused the terms of the treaty, and the anger turned into a passionate belief that the loss of the acreage and the islands amounted to a land grab of criminal proportion.

For the last two hundred years, the State of Maine had operated the reservation in a cavalier manner, selling land and timber rights to the Great Northern Nekoosa and Boise Cascade paper companies without any consultation with the tribe members. The proceeds from the sales did go into tribal trust accounts, so these sales couldn't be fully classified as stealing. On the other hand, tribal bank accounts were held not at the reservation but at the state capital in Augusta, some two hundred miles south of the reservation lands. State-appointed overseers controlled the money, not the Passamaquoddies, and what officials spent on the Passamaquoddies was not always with consultation. The 300 or so members of the tribe were among the poorest inhabitants of Maine. Unemployment was nearly 80 percent, and virtually everyone was on some sort of state dole. The 1950s was not a period when Indians were made to feel proud of their heritage, nor an era when whites considered it politically correct to be supportive of Native Americans. Stevens could not find an established attorney who would even consider suing the state and the paper companies to regain their land.

Many of the indignities suffered by the Passamaquoddy tribe were personal. They were not welcome, for instance, in the barber shops and beauty parlors of Princeton, the nearest town. Still, compared to the one-member Pequot tribe, they at least were a real tribe with a continuous and documented history. As a marginalized part of Maine society, many Passamaquoddies feared that if they were to complain to the state, the legislature might decide to simply do away with their reservation altogether. There were plenty of people at the Bureau of Indian Affairs in the mid-1960s who opposed the concept of reservations in and of themselves. Eastern Indians, they believed, should be integrated into American society. It was a combination of the Passamaquoddies' dependency on the state coupled with their fear of "termination" that led to their lack of activism in pursuing the injustices over which they privately seethed. But eventually, that lethargy would disappear.

In February of 1964, George Stevens, John's brother, was awakened by the grating sound of a chain saw. A member of the town council, George couldn't recall that any of the tribe members had been granted a permit to cut wood on that particular morning. So he slipped on his clothes and went outside to investigate. There he found one of his Indian neighbors, who told him that he had been hired by a non-Indian named William Plaisted to clear some land for a new road and some lakefront cottages.

Though angered by this invasion, George didn't do too much about it except complain to his brother John. It was just the latest example of encroachment, and George felt helpless about how to put a stop to it. John decided to call a town meeting the next night. A crowd of about thirty gathered, mostly to vent their familiar complaints. But the latest incident added fuel to the fire, and this time a decision was made to go ahead and seek legal aid, regardless of what bad consequences a loud protest might bring. The meeting ended with a unanimous vote to seek a meeting with John Reed, then the governor of Maine.

Two weeks later, the two Stevens brothers traveled to Augusta for their appointment with Reed, but the session did not go well. After keeping the Passamaquoddy leaders waiting for nearly the entire day, Reed simply passed them off to the attorney general, who listened to their complaints but made no promise to intervene. "If you decide to go to court," he said smugly, "I wish you well." When Stevens reported this insulting treatment to his fellow Passamaquoddies the next day, they were understandably incensed. The Passamaquoddies had rarely stood up to the state overseers, but the time to do so had clearly arrived. The following morning, 75 members of the tribe blocked construction of the road that Plaisted was building. The placards and signs they carried ordered him to "cease and desist." Plaisted retorted he had won the property in a poker game and the land for the cabin was now his. He then called the state police, who arrived promptly and arrested nine of the Passamaquoddies who were blocking the road. After posting $75 bond for each of the arrested tribal members, Stevens headed straight to the legal aid office in Eastport and asked Gellers to represent them. Gellers agreed and worked out a settlement that resulted in the trespass charges against the protesters being dropped. He then persuaded the Maine district attorney in his county to agree that neither the Passamaquoddies nor Plaisted would occupy the disputed property until a court had conducted an investigation and made a ruling on who owned it. This was the first step in a long-running federal case that would eventually reverberate from the Canadian border all the way to the tiny Mashantucket Pequot Reservation some 440 miles to the south.

THE CASE OVER THE disputed piece of Passamaquoddy reservation land led Gellers to a three-year investigation into the claims of John Stevens, an inquiry that introduced him to the treaty that had so long been locked away in a shoe box.

On March 8, 1968, four years after the roadside confrontation, Gellers filed suit in Massachusetts seeking $150 million in compensation for what he, and the Maine tribe, claimed was past mismanagement of the tribal trust fund, as well as for the "theft" of the missing 6,000 acres of Passamaquoddy land. Maine did not become a state until 1820, so Gellers felt the suit had to be directed against Massachusetts, whose governor had signed the treaty in 1794. But Gellers's theory, that Maine lawmakers had violated the provisions of the treaty, would never be tested in court. Three days after the case was filed, Maine narcotics agents raided Gellers's home and arrested him for possession of marijuana. Gellers jumped bail and fled to Israel. In his absence, the Passamaquoddies' lawsuit languished without ever coming to trial in Suffolk Superior Court in Boston.

Luckily for the Passamaquoddies, this was where young Tom Tureen came into the picture. The attorney was now working for the Indian Services Unit of Pine Tree Legal Assistance, a legal services office funded by the U.S. Office of Economic Opportunity, one of the nation's best-known poverty programs of the post–Great Society era. Tureen had a lot to learn about eastern Indians. Most of the work he had done since arriving in Maine was involved with setting up organizations and Indian corporations that would enable New England Indians to start taking advantage of the same types of BIA programs available to western tribes, with which he was more familiar. Tom was more than a little surprised to learn that the Passamaquoddies had never once received any financial assistance from the Bureau of Indian Affairs prior to his arrival at Eastport. When he queried sources at the BIA in Washington, he was told that BIA money only went to tribes whose land was held in trust by the federal government. Thus, the hundreds of little state-recognized tribes located in the thirteen original colonies virtually never received BIA grants or assistance.

Tureen's research into the federal-aid question led him to a law-review article written by Francis O'Toole, a Dublin-born University of Maine law student. O'Toole had focused his attention on an act passed by Congress in the late eighteenth century entitled the Indian Nonintercourse Act of 1790. This act stipulated that no transaction involving Indian land was valid unless it was achieved by means of a federal treaty approved by Congress. Tureen was mesmerized as O'Toole brought to his attention that the Passamaquoddy Treaty with the State of Massachusetts, which Gellers had tried to claim the State of Maine had violated, wasn't negotiated until 1794—four years *after* the passage of the Nonintercourse Act. As a treaty negotiated by the newly created State of Massachusetts, the Passamaquoddy agreement had never been submitted to the new nation's Congress for a vote, as would have been required by Congress. Neither O'Toole nor Tureen could find any legal justification for the commonly held assumption by most bureaucrats that the Nonintercourse Act did not apply to tribes living in the original colonies. Tureen was ecstatic as he came to realize that the 1794 treaty itself was illegal, since it violated a more supreme federal law.

Tureen felt like he had a bombshell, and he showered lawyers at the Interior Department in Washington with letters demanding that they accept O'Toole's thesis and begin to think about paying off the Passamaquoddies for the stolen land. In letters back to him, however, officials accused Tureen of ignoring the legislative history of the Nonintercourse Act, which showed that the act's intent was to protect the claims of western Indians and had no force whatsoever with regard to New England, where the interrelationships between tribes and colonial governments predated the country itself. Many of the western tribes roamed over state boundaries and most were in territories where state governments did not even exist yet. Hence the need for the Nonintercourse Act. The history of the New England Indians, as had been the case with the Pequots, was that they were simply subject to state authority and state-appointed Indian agents or overseers.

Until Tureen put O'Toole's academic thesis into practice, nobody had ever thought to question state authority over indigenous tribes in the eastern states. In an article coauthored with O'Toole in the 1971 edition of the *Maine Law Review,* Tureen forcefully made his argument. But there was no immediate indication that anyone was paying any attention, or taking Tom seriously.

Shortly before Christmas in 1971, Tureen decided to raise the stakes. He suggested that the Passamaquoddies drop their federal law suit asking for 6,000 acres and, instead, sue for the entire territory that their ancestors once roamed, over 1,000,000 acres of woodsy, bucolic, beautiful Maine. After all, if the 1794 treaty was invalid, then they had never signed away either their ancestral lands or their fishing rights. There was no point claiming that Maine had violated the treaty by selling off the 6,000 acres. As far as Tureen was concerned, there was no treaty.

Tureen's comrades in legal services thought his theory was a stretch at the very least and whispered among themselves that Tom was either a genius or a lunatic. None of this bothered Tom, who threw his energy into convincing tribal leaders themselves that what he had once described to his wife as a "neat theory" could in fact justify the return of the entire state of Maine to the tribe. Tom worried that it would be hard to persuade the Passamaquoddies to embark on such a large case, one that threatened the very existence of the state of Maine, whose residents and legislators were not likely to go quietly into the night. When Tureen presented his idea at a meeting of the tribal council, he was met at first with a stunned silence. But then, without a word being spoken, the tribal council members stood and began applauding furiously and spontaneously. A few moments later, Tureen had his go-ahead to proceed by a unanimous vote.

Tom's argument seemed so convincing that he was approached by representatives of the neighboring Penobscots, whose ancestors in 1796 had traded 5,000,000 acres for some groceries, rifles, and ammunition. The Penobscots asked Tureen to file suit for them as well. Tureen began building a legal team. He paid a visit to Arthur Lazarus, one of the nation's leading Indian rights attorneys at the New York law firm of Fried, Frank, Harris, Shriver & Jacobson. Lazarus believed that the case would not warrant the time or money spent on litigation. When Tureen laid out his theory about the Nonintercourse Act, Lazarus just shook his head sadly. He later told his law partners that he feared Tureen's plan would do lasting damage to the Maine Indians. He worried that Tureen would stir up bad feelings and prejudices that might subject Indians to hate crimes.

Tureen was nonetheless able to enlist several enthusiastic young attorneys. One was Barry Margolin, a law student at Northeastern University in Boston. Another was David Crosby, who had been an attorney for California Indian Legal Services. He also landed the help of Stuart Ross from the Washington, D.C., firm of Hogan & Hartson. Ross signed up on a pro bono basis, meaning he would work on the case for no fee. To pay the salaries of himself, Margolin, and his staff, Tureen in the spring of 1971 got funding for the suit from the Boulder, Colorado–based Native American Rights Fund. Of one thing Tureen was certain: they wouldn't win on sympathy.

Working out of an office in the town of Calais, Tureen awoke every morning at 5 A.M. to begin meetings with landowners and tribal members. Covering such a broad expanse of Maine proved to be a difficult problem, and eventually Tureen got a pilot's license so he could fly his own plane. The chief problem now was how to convert his theory into a political reality.

THE BIGGEST LEGAL OBSTACLE in Tureen's path was the Eleventh Amendment to the United States Constitution, which prohibited private parties from suing a state in federal court. In order to sue the State of Maine for violation of the Nonintercourse Act, the young lawyer needed to find some legal precedent. He also worried about other possible technical obstacles relating to a legal doctrine called "laches," which, simply put, meant the claims were too old to be seriously considered by the court. Tureen decided that if his client had no legal standing to sue a state in federal court, he would have to force the United States itself to intervene on his behalf.

In February 1972, tribal leaders under Tureen's guidance wrote a letter to Louis Bruce, the commissioner of the Bureau of Indian Affairs, stating the grounds on which their suit would be based. They demanded that Bruce request that the United States Department of Justice initiate a lawsuit seeking the return of 1 million acres of Indian lands as well as payment of unspecified monetary damages. The letter requested that this be done before a July 18 deadline, which Congress had established for the extinguishment of all claims on the wrongful use of Indian land. Bruce, a Mohawk Indian, was sympathetic to the request and sent a memo up the chain of command at the Interior Department endorsing the idea of filing the suit. But his memo landed on the desk of

William Gershuny, associate solicitor for Indian Affairs, where the paper sat for several months. Tureen flew to Washington to spur some action, but Gershuny gave little time to the cocky, cigar-puffing, twenty-eight-year-old attorney. He needed time to study the memo, Gershuny protested, shooing Tureen out of his office. As that July 18 deadline approached, Tureen began firing off impatient telegrams to Washington. Gershuny would only say that the request was under advisement.

In mid-May, Tureen met with a number of state politicians anxious to show that they were sympathetic to the plight of the Indians. The idea that the Indians would lay claim to two-thirds of the state hadn't really registered, nor was it taken seriously. No one expected Maine to simply hand itself over to Tom Tureen and the Passamaquoddies. So officials saw little harm in trying to appear sympathetic toward Indians. After Tureen visited Maine senator Margaret Chase Smith, she agreed to write a letter to Interior Secretary Rogers C. B. Morton. Senator Smith, who was up for reelection that year, also made calls to White House staffers and Gershuny. After the takeover by supporters of the American Indian Movement of the Bureau of Indian Affairs Building the year before, and the highly publicized shooting incident and standoff with federal agents at the Pine Ridge Reservation in South Dakota, public sympathy for Indian causes was building. Smith was anxious to show liberal Maine voters that she was doing something to help the downtrodden Passamaquoddies. But Gershuny, who was a civil servant, not a politician, bluntly told Smith that it was time that Indians recognized the facts of life. There was no way they could force the U.S. government to file a suit because of yet another legal principle, the "time honored" tradition of prosecutorial discretion, which left the decision to file a suit up to the Justice Department. The Interior Department couldn't be forced to do anything, and he considered the whole notion impudent. His stubbornness was a problem. If Tureen could not find a way to force the federal government to act by July 18, the case would become moot.

It was then that Washington attorney Stuart Ross came up with an idea. He pointed out that judges have unlimited power to preserve an issue once it is properly placed before the court. If Tureen could convince the court that there was a valid dispute over the meaning of the Nonintercourse Act, the court might allow the suit to be considered as filed just to avoid the mootness question, while Tureen and Gershuny continued to argue about prosecutorial discretion. In other words, they could get the suit started before the deadline, even though the federal government might not later win the right to sue. Tureen agreed that this was a good idea, and on June 2, 1972, Tureen filed suit on behalf of the Passamaquoddies and Penobscots against Secretary Morton and the Interior Department in federal court in Portland, Maine. He asked for a preliminary order compelling the United States government to file an action for monetary damages against the State of Maine, on behalf of the tribes. Tureen asked the federal courts to award $25 billion and 12.5 million acres, which would have cut Maine down to about one-third of its size. The legal action was unprecedented in U.S. case law.

Two weeks later, Tureen, accompanied by Margolin and Ross, was standing in federal court making an actual legal argument for the first time in his life. It would hardly be the last. He asked U.S. district judge Edward T. Gignoux to order the government to file the protective order on behalf of the tribe. At the conclusion of the hearing, Gignoux ordered the government to report within a week whether it would file the suit and to explain its decision. On June 23, a U.S. government attorney named Dennis Wittman conceded that the Nonintercourse Act applied to all the states. But he said the government had decided not to file the suit because the law applied only to tribes that had been federally recognized, and the Passamaquoddies never had been. Further, he said that the government's filing suit would "rupture relations" with its easternmost state. Gignoux observed that this was an odd argument in view of the fact that Maine's congressman and two senators were supporting Tureen's position

At this point Peter Mills, the U.S. attorney for Maine leaped to his feet and said he too wanted the government to file suit. Wittman, however, continued to argue that the federal government couldn't enter a suit on behalf of the Passamaquoddies because the tribe was legally extinct. In the audience were nearly a dozen tribe members. Gignoux smiled and declared a recess. When it was over, he ordered the United States to file the suit on the Passamaquoddies' behalf, and within a week

the Justice Department had filed twin suits for $150 million, one on be-
half of the Passamaquoddies, another on behalf of the Penobscots. No
federal judge in the history of American jurisprudence had ever before
ordered the federal government to file a lawsuit. As author Paul Brodeur
wrote in a 1985 book about the case entitled *Restitution:* "What was at
stake was simply mind-boggling, for if the case should be decided in favor of the Passamaquoddy, a staggering amount of real estate would be
resolved."

As the case went forward in 1973 and 1974, there was not a
tremendous amount of public interest in the litigation. The residents of
Maine, like the congressional delegation, were largely sympathetic, but
as measured by public opinion polls, they simply could not fathom or
take seriously the possibility that the courts might order two-thirds of
the state to be given back to the tribe. Still, on January 20, 1975, Judge
Gignoux rendered his opinion that while the Passamaquoddies were not
a federally recognized tribe, the 1790 Intercourse Act had established a
trust relationship between all tribes and the federal government. On December 23, 1975, the US. Court of Appeals for the First Circuit upheld
Gignoux's ruling. The State of Maine did not appeal to the U.S.
Supreme Court, and thus on March 22, 1976, Gignoux's opinion became the controlling law in the case. Tureen's "neat theory" had become
a recognized legal principle. But he was still far from actually taking
possession of the land or having the state write a check for compensation. Within a few weeks, the Bureau of Indian Affairs did announce,
however, that the Penobscots and Passamaquoddies were eligible for $5
million in federal housing benefits. While lawyers for the Interior Department now began to consider what to do next, Tureen felt the time
was ripe to begin to talk settlement.

But willing participants with whom to negotiate were hard to find.
The new Maine governor, James Longley, felt the request was frivolous.
The Great Northern Nekoosa Corporation, the paper company that was
Maine's biggest landowner, wasn't interested. Their actions reflected
that state officials still treated the request and the suit as something of a
joke. But laughs abruptly stopped later in mid-1976 when a prominent
Boston law firm, Ropes & Gray, issued a legal opinion that state bond

issues could no longer be backed with state property as collateral. After all, if the property belonged to the Indians, how could the state use it as collateral? The state was forced the next day to withdraw a $27-million bond issue. Overnight, Maine had no credit with which to build or complete schools, bridges, and roads. Rumors began to spread that landowners would find it impossible to transfer real estate or get mortgages. All those people who had approvingly thought that Indians were finally getting some long-delayed justice suddenly began to realize that this game was serious. A growing popular panic persuaded Maine's elected officials to introduce resolutions in the House and Senate directing the federal courts to refuse to hear any claim that might be brought for return of aboriginal Maine territory. Longley issued a public statement urging Tureen to restrict his claims to monetary damage and not to try to take people's homes. Noting that the real rental value of the state of Maine was probably more like $25 billion than the $150 million being asked for in the suit, Tureen reiterated his offer to negotiate an out-of-court settlement. But Longley and Attorney General Joseph Brennan still refused, claiming the suit was without merit and amounted to little more than blackmail.

On January 11, 1977, the residents of Maine were jolted when the Interior Department, now under the control of sympathetic appointees of Democratic president Jimmy Carter, suddenly issued a recommendation that seemed to favor ejecting the 350,000 non-Indians who lived within the disputed boundaries. Also threatened were the large paper and timber companies that had set up shop on the "stolen" property. As an alternative, Governor Longley proposed that the Indians be paid off, not for what the land was worth today but for what it was worth two-hundred years ago. Under Longley's plan, the sum would be determined by an antiquated Washington, D.C., board called the Indian Claims Commission. Attorney General Brennan asked the Maine congressional delegation to introduce a bill in Congress forcing the Indians to accept a substitute. Tureen commented on this request in a newspaper interview the following day: "The attorney general would have Congress unilaterally extinguish the Indians' property rights, lock them out of the federal courts, and shunt them into the Indian Claims Commission. Apparently he feels that the state need only live within the legal system so long as it doesn't prove burdensome, and that when it does, the state can either ignore the law or retroactively change it."

The Interior Department position was crystallized by Peter Taft, head of the Land and Natural Resources Division of the Justice Department. In a memorandum to Judge Gignoux, Taft, the grandson of President William Howard Taft, said the Indians had a valid legal claim to 5 to 8 million acres of forest land in northeastern Maine and that unless a settlement was reached by June 1 he would file suit against the principal landowners in the contested area. He described the coming lawsuit as "potentially the most complex litigation ever brought in the federal courts with social and economic impacts without precedent. . . ."

As state officials went to Washington to ask Congress to void the 1790 act, Tureen became the subject of hate mail and threats, and he felt the need to begin carrying a gun. In an effort to bring public opinion back to his side, Tureen launched a public relations effort designed at educating the public about the issue. He also had to calm down overheated members of the tribe, some of whom had convinced themselves that they might actually succeed in recapturing almost the entirety of the state. Tureen constantly had to remind them that they had to remain focused. What they would get would be compensation, he kept reminding them. Three hundred and fifty thousand residents of the state were not going to be moving out of their homes.

In 1979, President Jimmy Carter announced that he was creating a special White House task force to investigate the Passamaquoddy and Penobscot claims. Carter's entry into the fray came as Longley was becoming the darling of Maine property owners for his intransigent position against Tureen and the Indians. Longley's rising poll numbers encouraged Maine's Republican congressman William Cohen to take an increasingly hard stand against negotiating with the Indians. Resolved that he needed to do something dramatic to stem the tide of public opinion, Tureen contacted Archibald Cox, the avuncular former Watergate independent counsel who had been martyred, in a professional sort of way, when President Nixon fired him in the famous Saturday Night Massacre. After his Watergate ordeal, Cox, still basking in public popularity and respect, had returned to Harvard University to teach. After discussing the issue with Tureen over the phone, Cox suggested he come down to Boston to talk with him about it in person. Amazingly, Cox said he had been following the litigation. While Tureen was at first flattered, he later realized Cox had been following the legislation because his wife owned property in the state. Still, he and his wife were sympathetic to the claims of the Passamaquoddies, and Cox agreed to help out free of charge. The news that Archibald Cox had joined the case on behalf of the Maine tribes made headline news the next day.

Furious over the PR coup Tureen had achieved by luring Cox to his side, Longley held a press conference and accused Tureen of trying to "use the media" to force a settlement in the case. Longley then retaliated by hiring the nation's most famous private attorney, Edward Bennett Williams, to fight Tureen. Williams, name partner in the legendary firm of Williams & Connolly, had come to fame as the attorney for corrupt Teamsters Union chief Jimmy Hoffa and had represented a long string of famous clients in the most complicated litigation possible. In the next few weeks, settlement conferences were held at the White House between Tureen, Stuart Ross, Williams, Attorney General Brennan, and William Gunter, a special counsel appointed to the case by President Carter. Brennan presented "new evidence" that he said now disproved Tureen's theory that the Nonintercourse Act applied to eastern Indians.

Brennan's approach didn't really interest William Gunter, a no-nonsense former judge from Carter's home state of Georgia. He was uninterested in the technicalities of the issue, just wanting to settle the case and to find out how much it would cost to do so. Cox and Tureen suggested that the Passamaquoddy tribe be awarded 8 million acres. Gunter was startled by the demand, and on July 15, Gunter sent President Carter a four-page memorandum outlining his own solution to the controversy, which included a federal payment of $25 million to the two tribes. In addition, he suggested that the State of Maine come up with 100,000 acres to give to the Indians. He told President Carter that if the Indians did not accept the offer, then the U.S. government should "extinguish" the Passamaquoddies' claims.

Tureen felt that it was a good starting point for negotiations. One hundred thousand acres was more than any other Indian tribe had ever won in a land claim action, and $25 million was far more than had ever been awarded in a proceeding of the Indian Claims Commission. As for the claims being "extinguished," Tureen doubted Carter would ever adopt such a tough stand, which Tureen declared was a "tactic of the frontier days."

As Tureen had correctly guessed, President Carter himself showed little interest in threatening the Maine Indians. Instead, in 1978 he appointed a new task force to sit down and negotiate a figure.

Eight meetings, boycotted by all representatives from Maine, were held in the West Wing of the White House and the adjoining Old Executive Office Building. Tureen argued that 100,000 acres was simply not enough compensation and asked for 500,000 acres. President Carter's negotiators countered with an offer of 250,000, and the two parties eventually compromised at 300,000, the land to be purchased by the federal government from Maine's paper and timber company holdings. In return, the tribes agreed to drop all land claims against small homeowners and landholders, who were defined as anyone owning 50,000 acres or less. But what still remained in dispute was 350,000 acres of former Passamaquoddy land now owned by the State of Maine itself and another 3 million acres held by large timber and paper companies including Boise Cascade, Georgia Pacific, and Great Northern Nekoosa. Tureen agreed to dismiss his claims against the large paper companies in return for 300,000 acres of timberland. The claims for Maine-owned land would be dropped in exchange for an annual payment of $1.7 million a year for the next fifteen years.

Public reaction in Maine ranged from expressions of outrage to calls for violence. A legislator in the state capitol declared "somebody should get a gun and shoot these bastards." Longley called the settlement proposal the "second dealing of a stacked deck." The paper companies were joined by unions in opposing the settlement as potentially disruptive to the state's economy. The state's congressmen were divided. William Cohen, now running for the U.S. Senate against Democratic incumbent Bill Hathaway, said it was intended to pit small landowners, whom Tureen was letting out of the case, against the unpopular large landowners like the paper companies. While the elephants roared, Tureen urged the Indians to keep a low profile. It wasn't easy. Passamaquoddy and Penobscot children were harassed at school and called names. At sporting goods stores, there was a run on guns, and Tureen himself continued to be the subject of frequent death threats.

In early 1978, Cohen called for a Supreme Court ruling on Tureen's Nonintercourse Act claim. Tureen warned this might be a little risky. If the Supreme Court ruled in the Passamaquoddies' favor, Tureen's clients would then be totally justified in seeking return of the entire 12.5 million acres. In April of that year, Governor Longley and Attorney General Brennan suddenly declared they were ready to open negotiations with Tureen. Talks began on April 26, but conflict soon arose over the issue of whether or not the tribes should be exempt from state tax laws. Enraged by this demand, Longley insisted that the tribes were trying to establish a "nation within a nation." With the negotiations stalled, Carter's attorney general, Griffin Bell, turned up the pressure by announcing that the United States would sue the State of Maine for $300 million and 350,000 acres. But he said the state could not discriminate by suing the large landowners but not the small, as it was unfair to make a distinction between large and small landowners in claim suits. It was a distinction that would make it more difficult for Tureen to prevail. Then in the second week of September, Bell asked Judge Gignoux to grant the Justice Department a six-month delay in pressing the claim against Maine. In a letter to the judge, he explained that he still wanted time for Congress to settle the matter through legislation.

Bell's true motive was to buck up Maine's Democratic senator, William Hathaway, who was judged by voters as being too friendly toward the Indian side of the dispute. Republican Cohen was crossing the state saying that Hathaway was willing to turn Maine back to the Indians.

In an attempt to save his reelection, Hathaway announced a public understanding with Tureen in which the tribes agreed to accept $81 million with which they could buy back ancestral lands. In addition, the federal government would establish a $27.5-million trust fund, plus an additional $10 million to be used to purchase ancestral lands from the paper companies.

Hathaway's proposed settlement did him little good and Cohen was elected in a landslide. But it did provide the framework for ending the long-running dispute, which Tureen was anxious to bring to a close before Ronald Reagan took office. On October 10, 1980, Congress approved a settlement agreement between the tribes and the federal government. The Passamaquoddies and Penobscots would split an $81.5-million settlement, plus full federal recognition and benefits. It would result in each member of the tribe receiving $400 a year in an annual dividend payment. Another $900,000 was allocated to a smaller tribe of Maliseet Indians. In return, the tribes agreed to pay federal income tax, from which other tribes were exempt, and to be subject to state laws. It was the largest Indian land claim settlement in American history and it was signed by President Carter on December 12, 1980, one of his last official acts before turning the government over to President Reagan.

AFTER GIGNOUX HAD approved the theory of Tureen's case in 1975, Tureen sent his partners on a trip around the East Coast to find out what other Indian tribes might have had similar histories. It was in the course of this investigation that Tureen first became aware of the fifty-five Pequot descendants then living on the Mashantucket Reservation near Ledyard.

The Pequots were a state-recognized tribe that, like the Passamaquoddies and the Penobscots, had their tribal lands sold off by state officials after the passage of the 1790 Nonintercourse Act. Fascinated by their situation, the lawyers met with Hayward and his sister Theresa in the tiny living room of her Cape Cod–style home in North Stonington, Connecticut. Hayward was intrigued by this meeting. So far, none of the tribe's endeavors had brought much financial success, and the numbers Tureen was throwing around were impressive. Further, Skip had come to realize through his conversations with his mother that the state had taken more than Pequot land; it had taken a good chunk of Pequot history, but with no shoebox he was sure there had to be a way of questioning those land transfers, especially the sale of the 1,000-acre chunk in 1855. The lawyers from Maine were suddenly providing a concrete way to accomplish this. The conversation between Margolin and Hayward resulted in the decision to file a suit against the State of Connecticut and the thirty-five or so local landowners who had purchased what had formerly been reservation land over the years. At the core of the suit was the notion that a total of 2,000 acres had been sold off without the approval of the federal government.

It was early on a June evening in 1976 when Jackson King, a corporate lawyer in Norwich, received a frantic phone call. On the other end was a longtime friend and neighbor, Lois Tefft. Tefft, whose own family could be traced back in Connecticut to 1656, was in tears. That evening she, along with about thirty other landowners, had received a notice of *lis pendens,* a document stating that a claim was being made upon her property and suggesting that she in fact may not even be the legal owner.

King had always been aware of the existence of Indians living on the old Mashantucket Reservation in the vicinity of the Tefft farm. From interviewing Tefft, he learned for the first time of Elizabeth George Plouffe, who used to conduct annual expeditions onto neighboring properties, mostly to pick apples. She was never shy about telling her neighbors that the land on which they resided was actually Indian land. But there had been a bond between Elizabeth and Lois Tefft. Tefft had once come over to ask Elizabeth if she could ride her horse on the reservation. Plouffe was delighted. "You're the first person who has ever come and asked me for permission," Elizabeth had told her. It was the memory of those conversations that had made Lois Tefft so nervous. Elizabeth had always warned her that the Tefft property was really Indian land and now it seemed possible that her claims might be legitimate. At least that was what she told Jackson King in that first emotional phone call. King tried to settle her down, saying that he was confident that her property would be totally safe from the Pequots' claims.

That night, Tefft and her husband reviewed their land title documents at King's home, and the three spent the rest of the evening discussing the issues raised in the complaint. King's initial view was that Tureen was making a technical claim at best, and even if it had some validity a hundred years ago, the passage of time, the legal principle of laches, would surely prevent it from being asserted.

Gradually over the next few weeks, King began to realize that proper representation of the matter would require extensive legal research not only into the early history of the Indians in Connecticut but also into the early history of the Pequot tribe. The landowners barely had the resources to undertake such an extensive project, so King formed teams of volunteer researchers to go to Hartford and scour the state archives. The researchers learned that the Pequots had been massacred in the seventeenth century and ordered to disband forever. The few remnants of the tribe were, however, given a reservation in Noank about 10 miles south of Ledyard. In 1667, the colonists, recognizing the value of the Noank property, ordered that the Indians living there be relocated to Mashantucket. The original reservation at Mashantucket was about 2,000 acres. Over the years, it had been reduced through sales to a mere 200 acres. It became clear and then indisputable, even to attorney King, that there was a Pequot tribe and it had, in fact, occupied the reservation at the time of the passage of the Nonintercourse Act of 1790.

It was at this time that King learned about what had happened with the Passamaquoddy land in Maine. He first decided to create a network of defense attorneys throughout New England who would exchange memoranda, studies, and research in order to be of assistance to each other. It soon became clear to King, and to all the defense attorneys now involved in the suit, that the claims made by Tureen were not frivolous but had solid legal footing. Although King tried to get the notice of *lis pendens* thrown out on the basis of laches, the late timing of the suit, his arguments were dismissed by the federal court.

What had seemed unfathomable when King had first talked to Lois Tefft suddenly seemed possible. People who had purchased property, paid for it, improved it, and had what would appear to them or to any lawyer as a valid title were told that they could lose their property with no remedy whatsoever. Not only did the landowners have no title insurance, they basically had no suit against the real estate attorneys who had handled the purchases, as it was doubtful negligence could be alleged for failing to be aware of claims that had not been asserted for more than two centuries.

King himself was a native of New Haven, the son of an Irish railroad engineer. He had never ventured far from home, attending the University of Connecticut both as an undergraduate and for law school. After graduation, he had clerked for a judge on the Connecticut Supreme Court and was then hired by the most prominent firm in Norwich, Brown, Jacobson, Jewett & Laudone, a commercial litigation and real estate firm in a town that was economically moribund. King had done work in the past for Tom and Lois Tefft. Tom Tefft had known Skip Hayward back in the days when both had worked for Electric Boat. Lois had known Elizabeth George as well as any outsider could have. The two women had taken walks together and enjoyed long talks. Despite what they had learned from the legal documents, neither Tom nor Lois could believe that out of the blue this so-called tribe of people they had known all their lives was suddenly making a claim on their property.

King gathered together several other defendants, including the Holdridge family, who owned much of the land in question, to discuss what to do next. As they met in the conference room at Brown, Jacobson and discussed the problem of defending the suit, it quickly became apparent to all concerned that the cost of fighting Tureen would be far greater than the value of the property at issue. The land itself was among the least valuable in the state, which was precisely the reason the colonial government had given it to the Indians in the first place. Most of the people who had become the current owners of the old reservation property had acquired it at tax and foreclosure sales for an average price of $5 to $10 an acre. Except for the portion owned by Wendell Comrie, who operated a sawmill and harvested some timber on old reservation land, the property was so worthless that the owners had never even bothered to buy title insurance.

Still, the unexpected claim didn't seem right. At the meeting, King was showered with questions: "How could this happen in America?" "Where is the state government?" "Are they really going to drive me out?" But if the residents wanted to protect themselves, they would have to pay their attorney. They decided to divide the fees on a per acre basis.

King's primary legal defenses were based on time and adverse possession. Ordinarily, if you hold property for as many as fifteen years without anyone questioning your title, it is yours. But the judge who was presiding over the case promptly knocked out the time defenses, citing the precedents in the Maine cases. With all the work he had done on the Penobscot and Passamaquoddy cases, Tureen had turned virtually all the precedents to his own side. After the settlement with the federal government in 1980, Tureen was finally ready to turn his full attention to the Pequots. After several years in which the case simply hung in limbo, he finally contacted King and asked if he wanted to talk settlement. When Tureen suggested the possibility of a settlement that would place the burden of cost on the federal government, it didn't take King long to see that what had started as a potential landowner's nightmare might quickly turn into an unexpected gold strike. Under the theory that Tureen put forward, the landowners might be able to unload their virtually worthless property for up to twenty times its value. The tribe would get its land back; the federal government would pay for it all and as part of the settlement would probably pick up attorneys' fees as well, eliminating one of King's biggest stumbling blocks to working on the case.

Suddenly, King and the landowners turned from being Tureen's opponents into being his unexpected allies. This was a remarkable change of heart from an attorney who had originally been hired to fight against the Indians rather than for them. But the proposal made economic sense for all parties involved. The Indians wanted clear title to their historic reservation land. King's client-landowners were delighted to receive much more than "fair market value" for their property. King and Tureen were more than happy for the federal government to pay their legal fees. Working with the region's congressmen, as well as Senators Lowell Weicker and Chris Dodd, Tureen put together a bill that would clear the titles for the landowners who didn't want to sell, and allot $900,000 in cash for those who did.

King was amazed. Ignorant as to how to go about getting a local bill like this passed by the entire United States Senate, he merely stepped aside and let Tureen handle things. "I just took Tureen's word for it," King would later say, "that it could be done."

When King and his clients traveled to Washington to lobby for the bill that would legitimize the tribe as a federally recognized entity, Tureen gave him a list of key people to go see.

"How do you talk to these guys?" King asked.

"Fast," said Tureen. "They don't have a lot of time."

"Don't you have to have an appointment?" King asked.

"Of course not," said Tureen. "You just walk in."

The bill that was drawn up by Tureen and the Connecticut congressional delegation was to have settled—for all time—the land claims made by the Pequot tribe to their historic reservation. It would extend federal recognition to the tribe and require the Pequots to relinquish any other claims they might have to their historic hunting and shelling grounds. All lands purchased from the $900,000 settlement fund would be put into trust by the federal government for the benefit of the tribe. The sum was arrived at by Tureen and King because they felt that demanding $1 million or more for the scrubby little reservation might raise some red flags. "We were pretty much told up front," said Jackson King, "that Reagan would veto anything over one million dollars."

Hearings on the bill were held in 1982, at which time Hayward testified, "My people have never consented to the forced sales of their lands, nor has the passing of the years diminished our sense of injustice. Many times we have sought legal counsel only to be told that we could not obtain legal assistance because we could not afford the attorneys' fees. Were it not for the fact that our present tribal attorneys are representing us without charge, we could not maintain the pending federal court action.

"Since colonial times, the State of Connecticut has assumed the role of guardian of my people. We did not seek this relationship, which has so often been manipulated to our disadvantage. Although we have a legal and moral claim to the State's support in our fight to recover wrongfully alienated reservation lands, we had not sought public moneys to assist us in our battle.

"It was the desire of our predecessors that we hold and maintain the land. It is the desire of the Mashantucket Pequot people to continue to exist on its land as a tribe and be self-governing, and to maintain a good standard of living for its people," he said.

William Cohen, the same member of Congress who had fought so hard against the Passamaquoddies in his first election campaign, now sat as a member of the Senate Committee on Indian Affairs. Hayward's presentation impressed Cohen. "Sounds like you have a Harvard Law education," Cohen remarked.

At the end of the hearing, everybody was on board for the deal except for the one man with the power to stop it with the stroke of a pen. On April 5, 1983, President Ronald Reagan vetoed the bill. Reagan instinctively suspected that the recognition bill was a scam and doubted that the the Pequots were really Indians. "The government to government relationship between the West Pequot Tribe and the federal government that would be established by this bill is not warranted at this time," Reagan wrote in his veto message. He called for further investigation of the deal by the Bureau of Indian Affairs and insisted that the State of Connecticut, which after all had controlled the Pequots for three hundred years, be responsible for one-half of the settlement. Reagan's positions had been shaped by his interior secretary, James Watt, who told Reagan that in his opinion Indian reservations were examples of "failed socialism" that should be phased out of existence.

Reagan's veto caught everyone by surprise but hardly slowed the unflappable Tureen. By July, he had crafted a new bill that was basically like the original, except that it increased the portion of the settlement that would be sponsored by the State of Connecticut. Tureen also wrote into the legislation the requirement that the state build a road on reservation land, near some softball fields that had been built on it by the federal government.

In reality, however, the turning point for the legislation may have come when Tureen realized that King's law partner Vincent Laudone had grown up with Connecticut senator Lowell Weicker. Laudone called Weicker, and Weicker called Senate Minority Leader Howard Baker. Baker called Reagan and respectfully suggested that he change his position on the bill, especially if he wanted any chance of support on budget matters with the irascible maverick Republican senator Lowell Weicker. At Baker's request, Reagan pragmatically agreed to sign the legislation to keep Weicker happy. In October 1983, the bill was passed again and this time signed by President Reagan without comment.

The second bill contained everything that had been in the first bill, plus the additional commitment from the State of Connecticut to build a road on the reservation. That piece of pavement became known on the reservation as "the veto road." Hayward picked the name and believed that the road was worth the year's delay President Reagan had caused them.

With recognition now a reality, Skip Hayward awaited the check and the federal aid that would forever change life for the Pequots. His dreams for the future were suddenly within reach: a reservation with ample housing, a tribal administration building, a restaurant, a museum, a trading post, and an expanded maple sugar operation. The first thing he would do with the settlement money was buy the Mr. Pizza restaurant. But for the moment, on Thanksgiving Day 1983, he had more immediate plans: a feast of turkey, succotash, and cornbread to be served in a tent outside the house where his grandmother and Martha Langevin had lived. "This is the place," Hayward said as he raised a glass in a toast, "where the battle began."

Of course, Mashantucket wasn't really where the battle had begun. That was up in Maine where the Penobscots were already beginning to think about a different "light industry," one to which Hayward had not given much thought. The name of that business had five letters. Together they spelled B-I-N-G-O.

4

BINGO BILLIE

THE PASSAMAQUODDIES AND PENOBSCOTS had hit the jack-pot. Their amazing case had consumed fourteen years of litigation, most of it funded through the federal government's legal aid program and the rest of it through voluntary contributions from such sympathetic organizations as the Native American Rights Fund. Tureen and the legal team that had won the landmark settlement did not immediately share in the riches. Tureen and his partner Barry Margolin were not working on what is commonly known as a contingency, where the lawyer receives a portion of the legal fee, usually one-third. Instead, they had been paid by the federal government on an hourly basis. Nonetheless, Tureen figured out a way to make a profit from his victory. Within a year after the government cut the first check for the Passamaquoddies, he incorporated a company called Tribal Assets Management, signing a contract with his former clients to advise and manage their newfound money. Tureen's court victory had imbued him with an almost mythical image, at least in the eyes of the members of the Maine tribes. A decade earlier, when he had first taken over the lawsuit, it was suspected that Tureen was either a genius or crazy. Now the victory had convinced all but the most cynical that this native Missourian was most definitely a genius, and the Maine tribes trusted him implicitly. He had won them millions of dollars, and they were counting on him to invest it wisely.

In the years after the settlement, Tureen's Tribal Assets Management steered the Passamaquoddies into the purchase of an AM-FM radio station, a wild blueberry farm, and a cement factory. The Penobscots developed an ice-skating rink, a factory that built audio cassette tapes, and invested in a townhouse development. Both tribes also invested heavily in Schiavi Homes, a company that manufactured mobile homes. At first, it appeared Tureen might be as successful in business as he had been in law. The Passamaquoddies' purchase of Maine's biggest cement factory turned out to be highly lucrative. Dragon Cement was losing money when the tribe bought it, and it was turned into a profitable business. After five years, Dragon Cement was sold for $30 million, about three times the purchase price.

Many of Tureen's other investments lost money. Lumber prices plummeted after Tureen invested a substantial portion of the tribes' money in 150,000 acres of harvestable forest land. They spent $1.5 million on the ice-skating rink, but Tureen had underestimated the operating and maintenance costs. Nor did customers exactly flock to the building to skate, since many parents and local school administrators were nervous about letting their kids cross the narrow bridge that led to the reservation rink.

But it was the mobile-home investment that really took its toll on the tribal accounts. Acting on Tureen's advice, the two tribes had invested $5 million in Schiavi Homes, a mobile-home retailing company. It was a complicated transaction involving Key Bank of Maine, on whose board the Schiavi of Schiavi Homes sat. One of the requirements of the deal was that a Schiavi manager would continue to manage the business that was now 90 percent owned by the Maine Indians. After the tribes' entire stake in the transaction disappeared, the Penobscots filed a suit in federal court alleging that Schiavi and Key Bank executives had conspired to defraud and plunder them. According to tribal lieutenant governor Reuben Phillips, "We were victimized, manipulated, and lied to." For years, the suit remained caught like molasses in the federal court system. Their investment was never recovered, and it became clear that a great deal of the money won by the tribes had been lost. As the *Boston Globe* would summarize in 1994: "Through a combination of bad advice, bad judgment and bad luck, the Penobscot and Passamaquoddy investments never made enough money to lift the tribes out of poverty. And none fulfilled the foremost mission—creating large numbers of jobs."

There was one new Penobscot venture that did make money, and that was the nightly bingo game that the tribe had established about fifteen miles northeast of Bangor. Even in Yankee Maine, it seemed, elderly couples, farmers, even lumbermen, couldn't get enough of bingo. Canadians streamed across the border from New Brunswick. It was the one light business that worked.

BINGO SEEMS LIKE one of those games that has been around forever. The earliest version of the game as we know it was actually invented in Venice, Italy, around 1530. It became immediately popular throughout Europe and had numerous variations, the most common ones known as "loo," "housey-housey," and "lotto."

The bingo most familiar today, featuring combinations of letters and numbers on a square playing sheet, was enormously popular at country fairs in central Europe in the late nineteenth and early twentieth centuries. It was in Germany that a traveling American entrepreneur, whose name is lost to history, picked up some cards and a bag full of beans and carried them back to the little town of Jacksonville, Georgia, just south of Atlanta. He called the game beano, using coffee beans instead of little plastic or metallic markers to mark the spots. The caller pulled small numbered wooden disks from a cigar box and called out the numbers aloud. The players responded by checking their cards to see if they had the number called, and if they did, they placed a bean on the number. This continued until someone filled a line of numbers on their card— either horizontally, vertically, or diagonally. The winner yelled "Beano" and received a small Kewpie doll as a prize. In Georgia, the cards sold for about a nickel and the beano operator presided over twelve seats that were constantly filled. He gave a Kewpie doll worth about a nickel to the game's winner and pocketed the 55-cent profit, which wasn't bad for Depression-stricken Georgia in 1929.

One day, Edwin Lowe, a nineteen-year-old toy salesman, was driving back to his New York home from Florida when he happened upon the county fair where beano had become popular. The European-born son of a Polish Orthodox rabbi who had risked his life to come to

America, Lowe was part of an American generation determined to succeed, but the area that he was supposed to sell to was considered the bleakest sales territory covered by his company. For the most part, the Jacksonville fair wasn't all that spectacular, and there was little there that attracted Lowe's attention. He was just about to return to his gray-blue Nash Ajax and keep driving north on U.S. 1 when he noticed a long line waiting to get into the beano tent. As he would later describe it, "It was the only booth alive with smiles and whoops."

Lowe had to see what all the excitement was about. Just to get in and take a seat took him an hour, which he filled by seeing how far he could spit watermelon seeds. When he finally got a chance to play, Lowe never once got "Beano," despite his investment of nearly half a dozen nickels. But he did get something out of the experience. Lowe learned the details of how the game and the beano cards had been discovered at a fair in Germany, and he bought a handful of cards from the operator to bring back to New York. When Lowe got home, he created his own cards, bought some dried beans, and invited over a number of friends. He handed the cards out to his guests and called out the numbers he pulled from a cigar box, just the way the carney operator had done at the fair in Georgia. The most dramatic moment of the evening came when a young woman looked down and saw her five beans in a straight row across her card. Rendered dumb, she momentarily couldn't remember the name of the game. So instead of calling out "Beano," she began imitating the sound of a winning slot machine bell, yelling "Bing, bing, bing, *bingo!*"

In an interview years later, Lowe recalled that moment: "I cannot describe the sense of elation which that girl's cry brought to me, all I could think of was that I was going to come out with this game and I was going to call it Bingo." But before he journeyed off to the patent office to unsuccessfully register the Bingo trademark, Lowe showed his game to the parish priest of a Catholic church in Wilkes-Barre, Pennsylvania. The priest immediately saw the fund-raising prospects for such a game. His only complaint was that it didn't have enough possibilities. Lowe had come up with a twenty-four-card game, but that wasn't enough to suit the needs of the church. The priest had grandiose dreams of filling his church's social hall with bingo players. Acting on the priest's recommendation, Lowe found a mathematics professor at Columbia University, Carl Leffler, who helped him come up with many more number combinations. With Leffler's help, Lowe came up with 6,000 different cards, more than enough to satisfy the priest, who was anxious to open up the basement of his church to help raise money for the parish. Leffler became so obsessed with the numbers that when he died, friends claimed it was bingo that had killed him.

With the Catholic Church as a ready buyer, Lowe quit his job and dove headlong into the bingo business. Within a few years, he had 226 presses printing out bingo cards around the clock. By 1934, there were an estimated 10,000 bingo games a week across the United States, and Lowe's firm had 1,000 employees trying to keep up with the demand. He was never able to trademark the word "bingo," but he still became the dominant player in the industry and made even more money selling small plastic chess and checkers sets. In 1973, Lowe, who had also invented and marketed a dice game called Yahtzee, sold his company to the Milton Bradley Company of Springfield, Massachusetts, for $26 million. Lowe later turned to more adult pursuits, eventually buying the 322-room Tally-Ho Inn in Las Vegas, which later became the Aladdin Hotel.

In the intervening years, bingo had become a staple of church money-raising. By 1970, on Long Island alone, there were over five hundred separate bingo games taking place at any one time. In many Catholic parishes, it was credited with providing the funds for keeping parochial schools open. Bingo equipped volunteer fire companies, clothed football teams, and outfitted high school bands. By 1980, according to a government study, the total amount bet annually on bingo was $4 billion per year, and it ranked as the fourth-largest form of gambling in the United States, behind casinos, state lotteries, and horse racing. For the bingo maniac, the game was serious business. When law-enforcement authorities raided a volunteer fire department's two-cards-for-a-nickel bingo game in New Cumberland, West Virginia, in 1979, eighteen fire trucks carrying outraged players appeared at the courthouse the next day. They blared the sirens, wore "Bingo or Burn"

T-shirts, and chanted, "Bingo! Bingo! Bingo!" In 1986, a feud erupted among volunteer fire companies in the Pittsburgh area when one scheduled a new game that competed with another's. The same year, at a senior citizen apartment complex in Rochester, New York, a player was banned for winning too much. She hired an attorney to force her way back into the game.

Because bingo has been sold in a game box, often retailed at drug and toy stores, it has always been seen by legislators as recreation—as opposed to a form of gambling. When churches began charging patrons for cards and awarding small monetary prizes for winning, the game seemed completely harmless. It had become a passion for the nation's elderly. Nowhere in America was bingo more popular than in Florida, with its hundreds of thousands of retirees crowding into bingo halls to play games for as little as a dime per card. State law made sure the game remained penny-ante. Prizes were restricted to $25 per game. Bingo operators could offer games only a couple of times a week, and picayune laws of the Florida legislature even regulated the number of hours that a game could be played.

While the churches supplemented their operating expenses through bingo, Indian reservations across America eked out a living selling trinkets, running smoke shops, selling pencils and baskets, and getting small grants from the Bureau of Indian Affairs. Occasionally, the tribes also ran bingo games. Like the church games, these were mostly penny-ante, restricted by the law-enforcement authorities to the same time and prize restrictions as the churches. But due to a series of Supreme Court cases that appeared at first to be leading anywhere but to gambling, this would soon change. In the early 1970s, several cases concerning Indian sovereignty on taxes, licensing, criminal and civil jurisdiction, and balancing state and federal powers began being played out in federal courts. In almost every case, the courts expanded the sovereignty and increased the independence of Native Americans from the burden of state laws.

In 1975, for example, the Supreme Court took on a case of two non-Indians, Martin and Margaret Mazurie, who had opened up a bar on land they owned on the outskirts of a village that actually lay within

the boundaries of the Wind River Indian Reservation near the central
Wyoming town of Fort Washakie. The Wind River Reservation was occupied by both Shoshones and Arapahos, once bitter enemies now
driven together by their dire economic circumstances. Within the 20-
mile perimeter of the reservation lived 212 families of which 170 were
Indian and 42 were non-Indian or mixed. For decades, the federal government had prohibited the consumption of alcohol on reservations. But
in 1953, the U.S. Congress passed local-option legislation allowing Indian tribes, with the approval of the secretary of the interior, to regulate
the introduction of liquor into "Indian country." The Mazuries' Blue
Bull Bar resided noisily within the reservation but on land that the
Mazuries owned. In 1972, the tribal council of the Wind River Reservation passed an ordinance requiring that the Mazuries buy a license
from them to operate their bar. Although they had never had to get a license from the Wind River Reservation council before, the Mazuries applied for a tribal license, having been warned that they would be subject
to criminal charges if they continued to operate without one. The tribe
held a public hearing at which witnesses protested granting the license,
concerned about singing and shooting at late hours, disturbance of elderly residents at a nearby housing development, and the fact that the
Mazuries had allowed Indian minors into the bar. The application for a
license was thus denied. The Mazuries closed the bar for three weeks,
then decided to reopen and stay open until somebody did something to
stop them. The State of Wyoming, miffed over losing the right to regulate the bar itself, chose to do nothing about it. But after a year, the
"grace" period ended when federal agents came into the bar in 1973, arrested the Mazuries, and closed down the Blue Bull on behalf of the
tribe.

The Mazuries went to trial before a federal district judge who concluded that the bar was in fact located within Indian Country and that
U.S. government agents had jurisdiction to arrest non-Indians located on
privately held land within a reservation's boundaries. The bar was shut
down and both Martin and Margaret Mazurie were fined $100 each.
But a year later, a federal court of appeals panel reversed the ruling, arguing that since the Mazuries' bar was not on reservation land, it could

only be regulated by the state, not the tribe or the federal government. The appeals court found that the term "Indian Country" was too vague to make legally valid the law by which the tribe had denied the license. Therefore, it ruled the licensing law unconstitutional. In addition, the appeals court held that Congress had no right to "delegate" the licensing authority of the state to a tribe of Indians. It appeared to be a big victory for the states and a big loss for the reservations. But this was soon to change.

In 1975, the Mazurie case went to the United States Supreme Court, where it became one of the most highly anticipated and important cases on Indian tribal sovereignty in Native American legal history. In a unanimous ruling written by Chief Justice William Rehnquist, the Supreme Court declared that Congress could validly delegate such authority to collect fees and issue licenses to a reservation's tribal council and that while the Mazuries' bar might technically be located off the reservation, it was clearly within the definition of "Indian Country."

Rehnquist ruled that Congress did, in fact, have the power to delegate its power over liquor licensing to the tribe and noted that tribal courts had the legal right to exercise authority over non-Indians "insofar as concerns their transactions on a reservation with Indians." Rehnquist said it was immaterial that the Mazuries are not Indians. "The cases in this court have consistently guarded the authority of Indian governments over their reservations. Congress recognized this authority in the Navajoes in the Treaty of 1868 and has done so ever since," he wrote.

Rehnquist's decision ultimately took its authority from the Commerce Clause of the United States Constitution, "investing Congress with authority to regulate commerce with foreign nations, and among the several states, and with the Indian tribes. . . . "

In 1976, another case arose that would have widespread ramifications for Native Americans: *Bryan v. Itasca County*. Russell Bryan, a forty-four-year-old Chippewa man from Leech Lake, Minnesota, had bought a house trailer and hauled it to his home on the Chippewas' Leech Lake Reservation. Itasca County, in which the reservation was geographically located, assessed Bryan $147.95 in personal property taxes. Lawyers from the federally funded Legal Services Program filed suit against the county claiming they had no authority to assess county property taxes on the reservation. The county argued that a statute known as Public Law 280, passed by Congress in 1953, gave numerous western states authority to impose civil and criminal jurisdiction over reservation life. In this very important follow-up case to *Mazurie,* Supreme Court Justice William J. Brennan Jr. declared that Minnesota could not apply its personal property tax to a mobile-home owner whose trailer was within the bounds of the reservation. Brennan maintained that for the state to collect taxes on Bryan's trailer would violate Indian sovereignty. Brennan wrote of Public Law 280: "The law is not intended to effect total assimilation of Indian tribes into mainstream American society."

The 1975 and 1976 Court rulings on Indian sovereignty were being watched closely, but not just by Indians and their attorneys. For nearly three decades, a handful of Las Vegas operators had enjoyed a near monopoly on casino gambling. That was about to end in 1978 when the State of New Jersey legalized casinos in Atlantic City. But the idea of going into business with Indian tribes, who might be exempt from state regulation, seemed like a dream come true to an increasing number of U.S. businessmen, some of whom had close ties to mob-related organizations.

In no place was the interest more intense than in South Florida, which had long been home to mobsters like Meyer Lansky and Santos Trafficante. In Florida, as in Las Vegas, casinos were institutions with which mobsters felt understandably comfortable. Even legal casinos offered opportunities for money-laundering and loan-sharking that could prove lucrative in dealing with the increased number of drug and narcotics dealers who were setting up shop and even buying banks in Florida in the 1970s. Casinos offered even more opportunity for illegal activity than banks, since they were far more difficult to regulate. But the state of Florida, both its business community and its governmental side, were organized and sufficiently funded to stop progambling moves. When attempts to legalize gambling failed in the Florida legislature, progambling forces tried to put a referendum on the ballot. None of the efforts ever got close to being passed because of the objections of Bible-thumping Governor Reubin Askew and the ringing antigambling editorials of all the state's major newspapers.

But if gambling couldn't find its way into those big hotel lobbies in Miami Beach, where crap tables would have blended seamlessly into the decor, gamblers decided they'd be content to set up shop in Hollywood, Florida, where a federally recognized tribe of Seminole Indians resided in near abject poverty and desolation.

The Seminoles had lived in South Florida since well before the fifteenth century and no doubt many centuries before that. Their survival as an intact tribe with a history, traditions, and a language was an astounding accomplishment. Their experience of survival couldn't have been more different than that of the Pequots, who had lineal descendants scattered all over New England but no core group, no native language, and no institutional or even personal remembrance of any Indian traditions. But despite the miracle of their survival, reality of life for the Seminoles was dreary. Their businesses, like alligator-wrestling shows and swamp rides through the Everglades, were not particularly profitable, and it seemed that every few years a bad hurricane or storm would wipe them out financially.

In 1971, the Seminoles elected as their chief a man named Howard Tommie, who was determined to change the financial status of his tribe and himself. Tommie took the tribe into the business of selling cigarettes, which at the time could be sold on a tax-free basis. This proved to be a wise move economically. By 1976, the tribe's cigarette sales were grossing $4.5 million per year—hardly enough to break the cycle of poverty and alcoholism in which the large tribe's members were enmeshed—but Tommie had bigger dreams.

In 1978, he made a deal with newly created Seminole Management Associates, whose shareholders included associates of Florida crime boss Meyer Lansky, to introduce high-stakes bingo on his reservation. In 1979, Tommie resigned as Seminole chief to become a consultant and executive in the company. His place as head of the tribal council was taken by thirty-five-year-old James Billie.

Chief Billie, as he became known to the tribe, was born on a chimpanzee farm in 1945. His mother, Agnes Billie, was an enrolled member of the Seminole tribe of Florida, and her ancestors were part of the contingent that in 1820 had hidden in the swamps rather than surrender to an army commanded by Andrew Jackson. His father was an Irish-American Navy pilot stationed at a nearby military base, but the two were never married. When Billie was born on the reservation, he was subject to what then was the "standard procedure" for dealing with "half-breeds." Agnes was ordered to take young James and drown him in a creek, a method the Seminoles, unlike the Pequots, used to maintain their ethnic purity. But before the death sentence could be exacted, a tribal elder stepped in and took a long look at the baby. There was a possibility, he declared prophetically, that this child could have been sent to help the tribe, and he stopped the drowning. Baby Billie, by a stroke of good fortune, was allowed to live.

Billie's mother died when her son was just nine years old, and from that time on, Billie wandered among friends' homes and frequently slept in barns, haylofts, and the backs of cars. If he really needed to hide—and police and juvenile authorities did on occasion have reason to look for him—the teenager would flee into the swamps, where he had learned many tricks of survival and where he pretended to be his matinee idol, Tarzan. The only high school Billie attended was the Haskell Institute, a boarding school for Indians in Kansas, from which he graduated in 1964 at the age of twenty.

In 1965, Billie enlisted in the Army and went to South Vietnam as the leader of a long-range reconnaissance unit. He won a reputation as a fearless soldier and was frequently sent by commanders on dangerous missions behind enemy lines. It was said by the men under his command that while he was in charge his unit would always come back alive. If he could survive in the Everglades, he could survive in the Mekong Delta. "Just rice paddies instead of alligators," Billie would quip to his men. But in 1968, while Billie was on home leave, his Army Ranger team was trapped and mercilessly executed by Viet Cong forces. Billie was devastated and guilt-ridden by the massacre. When his second tour of duty was over, he returned to Hollywood, Florida, feeling that his life was without purpose or direction. Now he wasn't just a wayward youth growing up in poverty; he was a confused Vietnam veteran as well, who hopped from job to job and was in and out of jail for petty thefts. He worked at various Everglades tourist attractions, where he won some regional notoriety for his expertise in wrestling alligators. At one of those tourists dives, Native Village, Billie developed a reputation for being totally fearless, throwing alligators around as if they were puppies, although he would eventually sacrifice one of his fingers to his hobby.

But as he grew older, Billie also grew prouder as an Indian and more and more determined to do something to halt the cycle of poverty on the Big Cypress Seminole Reservation. He had spent more than a few afternoons in the tribal library and had made it a habit to keep up with the latest court decisions. While many of the members of the tribe were very reluctant to bank on something like bingo for the tribe's future, Billie had no qualms about it. Nothing could be worse than the current tribal budget, which was producing revenue of just $400 a year per Seminole. At this point, virtually the only industry on the reservation was selling cigarettes and sponsoring an occasional rodeo. The rodeos were so cheaply run that the tribe members would circle their pickup trucks to light the grounds because they didn't have enough money to pay for illuminating the rodeo ring at night.

When he resigned in 1979, Tommie asked Billie to run for chief to succeed him, and in a hard-fought election Billie emerged victorious, with a mandate to do what he could to use recent changes in Indian law to the tribe's benefit. Of his election, Billie remarked: "Some of 'em voted for me because they're old friends or members of my clan, some of 'em put me in because they thought I was the sorriest choice—except for all the others."

On the advice of a Miami attorney named Bruce Rogow, Billie became convinced that unlike state-regulated church bingo games, Seminole Reservation Bingo could set its own limits and hours of operation. This notion was based on Justice Brennan's ruling in the *Itasca* case, which had limited how much control states could impose on reservations. Together, Billie and Tommie decided to open a bingo hall on the reservation, setting their own hours and offering prizes far more valuable than those allowed at the churches, whose state law allowed only one $100 jackpot per night. Billie even planned to give away a Cadillac. Opening night was a huge success due to the tribe's widespread advertising that high-stakes bingo was finally coming to Florida. Attorney

General Bob Butterworth didn't share the public's enthusiasm, and ordered Florida state troopers to confiscate the bingo cards and numbers.

But the bingo hall didn't stay closed for long. Bruce Rogow went to federal court and won a quick ruling that stated that since bingo was a legal activity within the state of Florida, and since the Seminole's sovereignty had been federally recognized in 1957, the hours of operation and the size of the prizes could not be regulated by the state government of Florida. The attorney general's actions ironically provided the tribe with more publicity and free advertising than they could possibly have hoped for. The bingo hall reopened a few days later, and it seemed everybody knew where and what it was.

Within ten years of opening, Seminole High Stakes Bingo was earning over $100 million per year for the 2,200 members of the Seminole tribe. Eventually, Billie would run an empire that included five other bingo halls at various Seminole properties around the state, an investment in a Caribbean casino, a hotel in Tampa, a rope factory, and an airplane manufacturer. Billie himself became a licensed pilot with a fleet of luxury jet planes and three helicopters, which he used to hop around the state. His own favorite was a $9-million, eight-seat Turbo Commander once owned by Filipino dictator Ferdinand Marcos. Billie used the craft to fly himself to Tallahassee to lobby legislators, as well as to check on his various personal business enterprises, like Billie's Swamp Safari and the Chief's Beef Jerky, an all-natural beef stick sold at Florida's Winn-Dixie chain of supermarkets.

In general, Billie's strategy in dealing with state officials was the same one he had used in Vietnam: keep your battle plans secret. "There is no difference between the field of combat, where there were bullets flying, and politics, where you use words. It's all manipulation, how to outdo the other guy to get what you want," he would say. When Billie read one day that the City of Tampa had unearthed some 140 Indian bones in the building of a downtown parking lot, he quickly stepped in and demanded that construction be stopped on such holy ground. He then demanded that the tribe be given some property out in nearby Hillsborough County in exchange for his allowing the construction to continue. The City of Tampa agreed. The tribe then proceeded to build a giant tobacco store and bingo parlor on the property they had been given.

The financial success of Seminole High Stakes Bingo electrified Indian Country across the United States. Here was a historically impoverished tribe that had literally hit the jackpot. By 1998, the tribe's gaming revenues had risen to an estimated $500 million per year. Each of his tribe's 2,450 members received a monthly dividend check from the various bingo halls of $1,500 per month and the Seminole Management Associates earned an estimated $60 million a year from bingo and video gaming machines on the reservation. Tommie, in fact, had long since left the reservation for a luxurious $950,000 waterfront home in Fort Lauderdale. The enthusiasm of tribe members for their newfound wealth remained high, despite the fact that they had some unsavory friends to thank for much of their success. According to testimony delivered before a Senate committee by a mob insider in 1989, bingo had become one of the main industries of organized crime. The mob lieutenant, testifying behind a protective screen, revealed that Indian bingo was the easiest industry to penetrate, through management fronts or the purchase of supplies from mob-controlled firms. In some cases, the witness testified, the management company skimmed at least $600,000 to $700,000 a year from bingo profits—that on top of what they took openly, leaving "very little" for the reservation. Profits were skimmed through a variety of schemes, including padded payrolls, purchase of nonexistent supplies, and rigged games designed to ensure that large jackpots were won by someone other than legitimate players. The informant named the syndicate of organized crime figure Meyer Lansky, whose former associates had ties to the Seminole operation, as one of the big players in the mob bingo rackets. But nobody at the reservation was complaining.

IN 1983, at virtually the same time the Seminoles were suddenly cashing in on the bingo craze, a Maine court, where the legal situation was different from Florida's, ruled that high-stakes bingo was against state law, and the one lucrative enterprise the Penobscots had going, their bingo parlor north of Bangor, was shuttered. Unlike those in Florida, Indians in Maine had been made subject to state laws under the negotiated 1980 agreement that accompanied the federally financed settlement of their $90-million, 12.5-million-acre land claim. Tureen was sanguine about the court defeat. "The legal system has been good to Maine Indians, and the tribes in Maine have won a number of important decisions in the last eight years that made possible the largest settlement of its kind." Tureen told the press that the Penobscots would "obviously abide by the requirements of the law."

Tureen had reason not to be concerned. At the time of the ruling, he already had an alternative plan. The timing of the decision to close down bingo in Maine was coincidental with the successful effort of the Pequots to win their own federal recognition. If Maine wouldn't let the Penobscots run their bingo parlor in northern Maine, they would simply move the operation to Ledyard and run their bingo parlor in Connecticut, where he expected that there was no such legal impediment. He had been careful in negotiating the relatively simpler Pequot recognition bill not to agree to anything that might be interpreted as limiting their rights to run games.

Ledyard was a bit obscure geographically, but bingo fanatics always had a way of finding their games. The planning to open a Penobscot bingo hall in Connecticut was under way even before President Reagan got around to signing the Pequot recognition bill in late 1983. The Penobscots would go full bore into bingo as soon as recognition was complete. On November 22, 1983, Penobscot lieutenant governor Joseph Francis announced that the erection of a bingo building that could seat 5,000 people would begin as soon as the concrete slab could be poured.

When Hayward read Francis's comments, he was furious. But not as mad as some of his new tribal cousins, who had poured into Ledyard since the land settlement to take advantage of the free housing. Because most of them were either Jehovah's Witnesses or Baptists, they were not particularly gungho about bingo or any other form of gambling. The Maine Indians, many of whom were progambling Catholics, had no such moral qualms.

Penobscot governor Timothy Love had to do some quick backtracking. He admitted that officials of the Penobscots had talked about bingo games at Ledyard.

"We're only talking about helping the Pequots get started from the management point of view, and on the point of operations," said Love. "As for the ban on bingo in Maine, we've taken that in stride. We want to improve our relations with the state of Maine. There are many more things, other than playing bingo, that can be done so that we can make money, and we're looking at them."

Even as Tureen maneuvered to move bingo to Connecticut, Hayward told his family members that the Penobscot plan was ridiculous. "It's attractive in that it would create a large amount of money for the tribe," he said. "But 5,000 people—that's a lot of folks. It's not something that we would want to have in here." Privately, Love suspected it was only a matter of time before the Pequots came around. Joseph Francis, the Penobscot lieutenant governor, might have jumped the gun, he told Hayward. "But if I were a betting man, I would put money on the bingo parlor." Hayward called together a meeting of the family. In a stormy discussion, the fundamentalist religious factions of the family not only blocked bingo but made Hayward promise not to bring it up again for a whole year. They had not come this far to turn the tribe over to gambling and gamblers, said one of his mother's cousins, a woman named Phyllis Monroe. Hayward himself was skeptical enough not to push it. He lived in the community, and the gambling talk from the Penobscots had scared his neighbors. Even worse, it had alerted the state to keep an eye on the tribe's intentions. The great advantage that James Billie had always had with the State of Florida was that he had been a master of surprise.

No sooner had the meeting broken up than the State of Connecticut issued an official notice signed by the attorney general claiming that the state maintained full regulatory authority and jurisdiction over all bingo and any other gambling operations opened by the tribe. The Pequots would be required to live under the same rules and regulations as other charitable gaming operators in Connecticut.

Hayward responded to this notice with a nonconfrontational, appeasing letter that emphasized their claims of tribal sovereignty. He pointed out that the federal court decision in Florida, which would not necessarily be binding in a separate federal court circuit, was the controlling law as far as he was concerned. "I don't want to have any more tension with the state than we already have," Hayward told his cousins as he slipped the letter into an envelope. Hayward was still considering the idea of moving into gambling. After all, Tureen reminded him, in Maine bingo had been virtually the only industry that had produced real revenue for Indians. It was clean from an environmental point of view, and gaming had historic links to Native American history. Still, sitting in the back room of Mr. Pizza, Hayward worried that any gambling enterprise would attract the attention of the mob in Providence. "The mob only gets involved in illegal activities," Tureen assured him. "This will be completely legal."

Hayward was still skeptical, but he agreed to take a trip to the Seminole Reservation along with his cousin Bruce Kirchner. When they arrived at the reservation off of a busy section of Florida's turnpike, Hayward could hardly believe what he was seeing. The bingo hall was as long as four football fields and thousands of cars poured into the giant parking lot to buy bingo cards.

"How did you do this?" Hayward said to Billie, incredulous. "It was like somebody handed me a loaded gun and said if you want it, pull the trigger. I pulled it," Billie replied. When Hayward returned from the trip to Florida, according to one cousin, "He was full of flaming arrows." And he had reason to be. It was quickly becoming apparent to him that, as in Maine, the other more conventional business ventures simply weren't working out. His greenhouse, funded by federal grants, was supposed to bring $165,000 in gross sales by producing 6,000 heads of lettuce a week. After fourteen months, it was $54,000 in the red, and instead of delivering his product to restaurants, Hayward was unloading it at cheap grocery stores for almost nothing. He had obtained a $300,000 federal economic development grant with which to buy Mr. Pizza. But the restaurant was a financial disaster and never made a profit.

Skip was now sold on bingo, but he still had three big obstacles to overcome. One was to get the financing to build the bingo hall, the second was to convince his family to go ahead with the project, and the third was to overcome the state opposition, since the idea in Connecticut, as it had been in Florida, was to capture the bingo market by offering jackpots and hours that would be illegal for state-regulated charity bingo games. To try to get the financing, Tureen turned to his onetime legal adversary, Jackson King. King's firm was the best-known law practice in Norwich and was well connected with most of the local bankers. Tureen told King that they had incorporated a new tribal corporation to build a bingo hall, and he wanted King to approach local bankers and come up with about $3 million, which would be guaranteed under an economic development program offered by the Bureau of Indian Affairs. Hayward had worked hard to come up with the promise of a federal guarantee for the loan, plying the halls of the U.S. Interior Department for weeks. It was not without results. The twice-divorced Hayward befriended a raven-haired Chippewa Interior Department employee named Carol Defoe, who suggested that to ease his tension over the situation he go to a softball game with her. When Hayward left Washington a few weeks later, he had both the loan guarantee and a fiancée.

So for the second time, King began making the rounds on behalf of Hayward, Tureen, and the Pequots, and this time the task was actually something with which King felt he had some familiarity—calling Connecticut and Massachusetts bankers and getting a loan.

"Bingo in New England," scoffed one banker. "You must be kidding."

The general consensus among bankers was that high-stakes bingo was generally a bad idea and for staid Yankee New England a particularly bad idea. It didn't matter to them whether or not the state would try to shut the operation down. As far as the local bankers were concerned, it would never open in the first place. But Tureen himself finally found an audience for Hayward at the United Arab-American Bank in New York, where his proposal was listened to with more than passing interest. By the time he got to New York, Hayward was discouraged enough to expect nothing but the usual negative response. Sure enough, the loan officer said, "There is something wrong with this proposal."

"What do you mean?" said Hayward.

"Your hall will not be big enough. A forty-six-thousand-square-foot building will not work; it should be double that size."

The Arabs, of course, could afford to be generous, since the Bureau of Indian Affairs was prepared to guarantee 90 percent of the loan in case of default. Hayward decided to expand the building and take the loan. He then signed a four-year management contract with the Penobscots, who would come down to Connecticut to run the bingo hall on the Pequot reservation. After two years, the Pequots would buy out the contract and run it themselves.

In 1985, the 14,000 residents of Ledyard learned for the first time that a deal had been struck that would turn their little hamlet into what would eventually be the center of the New England gambling world. Mayor Mary McGrattan was among those shocked by the turn of events. Until this point, she had thought the town had a good relationship with Hayward and his family members. But she only learned of the plans for a bingo hall when Connecticut attorney general Joseph Lieberman called to let her know the state would oppose it. Although Hayward tried to downplay its significance, Lieberman was not fooled. "This is a large proposal," he told McGrattan. "Not because of the size of the project, but because it requires acceptance of the fact that there's a little piece of land in the state of Connecticut over which the state has little authority."

The state and the Pequots quickly squared off in federal court to decide what would be done. Connecticut fared no better than had Florida. Lieberman's objections were summarily tossed out by U.S. district judge Peter Dorsey. If the State of Connecticut could operate the lottery as a game of chance to raise state funds, he said, so could an Indian tribe operate a bingo parlor under their own rules. On July 5, 1986, Congressman Sam Gejdenson cut the red ribbon opening a bingo parlor with electronic scoreboards, closed-circuit television feeds, and fried-chicken dinners for the hungry. As had happened in Florida, thousands began pouring through the doors to play for the big prizes. Three centuries after they had supposedly been wiped off the planet, the Pequots were back in business.

5

A TRIBE WINS AT POKER

By the end of 1986, bingo profits were rolling into Mashantucket at a spectacular rate. The closing of the bingo parlor in Maine had been a fortuitous development for the Pequots. The Penobscots not only managed the bingo hall and handled training for the Pequots and their employees; they cooperated in bringing busloads of former customers through the rabbit warren of rural two-lane southeastern Connecticut highways to Ledyard.

The Mashantucket Pequot High Stakes Bingo Parlor itself was a squat one-story brick building facing lonely Route 2. In the entire state of Connecticut, one would be hard-pressed to find a commercial location more obscure. Even the dog track thirty miles away in Plainfield was at least off an interstate highway. Here, there was not only no major highway, but there weren't any signs providing a clue where the reservation was. But that hardly stopped bingo lovers or, for that matter, tour bus operators, happy to load up and deliver frantic bingo players to their destination.

But the competition was not universally welcomed. Civic groups like the Ledyard Lions Club had operated bingo games once a week for decades, and Lions Club president Wesley Johnson felt a certain hopelessness as he watched more and more vehicles rocketing past the Lions Club Hall to play bingo at the reservation. The Lions Club had been earning about $300 a week for charitable causes, buying clothes for needy children, or supplying smoke detectors to the elderly. But after just a year in business, an average of nearly 1,000 persons per day were patronizing Hayward's high-stakes bingo hall, and one by one the authentically charitable bingo games began closing down as players chased the big prizes and the more glamorous pots at the reservation. No demise was more unfortunate than that of the forty-one-year-old game at Sacred Heart Catholic Church in Groton. After raising roughly $450,000 for good causes over the years, players were suddenly vanishing and the game was discontinued. There was nothing the local parish priest could do. His prayers at Sunday mass asking that the game be maintained were apparently not answered.

The Ledyard state representative in the legislature, Glenn Arthur, complained that allowing the Indians to set their own limits on bingo games was "like setting up an independent nation within our nation." His sentiments were echoed by members of the town council. Several complained to Congressman Sam Gejdenson about the unfair advantage that Hayward's family had in running their game. Gejdenson simply referred their complaints to the Bureau of Indian Affairs. Eventually, the BIA shot back a perfunctory letter explaining that federal policy promoted Indian economic self-sufficiency through bingo.

Hayward was aware of his neighbors' concerns, but he had no intention of reversing his course. When a local newspaper wrote an editorial complaining about the possible negative effects of attracting disreputable outsiders to the quiet world of southeastern Connecticut, Hayward grew nervous. "I hope this isn't the common sentiment," he remarked to his brother Robert. But he took no action to allay anyone's concerns. Since the death of his brother Rodney, who on September 25, 1984, was fatally injured in a motorcycle accident while being chased by a Ledyard police officer, Hayward had little desire to speak to any of the town's officials and in fact determined that he would no longer refer to the location of the reservation as Ledyard but as Mashantucket. More importantly though, bingo was making more money for the tribe than he had ever seen, and there was no way Hayward was going to allow that to come to an end. Not a day passed that a bus company didn't call for directions from as far away as Boston; Manchester, New Hampshire; even Canada. Hayward, like many people who didn't play bingo, had no idea that there was such a huge bingo subculture with fanatics who would go to any length to find and play a big game. Though Hayward had been reluctant at first about establishing gambling on the reservation, the wonders he had seen at the Seminole High Stakes Bingo convinced him otherwise. Yet he still believed in 1986 that money made from bingo would not be an end unto itself but rather a means of financing his other businesses. In his dreams, he imagined that bingo would provide a new base of customers for Mr. Pizza, saving the restaurant that was rapidly swallowing up the $300,000 the tribe had paid for it. Hayward came to believe after purchasing the restaurant that its prior owners had kept a dual set of books and had misrepresented its receipts. He probably had paid double what Mr. Pizza was really worth. So he was counting on bingo revenue to even out for Mr. Pizza's losses, the same way Chief Billie had used revenue from the Seminole bingo parlor to run his roadside Swamp Safari.

Now Skip could afford to make pizza all night every night at a big loss. All projections for the Pequots' bingo revenue had been underestimated. By the end of 1987, the bingo parlor was on track to gross $20 million per year, of which 25 percent would be pure profit for the tribe. Skip loved to come home at night and do the math. In 1987, with about 100 members now in the tribe, bingo profits alone would provide a gross income equal to $60,000 per year for every man, woman, and child on the reservation. At the same time that Hayward treasured the feeling of making real money for the first time in his life, he remained deathly afraid of attracting the attention of Providence's Patriarca crime family. He had heard the rumors about the mob's involvement in other bingo operations, both in California and to a lesser extent in Florida, and was determined not to let organized crime get a foothold in his business. In conversations with Tureen, he made nervous jokes about getting "whacked" by Providence mobsters. Initially, he even went so far as to ban all coin-operated pinball machines from the bingo hall out of fear that the suppliers of these devices might have links to organized crime.

As the Pequots began raking in bingo money, government aid programs, made possible through the successful recognition battle, provided the funds for building an apartment building for new tribal members, many of whom were trickling in from Rhode Island's Narragansett community. Membership in the once extinct Pequot tribe was suddenly starting to look very attractive. Bureau of Indian Affairs policy allowed Indians to switch tribes. The question now became who was eligible to reap the monetary pleasures that bingo offered.

The reservation in 1987 had become a beehive of activity. BIA funding was providing more money than ever for homes, ball fields, and roads. Tureen and his partners were working virtually full-time on federal grant applications, to say nothing of the business and legal aspects involved in running an increasingly large business. The capital from bingo was providing funds to support a 120-person payroll that included all the employees at the bingo hall, the pizza restaurant, and the tribe's sand and gravel pit. Things, it seemed, were moving along just fine for the Skip Hayward clan, even though the newfound wealth pouring into Mashantucket would prove to be just a taste of what was to come. From 1985 to 1987, Hayward had inadvertently been helped by complicated and expensive lawsuits filed by the Passamaquoddies in Maine and then by the Seminoles in Florida. Other tribes had shouldered the legal battles, while the Pequots had taken advantage of the decisions. Since Tureen's salary was paid out of federal funds allocated to legal aid, Hayward rarely even had to pay a legal bill.

Now good fortune was about to strike again for Hayward. This time, the catalyst that would propel him and the Pequot tribe forward was a series of odd circumstances involving a small tribe of Indians who couldn't have lived farther away or been more different. They were known in California as the Cabazon Band of Mission Indians.

THE CABAZON INDIAN RESERVATION, located in the San Joaquin Valley just outside of Indio, California, had been established by the federal government in 1856. By 1977, it had a mere 25 enrolled members. Typical for inland western tribes, the Cabazon Reservation was dirt-poor. Located just twenty minutes into the desert from the palatial resorts of Palm Springs, the reservation had no paved roads, no running water, and no electricity.

In the early 1970s, while Indian nations were riveted by what Tureen and the Maine tribes were accomplishing, the two dozen members of the Cabazon Band elected a new chairman, Joseph Benitez. Elected first vice chairman was Benitez's half-brother Art Welmas, a trained barber with several years in the United States Marine Corps. After the Korean War, Welmas had become actively involved in tribal affairs, traveling to tribal meetings from his home in Escondido, north of San Diego. The two half-brothers frequently held discussions about using post–Great Society programs to bring some degree of economic self-sufficiency to their little reservation.

Prominent among those programs was the Indian Financing Act of 1974 by which Congress had appropriated $20 million for Native American loan guarantees. The Cabazons used the federal loans to establish a store on historic tribal land. There they sold liquor and cigarettes in a trailer whose cash register ran off a portable generator. From a desk in another trailer, they entered into pilot agricultural projects to grow jujube and sesame in conjunction with the University of California at Riverside.

The Cabazons then became the first tribe in the country to develop a mail-order business for cigarettes. It was so successful that the *National Enquirer* published a disapproving cover story trumpeting the claim that "Indians make $10,000 a day." The Cabazons were only wishful it was $10,000 a day. Actual net profit from the operation was rarely more than $3,000 per day. Benitez wasn't too happy about the *Enquirer* story, feeling that he had to explain to the tribe that the numbers were grossly overstated and that he wasn't just underreporting revenue and skimming profits. Still, there were quite a few tribe members who wondered who was telling the truth—Joe and Art, or the *Enquirer*.

Like many Indian tribes, the Cabazons hoped to use their tax exemptions to get a competitive edge in the selling of cigarettes and other tobacco products. But in 1980, the Supreme Court ruled in the case called *Washington State v. Confederated Tribes of the Colville Indian Reservation* that the exemption was unconstitutional, and the profits were virtually wiped out overnight. In a rare legal defeat for Native American lawyers, the High Court said a state's interest in collecting sales taxes from non-Indians was sufficient to warrant "the minimal burden imposed on the tribal smoke shop operators." The decision eliminated the biggest advantage reservations had in attracting non-Indian smoking customers to their stores.

With the smoke shop revenues decimated, tribal members got in touch with representatives of the now defunct Dunes Hotel and Casino, which had an interest in opening up a California "branch" of what was then their struggling Las Vegas operation. By September of 1980, plans for a small poker room were in high gear. The Cabazons opened their card room on October 15, 1980. A few days later, 35 members of the Indio Police Department, in helmets and riot regalia, moved in to close it down. They seized the tables, arrested a dozen people, and confiscated all the chips. The employees and customers were handcuffed, taken to the courthouse, and required to post bond.

Attorneys for the Cabazons obtained a court order releasing the tables and chairs and freeing the patrons and employees. They also won an order from the judge that allowed them to operate the card room while the case was adjudicated. Card rooms were legal in California, and quite a few, like Bell Gardens and the Normandy Club in Southern California, were quite elaborate and well known in gambling circles. Still, the state legislature required that for the Cabazons to be legal, they had to hold and win a referendum from the voters of Indio, where gambling was not allowed by local ordinance. The referendum was put on the ballot, but it was voted down by the Indio electorate.

The Cabazons' case was further weakened when attorneys for the City of Indio took affidavits from dissident tribal members. Some of them, who had never quite trusted their leaders' ledgers, testified that the card room and a bingo parlor, which was added subsequent to the card room, were crooked and that the tribe itself was being ripped off by the "professional" managers that Joe Benitez and Art Welmas had hired. In one of the affidavits, a former security guard, James Hughes, Jr., testified under oath that Welmas was forging expense accounts and paying hit men to carry out contract killings. Hughes testified that the Cabazons had put out a $30,000 contract on his life because he was "ratting" to authorities. Hughes also claimed that the bingo parlor operators were involved in gun-running missions to Central and South America.

Welmas told the *Los Angeles Times,* which extensively reported the charges and countercharges, that the allegations were fantastic and absurd. "We are very satisfied that we're running a clean-cut operation," he said. Maybe so. But the following year, 1984, an advisor to the tribe was jailed in a murder-for-hire plot after soliciting two police informants to kill several members of the tribe. It wouldn't have been the first murder in Cabazon history. In July 1981, the Cabazon chief of tribal security and two other persons had been executed gangland-style. Afterward, the murdered official's sister told police that her brother believed non-Indians running the casino were skimming gambling profits. He was apparently killed to keep him quiet, she told police.

The poker room case went quickly up to the federal appellate court for the western United States, the Ninth U.S. Circuit Court of Appeals. Despite its colorful leadership, the tribe got a favorable hearing from the three-judge panel that heard its case. The appeals panel ruled that Indio's ordinance against gambling was not valid because the 1,700-acre reservation could not be considered a part of Indio. As far as the Ninth U.S. Circuit Court was concerned, the Cabazons were pretty much free to manage their affairs as they pleased. But the battle was far from over. Though the reservation couldn't be cowed by city law, it still had to go up against the county government. Following the decision by the Ninth Circuit, officers from the county of Riverside raided the card room. A county supervisor said that while the City of Indio might have trouble proving their jurisdiction over the tribal land, the county had no such problem. The reservation might not technically be in Indio, but it certainly was in Riverside County.

Once again, the tribe got a temporary order allowing them to operate while the legal maneuverings were wending their way through the courts. In early 1986, the Ninth Circuit issued another ruling for the tribe. Citing "Public Law 280," the law that had already been interpeted not to affect "assimilation" by the states' right to deal only with the federal government, they declared that Riverside County had no right to prohibit gambling on a federally recognized reservation. The whole matter moved up the judicial ladder to the United States Supreme Court for the final determination. The case was argued on December 9, 1986.

On February 25, 1987, one year after the Mashantucket Pequots had opened up their high-stakes bingo hall, the Supreme Court handed the Cabazon Indians a total legal victory. The Court ruled that since bingo and card games were permitted in California, city, county, and state authorities had no right to stop or regulate them. Although federal law had given states authority to enforce state *criminal* statutes on Indian reservations, the Court reiterated what Brennan had said in *Bryan v. Itasca County:* that Public Law 280 was not intended to make Indian tribal operations subject to state and county gambling laws. Public Law 280 had specifically granted six states, including California, jurisdiction over criminal acts in "Indian Country," but the intent had been to provide relief to federal investigative agencies like the FBI and the U.S. Attorney's Office, whose personnel felt that working on minor crimes, just because they had occurred on a federally recognized reservation, was a waste of their time. The law had not been intended to make tribes subject to a state's civil code.

In an opinion written by Justice Byron "Whizzer" White, the Court declared that even if a state was legitimately concerned about organized crime, that was not enough to allow it to enforce gambling laws. Only the federal government, White declared, "has the authority to forbid Indian gambling enterprises on Indian Reservations." White added that Indian tribes retain "attributes of sovereignty" over both their members and their territory and that this sovereignty is dependent on and subordinate to the United States and not the individual states. "State law can be applied only if the federal government has expressly said so," wrote White.

California lawyers had argued that violating the state bingo laws was in fact criminal in nature, which would give the state the right under Public Law 280 to deal directly with the Cabazons. Their view was that it was contrary to the criminal law of California to operate a card game without local permission, which the Cabazons did not have. But California's argument fell apart in the exact same way that Florida's stand against the Seminole bingo operation had collapsed. Not only did California law not prohibit all forms of gambling, the state itself operated a popular statewide lottery. The gambling that the state attorney general now claimed was criminal was actually legal in many other contexts. White noted with irony that the state actually bought advertising to encourage its residents to participate in the lottery, the "criminal" activity that it was now so intent on stopping.

What White's decision meant was that while a crime such as prostitution, banned in all cases by California, could not be justified even on the basis of tribal sovereignty, gambling had to be treated separately. In addition, because the tribal gaming provided the sole source of revenue for the operation of tribal government—the Court having put an end to tax-free cigarette sales—White ruled that state regulation would impermissibly "infringe on tribal government." If a state allowed gambling, it could not restrict it on a reservation.

The Cabazon ruling blasted like a thunderbolt across Native America. The unequivocal ruling was exactly what lawyers like Tom Tureen had been awaiting for a long time. Cabazon was far and away the clearest declaration yet of how far the Court was willing to go to allow unregulated gambling on reservations. The State of Florida had never taken the Seminole bingo case to the Supreme Court out of fear it would lose and set a national precedent. Now the attorney general of California had done just that.

IN THE AFTERMATH of Cabazon, state officials began to clamor for congressional action that would blunt the effect of the ruling. After all, White had declared that gambling by Indians could be halted; it just had to be at the federal level. If states were basically helpless to regulate the burgeoning bingo halls and card rooms, their governors and attorney generals would just have to ask for federal action.

The state governors, including the influential chairman of the National Governor's Association, Arkansas's Bill Clinton, did not have to look far for help. The congressional delegation from Nevada, where entrenched gambling interests had the most to lose from new competition, was more than willing to take the lead. In speeches on the floor of the

House of Representatives in Washington, members from Nevada, California, and New Jersey, where gambling was legal, droned on about how organized crime would destroy the poor Indians. California congressman Tony Coelho remarked: "Indian tribes certainly have the right to engage in gambling if they wish. But the states also have a sovereign right and responsibility to protect their citizens from the threat of criminal activity."

Blunt-speaking Arizona senator John McCain, a huge supporter of the Indians, saw through the self-serving righteousness. "At the core of this debate," he said, "is simply the casino industry's fear of economic competition." Congressman Morris Udall of Arizona similarly had a more objective view than Coelho. "The Indian opponents that are instructing us in the evils of organized crime are the gambling casino operators of Nevada, the Horse Track Owners Association, and the American Greyhound Track Operators Association," Udall said. "Let us be candid. This debate is not based upon high moral ground, crime control, and a level playing field. It is quite simply economics. The gambling lords of Nevada and the racetrack owners of this country perceive an economic threat to their profits from the bingo game on the little Tulalip Indian Reservation in Washington and the card parlor on the Cabazon Reservation in California."

Despite such sentiments, there was enough post-Cabazon hue and cry that Congress felt the need to do something, even if there was no clear consensus on what exactly that was. The gambling industry, whose enormous campaign contributions fueled the successful election of many senators and congressmen, was calling in all its chits. Ecstatic over their landmark victory in the Supreme Court, attorneys for the Indians didn't want any legislation at all. But legislators, flush with casino-industry political contributions, were expected to do something. Newspaper editorialists, alarmed that the Cabazon decision would lead to untrammeled and unregulated casino frenzy also called for action. In the time-honored fashion of Washington, it was important to let the casino industry look like it was getting action for all the money it was contributing to the politicians. At the same time, Congress did not want to come off as insensitive to Native Americans. Congressional leaders were in a bind.

A bill that was titled the Indian Gaming Regulatory Act was finally put together with the help of Senate Indian Affairs Committee chairman Daniel Inouye of Hawaii. The proposal was carefully crafted to appear to control Native American gaming, while in reality the terms were extremely lenient.

In Washington, the bill became known as IGRA, a rather awkward acronym. But the title reflected the degree of negligence that went into the proposed law. IGRA provided a federal statutory basis for Indian gaming—supposedly shielding the activities from organized crime—and insisted that games on Indian reservations be held "fairly and honestly." When it came to heavy-duty forms of casino gambling such as blackjack, craps, slots, and roulette, the proposed legislation said that before an Indian tribe could offer such games, it would have to negotiate a "compact" with the state in which its casino was located. If the tribe felt the state was not negotiating in good faith, it had the right to sue the state in federal court after 180 days of negotiations. The Indian Gaming Regulatory Act put the burden of proof on the state government to show the court that it was in fact acting in good faith. The legislation required that the court would ultimately have the power to compel a state to conclude a compact within 60 days or submit the dispute to a mediator. Either way, the tribe would get its casino or card room. The Indian Gaming Regulatory Act, passed by the Senate on September 15, 1988, and the House of Representatives on September 27, 1988, was a true compromise of interests. It was not supported by the Indian tribes and their allies; Nevada interests felt it didn't go far enough but that it was the best they could get.

Though White's ruling in the Cabazon case had made it clear that the federal government had the authority to regulate or ban Indian casinos, the tribes had a powerful ally in Senator Inouye, the chairman of the Committee on Indian Affairs. Inouye had collected and would continue to collect thousands of dollars in campaign contributions from Indian tribes, even though his seat was one of the safest in Congress and he was rarely even opposed for reelection. IGRA was Inouye's creation, and he argued that the law "balanced the need for strong enforcement of gaming laws with the strong federal interest in preserving the sovereignty rights of the tribal governments." The idea, he said on the floor of the Senate, "is to create a consensual agreement between two sovereign governments." The fact of the matter was that tribal sovereignty had been guaranteed by the decisions of the Supreme Court, and anything Congress enacted that failed to recognize that reality was likely to be struck down by the Court. As for guaranteeing the "strong enforcement" of gaming laws, they were hollow words. On the day the Indian Gaming Act was passed, two tribes, the Red Lake band of Chippewas and the Mescalero Apache tribe, filed suit asking the Court to declare it unconstitutional because it put restrictions on their sovereignty. The Supreme Court, however, quickly dismissed the applications, saying IGRA was a legitimate exercise of federal power.

In late 1987, the Fort Mojave Indian tribe on the Nevada border with Arizona and California became the first in the nation to voluntarily enter into an agreement with a state, getting Nevada's support for a small casino near the gambling town of Laughlin on the Arizona border. The Fort Mojave tribe agreed to state regulation in their compact, largely out of a desire to have good public relations and a desire not to project an image that its casino was any less legitimate than the state-regulated ones with which it would compete. For their part, Nevada was anxious to show that it could do something small for the tribe in order to allay criticism that the positions they had taken during the congressional debate were anti-Indian. And it probably didn't hurt that an influential state politician was awarded the tribal casino's management contract. It was not a big deal, just one more casino in a state that already had plenty.

No one imagined that the Cabazon case and the Indian Gaming Act would ultimately have so much effect on little eastern tribes like the Pequots. Outside of New Jersey, there were no northeastern states where casinos were legal. No one had paid any attention to the fact that there were charity card rooms in Connecticut, and those who did felt confident that, one way or the other, staid old New England would never go so far as to tolerate an actual casino. Among those who believed this was the old *Mayflower* descendant turned Indian chief, Skip Hayward. The bingo hall was initially about as far as he wanted to go in the gambling business, and so he too didn't imagine that the decision in the Cabazon case would affect him. But just as the Seminole bingo hall had made him see the potential riches from little square sheets and numbered balls, the card room at Indio showed the potential from playing cards.

Within just a few years of their casino's opening, the Cabazons had built their own fire and police departments. Once without electricity, now they became partners in a $138-million generation plant powered by agricultural wastes. Plans were under way for a housing subdivision, a resort hotel, and an amusement park. It was staggering to frugal Skip Hayward just how much cash people were willing to give away, especially considering how much the same people would squawk when their taxes were raised by a couple of dollars to support some BIA program.

Bingo hadn't worked out so badly, Skip told Tom Tureen one afternoon. Maybe the time had come for something more.

III

JACKPOT!

Skip Hayward holding up the cornerstone for
Foxwoods High Stakes Bingo and Casino

6

"DANCES WITH WOLVES"

IT WAS EARLY MAY 1986, and in Connecticut, as in the rest of the country, high school seniors snapped their cummerbunds and pinned on their boutonnieres. It was prom season. Girls put on their finest new dresses and waited nervously for their dates to pick them up, many in the snazzy new cars that their parents had just purchased for them as a graduation present. They sped to the proms and then sneaked out to the parking lots of their schools, pulled out their flasks, and drowned themselves in beer and liquor. When the prom was over, many headed to private parties and dances for even more drinking. In rural Connecticut, that was a risky routine. Landmarks were hard to find on the dark tree-lined, curvy roads. Most streets lacked even a basic yellow dividing line and road signs were often faded, impossible to read even when a driver was sober. With driving conditions such as these, no one was surprised each year when the prom-night highway death count exceeded that of the year before. But 1986 was particularly devastating. Nearly a dozen Connecticut teenagers were killed in car accidents after high school proms. Almost all of these accidents involved drinking, even though the legislature had already raised the legal drinking age from eighteen to nineteen, a cheaper and more politically popular solution than spending the money necessary to properly light roads or improve street signs.

Agreeing it was time to take action, the Connecticut chapter of Mothers Against Drunk Driving, an organization well known by its acronym, MADD, held an emergency meeting in Hartford to discuss the rising death toll. Obviously, there was no way to keep kids from drinking. Parents who believed that laws and lectures could make a difference were simply naïve. Ironically, according to studies, drinking children of nondrinking parents are most vulnerable to serious alcohol-related accidents and most susceptible to irresponsible drinking. The more realistic of those who came together to discuss the problem believed that the solution lay not in attempting to curb the drinking but in stopping the driving. A chaperoned activity, they believed, held at school after the prom—and an activity exciting enough to hold the kids' interest until the effects of the alcohol had worn off—was proposed as a solution. After much brainstorming, the mothers arrived at a consensus. They would try to initiate a postprom gambling night for high school kids, one modeled after the play-money casinos set up on fund-raising nights by civic clubs.

The idea of a charity casino was not a new one, although the twist of letting teenagers play roulette, blackjack, and craps did have a certain novelty. Connecticut had allowed charity bingo in the state since 1939. In 1955, Connecticut legislators expanded the concept to legalize raffles for fund-raising purposes. By 1987, there were, in fact, only five states in the country that didn't allow charity gaming—Arkansas, Idaho, Tennessee, Utah, and Hawaii. Utah and Hawaii have remained the only two states in the country that don't allow any form of gambling or lottery at all. Nationwide, the so-called Las Vegas or Monte Carlo nights sponsored at legion halls and Catholic churches were generating a gross handle of $7 billion per year.

But one had to be conscious of the fact that numbers such as these represented the *gross* revenue, not what was actually being raised for charity. According to a 1992 study done by the National Association of Fundraising Ticket Manufacturers, a fund-raising trade association, on average only 12 percent of money raised at charity fund-raisers actually went to any charitable cause. The rest was soaked up by operating costs and prizes for the players, and a good healthy amount was captured by graft and corruption. Even at respectable operations, such as volunteer firehouses, cash raised at charity fund-raisers was often skimmed. Instead of putting the money into a bright new hook-and-ladder truck, there were plenty of firemen more than willing to use it to pave their own driveways or build new additions to their homes. Nowhere was the system more corrupt than in Prince George's County, Maryland, where "charity" poker, roulette, and blackjack were legal year-round. A main feature of this schedule was the regular raids of charity casinos and the brief jailing of the charity chieftains. The games were eventually banned by Maryland's governor in 1997. In the state of Tennessee, the corruption was also bad. Of the $50 million raised annually through bingo and other gambling games, only $1 million actually found its way to a worthy cause.

Nonetheless, by 1987 the Connecticut Mothers Against Drunk Driving decided that if their kids couldn't drink and drive, then they would just have to learn to gamble. MADD first petitioned Connecticut attorney general Joseph Lieberman to issue a ruling allowing casino nights after high school prom and graduation exercises. Existing charity gaming laws, however, restricted the age to eighteen and above. Lieberman said that if MADD wanted to expand the casino nights for their children, it would have to be done through legislation.

Needless to say, many legislators were dumbfounded when they discovered the bill on their statehouse desks during the 1987 legislative session in Hartford. Bible-thumping state representative Jerry Patton of Milford declared incredulously, "We've taken prayer out of the schools and now we are putting slots in." Though slots weren't part of the legislative package, blackjack, craps, roulette, and poker were. State representative John Savage was among those most offended. "There's a disease, an addiction in gambling that's sometimes as serious as a liquor addiction can get," he protested on the floor of the House. But MADD was a popular legislative force. Once the battle was cast as a do-gooder effort to save the lives of schoolchildren, the opponents never really had a chance. The bill passed the Connecticut House of Representatives by an 87-to-50 vote and was sent to Governor William A. O'Neill for his signature.

O'Neill viewed the vote skeptically but did not object. While encouraging teens to gamble seemed crazy on the surface, there were mitigating angles to the controversy. The bill as passed by the legislature didn't technically allow gambling as people usually think of it. The high school seniors and their dates would have to use play money that could only be redeemed for door prizes, and the law made it specifically illegal for anyone to turn the door prizes into cash. The key part of the bill, the sine qua non as far as MADD was concerned, was that no drinking was allowed at the teenybopper casino. O'Neill blithely signed the bill and thought no more about it. Connecticut now had the most liberal, expansive charity gaming law in the country, but if it involved playing for stuffed animals, who could object?

The after-school casinos ultimately did little to stop drunk driving accidents, which continued at a high rate every May. But they did wake up one driver. Tom Tureen immediately saw the possibilities this legislation had created.

ON MARCH 30, 1989, two years after O'Neill signed the bill, and about a year after passage of the controversial Indian Gaming Regulatory Act in Washington, Tureen and Jackson King jointly wrote a letter to Connecticut state authorities formally requesting negotiations for a Type III, full casino license in accordance with the provisions of the gaming law. Since the state now allowed full-scale charity casinos, it would have to allow the Pequots to run their own.

Governor O'Neill was surprised at the breadth of the request. The tribe already had bingo, and he was disappointed to learn that Hayward, whom he had helped during the Pequot fight for federal recognition, now wanted to expand to full casino-style games like blackjack and craps. Few games in the world could generate more adrenaline than craps, and in few games could there be such stupendous action coupled with wild swings and the opportunity for quick winnings and huge losses. O'Neill knew well that allowing craps with real money—not high school scrip—represented a big escalation in the battle over Indian gaming. In the entire East Coast of the United States, the only place where one could find a real legal craps table was in Atlantic City. Not even in wide-open Prince George's County in Maryland, where it seemed almost anything could go, did the authorities open the door to this superaddictive, roller-coaster battle of man versus dice.

For several weeks, the letter remained on O'Neill's desk in Hartford. At first, he simply was at a loss as to how to respond. But as he talked to local priests and representatives of various charities, he became convinced that allowing a full-scale casino in Ledyard could have unfortunate financial consequences for many established churches and charities. Already, in the proximity of the Indian bingo hall, charity bingo was drying up. American Legion members, Lions Club people, and Elks Hall patrons all urged him to resist.

In addition, it appeared there was no way the state could benefit from a full-scale casino. The state had the authority to tax the revenue of traditional charity gaming operations, but the Indian Gaming Regulatory Act had spelled out that Indian casinos on federally recognized reservations could not be subject to state taxation. The language of IGRA made it clear that if a state even attempted such taxation, the courts should interpret this as a sign of "bad faith" on the part of the state government.

On May 1, 1989, four weeks after receiving Tureen and King's letter, O'Neill referred the matter to Clarine Riddle, who had just become the state's acting attorney general. O'Neill asked Riddle to come up with some theories as to why the state should not have to comply with the request to grant the Pequots a full-fledged casino. Riddle was a good liberal Democrat whose husband taught at Yale University. She was sympathetic to the plight of Indians and anxious to do whatever she could to make amends for the generations of genocide and discrimination against Native American peoples. In the past, she had supported requests for sweat lodges at state prisons as well as various measures to preserve traditional burial practices at Indian graveyards. But Riddle had no problem drawing the line at casinos. After considering the issue, she concluded that the charity gaming statute just passed by the legislature was completely different from the ones that had been involved in the Seminole and Cabazon cases. In the case of Connecticut, the state had established play money and stuffed animals as prizes that couldn't even be redeemed for cash. She told O'Neill, "There is no way that Las Vegas Nights can justify the legalization of full-scale casinos." Further, she added, the request was illogical and certainly not the intended result of the Indian Gaming Regulatory Act. Real casino gambling, with actual money, Riddle concluded, was not allowed in Connecticut and provided no opening for the tribe's request to be granted.

O'Neill was delighted with the report. On July 19, at O'Neill's direction, Riddle informed Tureen that the state was under no obligation to negotiate with him or with any other representative of the Pequots. They had their bingo and they would just have to be content with it. Case closed. She, of course, had not dealt with Tom Tureen or his young partner Barry Margolin before. If she had been more familiar with the whole history of the Maine tribal litigation, she might have known immediately just how hopeless her position was. Tureen took letters like Riddle's as a challenge, and he was supremely confident that the State of Connecticut would pay for its failure to give the Pequots what he wanted.

Brilliant and precise, Margolin was the visionary Tureen's perfect complement. In 1985, they had moved from Eastport in northern Maine to Portland and established the law firm known as Tureen & Margolin. In many ways the two partners were perfect opposites. Tureen now flew his own plane from reservation to reservation; Margolin hated flying, even as a passenger. Once an antiwar activist at Harvard University, Margolin initially had no special interest in Indian law. He had joined Tureen in 1972 on the recommendation of a friend who had interned at Tureen's Pine Tree Legal Assistance program. When he arrived there, Tureen was just about to file the Maine land claim. Margolin had arrived in Maine on a Greyhound bus and spent his whole first night writing the brief, getting it typed, and flying it to federal court the next day.

The two had certainly come a long way from the days when they scraped by on $30 an hour from legal aid work. Since 1972, when Tureen hired Margolin as his summer associate, the two had been personally responsible for putting six Native American tribes on the map. They had a map pinned to their office wall and the portion of New England land occupied by their tribes they had covered in pink. Margolin loved seeing the pink areas grow larger and larger. Like the Mashantucket Pequots, several of the tribes had been virtually created where little more than a memory had existed.

The Indian Gaming Regulatory Act had set a time frame of two hundred days for the state to begin its negotiations for a gambling compact, a stipulation O'Neill ignored. On exactly the two hundredth day after sending the original letter to the governor, Tureen and Margolin filed suit against the State of Connecticut in federal district court in Hartford. The suit demanded that the federal court compel the state to grant the Pequots a gaming license. O'Neill held on to the hope that public antipathy and pressure against gambling in Connecticut would ultimately force the Pequots to relent. But he was up against stubborn and well-prepared foes.

The case was assigned to U.S. district court judge Peter Dorsey, the same judge who had previously ruled for the Pequots in the bingo case. Riddle argued to Dorsey that Margolin's request was improper because the tribal council itself, of which Skip Hayward was the chairman, had never specifically voted for a tribal ordinance on gambling. She also claimed that neither the Seminole nor the Cabazon decision could be used as a precedent because neither had dealt with a full-fledged casino. The Seminole case was about bingo and Cabazon was about a poker room. But as confident as Riddle sounded at oral arguments before Judge Dorsey, Riddle and Margolin shared one opinion in common. They both knew that she was going to lose. In the privacy of the governor's mansion, she acknowledged as much to O'Neill. Even before a ruling was made by the judge, they began to discuss other possible options. Eventually, Riddle suggested that the only way the Pequots would be stopped was for the state legislature to repeal its 1987 charity gaming law. Everything the state permitted, down to the paper scrip and stuffed animals, had to go. If there was nothing that even resembled a casino in the state, the Indian lawyers would have nothing upon which to stake their claim to a legal gambling palace.

O'Neill didn't think this was a very good idea. Such a shift in tactics would look like a dirty trick, as if the state was once again pulling the rug out from under downtrodden Indian peoples. Second, he told Riddle, it probably wouldn't work. Because of rising public sympathy for the Indian cause, the legislature would not go along. Third, and most importantly, he worried that Judge Dorsey would interpret such a move as evidence of bad faith and sock the state with penalties and sanctions in addition to giving Tureen and Margolin everything else they wanted.

On May 15, 1990, Judge Dorsey finally issued his ruling in the state's case. It surprised no one that he ordered the governor to continue negotiations with Tureen and Margolin on behalf of the tribe—through an impartial mediator. The state did not have a choice as to whether or not there would be a casino, only as to how it would be regulated. The Pequot legal camp was joyous. The lawyers prepared to wrap up their negotiations and install the blackjack, roulette, crap, and baccarat tables that would define a new era in profit. The only thing denied to the tribe was slot machines, which the legislature had decided weren't suitable for teenagers. The highly addictive slots were not legal even at charity gaming nights and thus could not be part of the Indian casino either.

O'Neill was not ready to give up completely, and he appealed the case to the Second U.S. District Court of Appeals in New York. On September 4, 1990, a three-judge federal panel unanimously upheld Judge Dorsey's ruling. Noting that Connecticut permits "games of chance," it seemed obvious to the appeals court that "such gaming is not totally repugnant to the state's public policy." The state appealed again, this time to the United States Supreme Court. But this appeal would prove to be just as fruitless and eventually it would be denied.

ULTIMATELY, THE CASINO ISSUE would not be O'Neill's problem. Having presided over a state with a stagnant economy and a large budget shortfall, and with virtually no chance at reelection, O'Neill had wisely decided not to seek another term.

Meanwhile, after losing his Senate seat in a hotly contested race against Democrat Joseph Lieberman in 1988, Weicker had set his sights on the governorship. In November 1990, he ran for governor as an independent, winning 40 percent of the vote in a three-way race. Weicker was well known in the state for his arrogant, often brutal political manner. Weicker was a child of privilege, descended from the founders of the Squibb drug company fortune. He had become best known nationally in the U.S. Senate as a member of the Senate Watergate Committee that exposed many of the excesses of President Richard Nixon in 1973–74.

Despite the fact that Weicker owned racehorses and was a frequent visitor to the little Rosecroft Raceway in corrupt Prince George's County, he came into office as an outspoken and visceral opponent of Indian casinos. Part of his opposition stemmed no doubt from the fact that the pari-mutuel racing industry, with which Weicker was associated, greatly feared the competition that a casino would bring. (While a senator in Washington, Weicker had even kept pictures of his racehorses on his office wall.)

The attorney general elected with Weicker was a young up-and-coming lawyer named Richard Blumenthal. It would be Blumenthal who inherited the case as it rose to the level of the U.S. Supreme Court. In a slight shift of the state's position, Blumenthal drafted an anticasino brief, returning to the theme that the casino would bring in organized crime. This had already been the losing strategy in the Cabazon case, and Blumenthal fared no better.

Connecticut could not even get any help from such a moral gentleman as U.S. solicitor general Kenneth Starr. The parsonlike attorney who would later go on a moral crusade to expose President Clinton's sexual proclivities found nothing to object to when it came to casinos. In fact, he intervened to ask the Supreme Court to rule in favor of the tribe. "The games of chance at issue here are not prohibited in Connecticut but instead are permitted subject to extensive regulation and limitation," Starr said. He noted that federal law "does not entitle the state of Connecticut to refuse to enter into any negotiations" over the gambling proposal.

Meanwhile, the U.S. Department of the Interior announced it was going to implement the plan of a court-appointed mediator and approve the compact. The conclusion was almost foregone, and the Pequots didn't even wait for the official word of their victory at the Supreme Court before they began taking steps in early April of 1991 to expand the bingo hall into a casino. A team of casino experts was already in place to operate the establishment that was to be called Foxwoods, and unbeknownst to anyone, the tribe had already come up with an exotic financing scheme. At the time, no one really knew the details of what was happening back in Ledyard. Hawyard and Margolin wanted it this way, certainly until they got the official go-ahead from the High Court. On April 22, that go-ahead came. The Supreme Court would not hear Connecticut's appeal. By a unanimous verdict, it decided to let the U.S. appeals court ratification of Dorsey's original pro-Pequot decision stand.

Inside the statehouse, the mood was sour. Although it seemed like the fight was over, Weicker was not yet ready to surrender to the resurrected upstarts from Ledyard. He huddled in his office with Chief of Staff Stanley Twardy, a former U.S. attorney in Connecticut with deeply held beliefs about gambling and mob activity. "I've seen what the mob can do," he told Weicker. "Even those with good intentions can get run over." Twardy should know. As U.S. attorney, he had helped bust the New England–wide operations of Rhode Island's biggest organized crime syndicate, that of Raymond J. Patriarca, Jr. Even as twenty-one members of the New England crime syndicate awaited trial, New Yorker John Gotti of the Gambino family and Vincent "the Chin" Gigante of the Genovese family were chomping at the bit to fill the void in the region that Twardy's successful prosecution had helped create. Twardy was anxious not to give either Gotti or Gigante an excuse or reason to expand into Connecticut.

Certainly, there was nobody in the Pequot camp, not Hayward and especially not Tureen, who was really equipped to deal with organized crime. Twardy advised Weicker not to give up the fight against the casino. There was still one last option, the one that William O'Neill had rejected a year earlier. On the morning of April 30, 1991, Weicker called a meeting with Hayward, Margolin, and other members of the tribe's legal and lobbying team at his office in the statehouse in Hartford. The governor and the chief sat down on opposite couches and Weicker, in his characteristic blunt manner, got right to business. "The mob will eat you alive," Weicker said, leaning forward into Hayward's face. Then he turned to one of Hayward's advisors, who was introduced as being from Atlantic City. "I don't care who he is," Weicker barked. "I wouldn't take my dog to Atlantic City."

Personally, Weicker was drawn to Skip. Both men knew that Weicker's intervention in 1984 had been instrumental in persuading President Reagan to reverse his veto of the Mashantucket Pequot land settlement claim. Without the $900,000 settlement, Skip's effort to resurrect the tribe would have failed. Skip and his cousins would have been forced by economic circumstances to leave the reservation. Skip couldn't believe what he was now hearing from a man he had assumed to be on his side. Worse, Weicker was a very good friend of Vincent Laudone, Jackson King's law partner whose call to Weicker six years earlier had resulted in Weicker's successful intervention in the case. Hayward had assumed that as long as Jackson King and Vinnie Laudone were on his team, the tribe was in good hands. Now Skip was very concerned, as Weicker continued his lecture.

"They will eat you alive," Weicker repeated, his deep voice rising with each syllable. "They are too sophisticated for what you are trying to do." The governor couldn't have hit a rawer nerve with Skip. Everyone in the room noticed that Skip grew white and shaky every time the mob was mentioned.

Margolin tried to step into the awkward situation, talking about the compact he had tried to negotiate over the previous eighteen months, referring to it in favorable terms that would benefit both the tribe and the state. Weicker agreed it was a great compact. "You did a hell of a job," he told Margolin. "The state did a shitty job."

The assistant attorney general for the state, Richard Sheridan, who was present at the meeting, burned red with embarrassment at the language. Then Weicker leaned forward, rubbed his hands together, and declared, "We're not going to have gambling in Connecticut."

Skip was shaking when the session ended. Weicker left his office and announced to the press that he would send a letter to the legislature asking that the charity gaming laws be repealed. "I do not want casino gambling," baritoned Weicker in his best gruff bluster. "The statistics are irrefutable as to crime, organized crime, as to prostitution, drunken driving."

Weicker began telling the public and the legislature that in order to stop the Pequots the state's charity gaming law would have to be repealed. At this late stage, he said, nothing else would work. The state would be working against a deadline. Secretary of the Interior Manuel Lujan, whose agency was supporting the tribe, could not legally grant the federally approved casino license until May 17. Weicker's plan was to have the charity gaming laws revoked by that date. Then the state would send a new petition to Lujan asking him, in light of developments, not to grant the federal approval.

Hayward was stunned by Weicker's turnaround. By now, the tribe had put nearly $1 million into the effort to get the casino approved. Plans had been drawn, color schemes selected, management chosen, and lawyers and lobbyists and PR people had been hired. Hayward launched into a bitter denunciation of Weicker, telling Tureen and Margolin that when the casino was finally built, Weicker would never, never be invited to set foot in the place. In a public statement, Hayward could not contain his anger and disappointment. "Indian people have faced a long and tragic history of broken treaties," he said. "It could be very sad if Connecticut added another chapter to that history. We cannot believe the state would do this to us now."

But it seemed, of course, that the state was doing it. Weicker got immediate support from influential Republican congressman Chris Shays. "I want to to help our state do everything it can to prevent casino gambling from coming in," Shays said. "If the law says we have to allow casino nights because charitable organizations have casino nights, then the law has to be changed." Shays was already regretful that the state had allowed dog racing and jai alai, two gambling games rife with dishonesty and mob involvement. "With casino gambling you make a quantum leap backward," he said, adding that he found it "bizarre" that the state had to allow a casino simply because charities hosted Las Vegas Nights with play money.

Bizarre or not, this was the situation in which Connecticut found itself, and it continued to get no help from the federal government. The Interior Department quickly came out against making any changes in the newly passed IGRA; no one wanted to reopen that legislative fight, and Interior Secretary Lujan observed that Shays's distinction between real money and play money had no legal weight because play money could still be redeemed for a prize, which had some value, even if it was just a cheap stuffed animal.

The Interior Department made it clear to Weicker that it wasn't going to halt the casino permit because of the governor's eleventh-hour sneak attack. Even if Weicker won, this would not be the end of the casino but would put the matter back into the courts one more time.

To prepare for the legislative battle, Margolin and Gips enlisted the aid of Charles Duffy and Keith Stover, two savvy Hartford lobbyists. Duffy was a Georgetown University graduate and a former classmate of Bill Clinton. Once when Duffy went with his parents to visit Hot Springs, Arkansas, Clinton set Duffy up on a date with a beauty pageant winner. Duffy had been hired by Margolin in September of 1990, when the tribe had become certain, as a result of the U.S. Court of Appeals ruling, that the casino was inevitable. Up until now, Duffy's contributions had been minimal. He had been hired to be the tribe's "eyes and ears" in Hartford and to alert Margolin if there were any problems with legislators. The last thing Duffy had expected was a full-scale lobbying war. Like everyone else, he had thought that the Supreme Court case was the final act. In his many discussions with the state, he had not encountered anyone who had predicted that the legal battle would spill over into a legislative and political one. But Duffy was ready for the fight.

What he didn't expect was that almost immediately Weicker would win the support of the powerful *New York Times,* which editorialized, "Mr. Weicker's strategy may be shaky, and it is certainly unpopular with some vocal constituencies. But his instincts are sound. If anything, Connecticut needs less gambling, not more."

Though the *New York Times* was influential, there were still some forces with which it could not compete. Earlier that year, Kevin Costner's film *Dances With Wolves* won the Oscar for Best Picture. *Dances With Wolves* was a powerful indictment of how the United States had brutally dealt with American Indian tribes, with Costner playing a U.S. soldier on the American frontier who realizes over time that the Indians are much more humane than the government he represents. Most residents of Connecticut were eager to identify with Costner's on-screen character, and Margolin and Gips even made some exploratory calls to see if they couldn't get Costner into the state to pose with their clients.

In Ledyard, feelings were mixed. "I'm caught in a bind," said State representative Glenn Arthur, a Republican who represented the town in the legislature. In principle, Arthur was opposed to the casino, but on the other hand, he did not want to hurt nonprofit groups and had doubts about whether changing the law would be constitutional at this point. The state legislature too was both conflicted and confused over the Weicker proposal. Connecticut was already wrestling with a huge shortfall in revenue, to say nothing of one of the biggest recessions in the state's history. In his zeal to halt the casino, Weicker would be depriving nonprofit groups of a proven way to raise funds when voluntary charitable contributions were slipping and when the need for such services was rising. He would be slamming the door on what proponents of the casino claimed would be 1,900 new jobs in his state at a time when Pratt & Whitney, Electric Boat, and General Dynamics were laying people off by the dozens. And what would happen if the state killed off charity gaming, only to find that the casino was allowed by the courts to open anyway? Connecticut would end up with a giant casino that it couldn't tax and would have done away with all the harmless little gambling halls that it could and did assess.

The Speaker of the Connecticut House of Representatives, Richard J. Balducci, noted at a news conference that he had participated in Las Vegas Nights himself to raise money for a football team in his town. He said he was not convinced that repealing the charity gambling laws was desirable. Though the state would not derive any tax revenues from casino profits, according to the president of the Chamber of Commerce of Southeastern Connecticut, William D. Moore, the casino would make the Pequots the fourth-largest employer in the county. In just the week since the Supreme Court had announced it would not hear the state's appeals, Moore had received calls from four developers who wanted to talk about building hotels in the area. "There is considerable amount of business support for the casino—considerable," Moore remarked.

But before the issue ever got to the House, it had to pass the thirty-six-member Connecticut Senate. It became a put-up-or-shut-up situation for Governor Weicker. He had come off to a lot of legislators as something of a bully, and his co–chief of staff, Thomas D'Amore, was pulling out all the stops to avoid a Weicker humiliation in the first high-profile battle of their new administration.

Starting with just eleven out of thirty-six senators on their side, D'Amore, Twardy, and Weicker feverishly worked the corridor, the chamber of the Senate, and the cloakrooms. Duffy and Stover stood outside the door as the ninety-minute debate roared on inside. "Before we know it, Connecticut will be the Atlantic City of New England," bellowed Senator James T. Fleming. "That's not a compliment in my opinion." But a senator from Uncasville, about 15 miles west of Ledyard, endorsed the Indian position and pointed out how badly the area needed economic development. "Ledyard will never be Atlantic City," he said naïvely. When the votes were cast, Governor Weicker had won by a vote of 19 to 17. The battle moved to the Connecticut House of Representatives, where a vote was scheduled the next day. Twardy was confident of victory. And Duffy and Stover, two shrewd old-time Hartford hands, knew the odds were now against them. They got the vote delayed for a day and went to work, reminding legislators just how bad it would look to take this little casino away from the downtrodden Native Americans. More importantly, the lobbyists were able to enlist the key support of the state legislature's black caucus. Duffy urged Kenneth Reels, the leader of the Pequots' Narragansett faction, to visit key black legislators and ask for their support. Reels told them that much of the opposition to the Pequot casino was due to the fact that 75 percent of the tribe members were black. Couching this issue as a racial matter began to make many legislators very uneasy. Now a vote for Weicker might well be seen as the latest example of the Indians' being taken advantage of by the white man. During the twenty-four-hour delay, House members received numerous calls and telegrams from church groups and pastors who didn't want to have their own sources of funding cut off. The delay seemed to be working to the Pequots' advantage.

In four hours of emotional debate on the floor of the statehouse, the representatives argued the pros and cons of the potential casino, one suggesting disgustedly that "we might as well move a craps table into the well of the House." Liberals were torn between their desire to be the defenders of the downtrodden and their desire to oppose a destructive vice like gambling. "One of the things that will never be rectified is what we have done to the Indians," said Edna Negron, a liberal Democrat from Hartford. "It's an issue of justice. They went through the process. They did it right, they won." Republicans railed against the evils of gambling and sin but at the same time agonized about the financial impact of eliminating bingo from their parish churches. The director of one senior citizen center came to Hartford and begged the legislature not to deprive her elderly residents of their "night of fun."

But the most emotional speech of the night came from Republican representative Kevin Rennie. He knew that many of his constituents had been deeply affected by *Dances With Wolves*. He rose on the floor of the legislature and proclaimed, "The Trail of Tears stops here in the Connecticut House of Representatives." No sooner were his words out than the gallery burst into tearful and spontaneous applause.

As the members sat down for the vote, four television cameras rolled. The House voted 84 to 62 to keep the charity gaming laws. The vote might have been closer, but when the majority was clear, several House members switched their votes to go on the record with the winning side. This made the margin seem larger, and it obliterated the state's last possible hope of stopping the Pequots' casino. When the vote was over, Duffy admitted that his role in the victory had been much less significant than Kevin Costner's.

Weicker took the defeat with aplomb. His decision to push for repeal instead of trying to use his clout to get concessions from the tribe had ultimately worked against the state, allowing the Pequots to operate largely free of Connecticut supervision, as well as state taxes. And they made no agreement to pay the state any percentage of the profits, as they might have been willing to do if Weicker had taken a more conciliatory tack. Nonetheless, Weicker announced after the vote that he would immediately begin to implement the terms of the compact that had been negotiated by the mediator. In a meeting with Hayward and

Duffy, he said, "You won fair and square." He assured them, "I could make your lives miserable, but I won't."

Weicker instructed Attorney General Blumenthal to make sure the compact was enforced and the casino honestly run. The compact didn't do a lot for the state, favoring the Pequots, as Weicker had colorfully observed earlier. But the compact did give the state authority, among other things, to do background checks and to require state-issued licenses for the people who would be getting jobs at the casino. "We were opposed to it," Blumenthal said of the new casino. "But now that it's a reality, we want to insure that any prospect of criminal activity will be kept to a minimum."

Despite the inflamed rhetoric of the legislative debate, residents were hardly alarmed. Arnold Danielsen, president of the Eastern Connecticut Chamber of Commerce, whose 500 members include business owners in Ledyard, Preston, and North Stonington, observed, "It certainly is important to the Indians, if not more important, to maintain the area's beauty and tranquility. We're talking about a small casino on a reservation where people will be able to look out the windows and see the forest." The Pequots' tribal affairs coordinator, Skip's sister Theresa Bell, confirmed that the Indians were dedicated to maintaining the serene atmosphere on their land. "We live here, and our children live here," she said. "We don't want the area to become another hamburger alley. It's going to be up to the towns to make sure that doesn't happen. We have a lot of pride and love for our land. We intend to keep everything at the highest possible standards," she said.

Still, there were skeptics. State representative Robert Farr predicted that Ledyard would turn into the "Kuwait of Connecticut," a description that would prove to be more apt than most. Arthur Dawley, whose family had lived on several hundred acres of farmland near Ledyard, expressed fear that the town's "peace will be shattered" when the casino opened. "I think it's going to change the whole area," he predicted. So did Gerald Grabarek, chairman of the Town of Preston's Planning and Zoning Commission. "This is going to change the town a lot more than anybody realizes," he said. "But I'll tell you something, I don't think this is going to help businesses here all that much. People are going to come here to gamble. They aren't coming to see our town."

Other local residents said they were worried that Route 2 would be constantly clogged with traffic. "The greatest impact on the area will be the increased traffic flow," said Preston's first selectman Parke C. Spicer. "Those roads were never designed for the kind of traffic this casino is going to generate. Something is going to have to be done about that."

But optimism prevailed among most local merchants who agreed there would be big changes and looked forward to them. "This has been a sleepy part of the state for many years, and now that's going to change," said Wayne Henson of Holdridge's, a nursery and greenhouse in Ledyard. "We're going to be seeing a lot more people around here once the casino opens, and that's got to be good for business."

On May 17, Manuel Lujan, the secretary of the interior, sent by courier to Skip Hayward the official okay to go ahead and start up the gambling. Hayward was still steaming over the unexpected sideswipe by Governor Weicker. But his promise to keep the governor out of the casino would not last any longer than the broken vows of his enemies. In a very short time, Hayward and Weicker would both come to realize that each could be the answer to the other's biggest problem. Before they knew it, their mutual interests would come together.

7

THE LAND BRIDGE TO ASIA

LOWELL WEICKER and his top assistant, Stanley Twardy, had worried endlessly about organized crime getting its hooks into the Pequots. But as Twardy would later come to admit, his fears were largely unwarranted. Crime figures shared the view of many of the residents of Ledyard, that the new casino wouldn't amount to much. Their business was running illegal gambling games, and they quickly dismissed the idea of even investing in this legal casino, the newest competitor to their numbers, football betting, and illegal horse books.

Twardy, the former federal prosecutor, had only himself to thank for the mob's lack of influence in New England. As the U.S. district attorney in Connecticut before hooking up with Weicker, Twardy had been part of the prosecution team that in March of 1990 had indicted twenty-one members of the Raymond Patriarca crime family, a sweep that spread out over Connecticut, Rhode Island, and Massachusetts. Weicker had warned Skip Hayward that the Pequots did not have the muscle to deal with organized crime. But not even Weicker was aware of just how anemic the Providence organized crime family had become by 1991. Twardy's prosecutions of key mob members, and the incarceration of Raymond J. "Junior" Patriarca, the head of the family, had severely depleted the family's criminal operations. One prosecutor noted, "We've come as close as ever to destroying the Patriarca family. I'd be close to declaring victory on this one." Nor did Foxwoods have to fear threats of shakedowns or extortion from Patriarca's rival, John Gotti, the head of the New York–based Gambino family, one of the five powerful New

York City crime families. Gotti specifically rejected a proposal that his operation get involved in Foxwoods, telling underlings that they could make as much money loan-sharking to individual losing gamblers at the casino as they could trying to shake down or intimidate the owners. Indeed, the casino provided an unexpected bonanza for mob operations in a totally inadvertent fashion. When gamblers run out of money, they can't usually get help from the loan officers at Chase Manhattan. Mobsters would be the venture capitalists who kept the money flowing into Foxwoods' gaming tables.

Though neither Gotti nor Patriarca may have been interested in a legal gambling palace in Ledyard, halfway across the globe—in a tall glass-enclosed skyscraper in Kuala Lumpur, Malaysia—someone else was. It was here in his headquarters in Kuala Lumpur that an eighty-year-old industrialist named Lim Goh Tong had thirsted for decades to own a casino in the United States. But until the Pequots went to court to win the right to open a gambling palace, it seemed to be the only thing he wanted in the world that he could never have. Lim's involvement with the Pequots had its genesis in September 1990 when the U.S. court of appeals had upheld federal judge Peter Dorsey's order that Connecticut negotiate a casino-gambling compact with the Pequots in good faith.

At this point, Barry Margolin had decided it was finally time to put the wheels in motion to begin construction of the casino, as well as to put together an operating team. In his mind, there was no doubt that the federal court ruling would be upheld by the United States Supreme Court. Neither he nor Tureen had predicted Weicker's ultimately unsuccessful and desperate effort to have the legislature kill the charity gaming laws.

Rob Gips, a young Tureen-hired lawyer from New Jersey with some connections and some expertise in gambling laws, was given the assignment of trying to find somebody who knew how to set up a casino and who could advise them on perfecting the required "compact" with the state. The customary thing to do would have been to hire a management company to operate the casino in exchange for a half-share of the profits. That was the arrangement many tribes, including the Cabazons and the Seminoles, had made in the past for their own gambling operations. Management contracts made sense for the tribes, who simply lacked the experience and expertise to run something as complicated as a casino. Even though Las Vegas casino owners had fought to ban Indian casinos, now that Foxwoods was here to stay, their executives were more than happy to get whatever piece of the action they could. Half a small fortune was better than none, and it wasn't long before Margolin and Tureen were getting calls from representatives of casino moguls Donald Trump, who owned the Taj Mahal in Atlantic City, and Stephen Wynn, of the Mirage in Las Vegas, almost every day. Both Wynn and Trump had their sights set on helping to operate the Foxwoods Casino, for a percentage of the profit.

Skip, however, was nearly as nervous about a Las Vegas connection as he was about mob involvement. "Sure, we could let some company come in here and build the casino," he told Margolin. "But it wouldn't be ours." Skip already had his own vision of how the casino would look and feel, and he wanted to make sure he didn't lose control over his concept. He had agreed to build a casino and he had agreed to sell the idea to the tribe. But he absolutely would not, he told Margolin and Tureen, put the newly revitalized Pequots at the mercy of Las Vegas casino operators. Tureen could hardly protest. An iconoclast himself, he admired Hayward's independent streak, even when it made his own life difficult. How could he ask Skip to do anything else but to follow his own path? Besides, Tureen wondered with his own midwestern naïveté, how hard could it be to run a casino?

Tureen, Margolin, and Gips thrashed out the problem of accommodating Skip's concerns at their office in Portland, Maine. Between the three of them, they knew about as much about casinos as Skip, which was next to nothing. Still, Tureen was anxious to move ahead. His projects on behalf of the Passamaquoddies had involved too much heavy, polluting industry. Mobile-home manufacturing and the operation of a cement factory had been giant headaches, especially from an environmental and regulatory point of view. The casino needed to go up as soon as possible, and they needed to find somebody trustworthy to run it for them. Unfortunately, the team had few contacts in the business.

Gips recalled that a year earlier on a Continental Airlines flight to a gaming conference in Atlantic City, he had heard a businessman directly across the aisle practicing a speech on the Indian Gaming Regulatory Act and its possible effects on casino regulation. Gips introduced himself to the man and excitedly began telling him how he represented an Indian tribe that one day might want to open a casino. Gips was eager to make a contact in the business, but the other passenger didn't quite know what to say and seemed anxious to keep working on his speech. After his arrival, the other passenger remarked to friends how he had the misfortune of being seated next to a "crazy guy" jabbering away about an Indian tribe that might one day need some help.

The only other contact Gips could think of was a lawyer for whom he had worked during law school, John Degnan. Degnan had been chief counsel to New Jersey governor Brendan Byrne in 1976, the year New Jersey voters approved a referendum permitting casino gambling in Atlantic City. Degnan was appointed attorney general in 1978, the year Resorts International became the first Atlantic City casino to open its doors. Gips called Degnan to see what he could find out and express the tribe's special concern that they find someone to run the casino who was totally clean of mob ties. His hope was that he might be able to persuade Degnan himself to come to Connecticut and provide advice on what should be written into the compact.

Degnan was not prepared to go that far. But he sympathized with Gip and referred him to the former chief enforcement officer at the New Jersey Casino Control Commission, a fellow lawyer named G. Michael "Mickey" Brown. Brown's dream, Degnan said, was to one day run his own casino. Degnan endorsed Brown unreservedly. "If there's any one person you should talk to, it's Mickey Brown," he said.

Until he made an appointment to see Brown and walked into his office in Princeton, New Jersey, Gips had no idea this was the same man he had pestered a year earlier on the airplane. When Gips walked in the door, Brown did a double take and exclaimed, "Hey, aren't you the guy from the airplane?" Gips turned red with embarrassment before admitting that that "guy" had indeed been him.

Born into a tough Irish-Catholic family in northern New Jersey,

Brown had attended St. Benedict's Preparatory School in Newark, then enrolled at Franciscan College in Steubenville, Ohio. After college, he enrolled in law school at Seton Hall University back home in Newark, where he spent weekends in a National Guard unit. In October 1968, after graduation from law school, Brown was sent to Fort McClellan, Alabama, for a year of active duty. His job was driving a military supply truck. After the year in Alabama, Mickey got his orders to go to Vietnam, to carry supplies and weapons at the height of the war. Between land mines and Viet Cong ambushes, this was about as dangerous an assignment as a soldier could have. In the fall of 1969, Brown arrived at Bien Hoa Air Force Base, 15 miles east of Saigon, and made his way to the Long Binh headquarters of the U.S. Army command. On his first day there, Brown walked over to the office of the adjutant general, a Colonel Greenberg, and stood outside the entrance until Greenberg showed up.

"Who are you?" Greenberg asked.

"I'm a lawyer," Brown replied.

"I've been looking for a replacement," Greenberg said. "You got the job."

So instead of driving a truck, Brown took over the legal office at the U.S. Army headquarters at Long Binh, recommending court-martials, arguing drug cases and desertions, and prosecuting or sometimes defending soldiers charged with illegally selling goods on the black market. Fortunately, his unit was called back to the States after just a year, and Brown resumed his legal career at home in New Jersey. He first took a job as an assistant attorney general in the New Jersey Division of Criminal Justice. In the spring of 1980, Brown was assigned to handle a landmark criminal case intended by Attorney General Degnan to prove to the world that organized crime did, in fact, exist. At the time, although the existence of a "mafia" was established in American folklore, movies, and books, its existence had never been proven in court. Degnan had decided not only to put the leading members of New Jersey's best-known crime "family" in prison, but in the process to establish— for the legal record—that there was a national crime conspiracy. With Brown doing much of the legwork, Degnan developed testimony from a New Jersey painting contractor, who claimed that members of the Vito Genovese crime family, led by an eighty-eight-year-old gardener named Richie "the Boot" Boiardo, had left him bankrupt through extortion and the charging of usurious interest rates. Brown eventually elicited the co-operation of Anthony "Little Pussy" Russo, who had been the chauffeur for the legendary Genovese, a one-time henchman for Lucky Luciano, who became the powerful don of one of New York's most dangerous crime families. Brown was able to indict seven of the leading organized crime figures in New Jersey on charges of murder, extortion, loan-shark-ing and bookmaking. Even though Russo was gunned down before he could testify, Brown was able to convince a jury that an organized crim-inal conspiracy the members referred to as La Cosa Nostra, a phrase translated into English as "This Thing of Ours," was in fact a reality. The word "mafia" was never used in the case. On June 4, 1980, after a three-month trial, Brown won guilty verdicts against four of the defendants, although Richie "the Boot" was excused by the judge on grounds of ill health. To the press and the legal community, the real significance was the establishment of the existence of La Cosa Nostra and the possible impact that would have on future government prosecutions of organized crime figures. The defendants were more skeptical about the dent Brown had put in the mob's operations. After leaving the courtroom, Anthony De Vingo, convicted of loan-sharking and of participating in a criminal conspiracy, observed: "Ford may have closed its plant in Mah-way, but the company didn't go out of business."

Brown's success pleased Degnan, who later in the year was looking for somebody to take over the state's new Division of Gaming Enforce-ment at a time when the boardwalk casinos were all just starting out in business. Brown played a key role in writing the bylaws by which New Jersey would regulate its casinos, and he set about making sure they were enforced. When a new casino owner came into town, it fell on Brown to do the background check and to recommend to the state Casino Control Commission whether that person should get a license. After two years in this new post, Brown left government work, and in 1982 he formed a consulting firm representing gambling companies. Brown was not the kind of lawyer to idly chat about his work, so not too many people knew exactly whom he had represented, just that he seemed to travel a lot and was logging a lot of hours in Australia. But what people like Degnan were confident of was that when it came to setting up a casino, Mickey Brown was dependable, smart, and tough.

While the Pequot representatives were fighting with Governor William O'Neill over their letter requesting a casino, Gips and several members of the tribal council traveled to Princeton, New Jersey, where Brown had an office, to ask for his advice. They simply weren't sure what functions they should let the state perform and what duties they should retain as a matter of tribal rights. On many matters, Brown recommended letting the state take a lead role. He talked to them about the licensing of employees and suggested that the tribe entrust the state police with the responsibility of running background checks on all casino workers. Since one of the biggest problems in running a casino was dishonest dealers, they would need the help of the state in identifying corrupt job applicants. He also suggested that the Pequots voluntarily comply with the state liquor laws and, since the tribe at that time did not have a police force, that they authorize the Connecticut State Police to enforce criminal laws inside the casino. It was clear to Brown that neither Gips nor the tribal council members really understood the gambling business all that well. When the meeting ended, Gips asked if Brown would come up to Ledyard to meet Skip. They were definitely interested in hiring him as a full-time consultant.

Brown was more than happy to oblige, although cooperating with an Indian casino in Connecticut was professionally risky for him. New Jersey casino operators would immediately view such a relationship with suspicion. They would not appreciate a New Jersey native's involvement in helping what could turn out to be serious competition.

But Brown went up to Ledyard anyway, and he and Skip hit it off immediately. Like most people, Brown found Skip likable, enthusiastic, and engaging, and they shared a common love of fishing. Skip took Brown on a tour of the bingo hall, which was filled with folding bridge chairs and cheap-looking fluorescent lights, pointing out where the casino would be, where a hotel might stand, and where he hoped one day to put a tribal museum. Though Skip had some ideas for his casino that Brown didn't favor, his enthusiasm was contagious and he envisioned creating a building that would blend into the neighborhood, provide jobs for his family members, and create a small zone of economic prosperity on the reservation. He had even come up with the name for the future casino complex, Foxwoods, based on the popular legend that the Pequots had once been known as the fox people. Skip himself created the casino's emblem, a fox under a tree, supposedly based on a drawing by a descendant of the eighteenth-century Pequot chief Robin Cassacinamon that he had found in his grandmother's papers. Ironically, none of the actual lineal descendants of Cassacinamon, who were plentiful in the region, were allowed to join the tribe, since their ancestors had not lived on the reservation in the last century and thus were not listed on the 1900 or 1910 census forms for the reservation as Skip's grandparents and aunts had been.

When Skip got going about his plans for the casino, it was pointless to try to cut him off. He could move into a conversational zone that was spellbinding. Brown immediately sensed his sincerity and commitment to the tribe. Whether Skip and his band were or were not really descendants of the original Pequots was totally irrelevant to him, and he wasted little time worrying about it. Skip had the recognition from the BIA and that was all that mattered. Brown immediately decided he was interested in the project. The word that kept running through his mind during that first visit to the reservation was not "authenticity" but "exclusivity." He couldn't have cared less if Skip and his family were not really Indians. What mattered was that if the Pequots could get their application through, they would have the only casino in New England. Of all the people who knew about the casino, from the townspeople to the legislators, even to Skip himself, Brown was the one person who instinctively sensed exactly how powerful and profitable it could be.

If Brown were hired, he would have to help find financing to build and operate the Foxwoods Casino. Tureen and Jackson King had already approached twenty-four northeastern banks and lending institutions looking for someone willing to give them the estimated $60 million necessary to expand the bingo parlor into a casino complex. All had turned them down. Under federal law, the lender to an Indian tribe could not take any reservation property as collateral. The Ledyard reservation, like all federally recognized reservations, was land held in trust for the tribe by the federal government and could not be seized if the Pequots were to default on the loan.

But what really sank the enterprise as a magnet for local financing was the prevailing view that a casino in Yankee New England would not be economically viable. Never mind that this argument had already made the rounds and been discredited with regard to the bingo hall. Bingo and blackjack were two completely different things, and not even the Arab-American Bank, which had tendered the federally backed loan for the bingo hall, was willing to make the leap when it came to hard-core casino games. Besides, Foxwoods wasn't really a full-fledged casino anyway because slot machines were not part of the package. The few bankers in Connecticut who understood the gaming industry knew that it was slots that drove a casino's profits. But there were to be no slots at Foxwoods and Governor Weicker was adamant that there never would be.

Without collateral, Foxwoods was a risky bet for a banker to make. What if people didn't want to drive the 124 miles from New York or Boston just to play blackjack? What if the Pequots couldn't repay the loan? The bankers, clearly, knew nothing about gamblers or the compulsion that fuels the addiction. Luckily for the Pequots, Brown knew somebody who did. When Mickey Brown left government service in 1982, he was approached by representatives of Malaysian billionaire Lim Goh Tong and asked to evaluate the chances of Lim's entering the American casino market. Brown could offer little assistance to the Malaysians, at least in terms of getting into Atlantic City. State and local regulations made it almost impossible for a foreign owner to buy or establish a New Jersey casino. Yet Lim would not give up his dream of owning an American casino.

Lim had been born in China's Fukien province in 1918 as one of nine impoverished children, but he left China as a teenager in 1937 to avoid being conscripted into the Army. He found an uncle in Singapore and began making a living as a carpenter and construction worker. Before long, he began using his wages to buy and sell small parcels of real estate. Eventually, these parcels grew larger and larger. By his early twenties, Lim had gained a reputation as one of Malaya's cleverest and most politically astute property developers. When Malaysia became an independent nation in 1963, Lim was already recognized as the sugar daddy of the United Malays National Organization, the ruling party that would organize and form the first national government of the former British colony. In 1969, Malaysia's first president, to show his gratitude, gave Lim Goh Tong the first and only gambling license ever issued by the Malaysian government.

For the next thirty years, Lim would continue to receive the renewed licenses, carefully issued in three-month permits. In 1964, Lim built Genting Highlands, which started as a thirty-five-room hotel, and over the next decade it grew into a luxury casino-palace. To a large extent, the casino depended on the patronage of the 7 million non-Muslim Chinese who made up about 35 percent of Malaysia's population. The country's Muslim majority was forbidden both by religion and by law from gambling, but the passionate Chinese more than made up for it.

Genting was located 6,000 feet above sea level on a mountaintop 64 kilometers from Kuala Lumpur, and its complex of sports and banquet facilities quickly made it the premier conference center for foreigners in Southeast Asia. Access could be gained through a series of gondolas that went high up into the mountain, although a steep winding road was the more common path. On average, Genting attracted 40,000 visitors a day, about 40 percent of them from Singapore. During the June and December school holidays, the figure swelled to 60,000 per day. Teenagers were particularly attracted by the casino's amusement park, which featured train and boat rides, high-tech virtual-reality video games, and simulated spaceship and runaway truck rides in a "cinema" with movable hydraulic seats. Lim also provided a child-care center so parents could spend large chunks of time at the casino.

Genting Highlands was a truly spectacular resort. But it made its real money by being the only casino in the country. Genting's exclusivity enabled it to function as a giant cash machine from which Malaysian politicians would frequently draw. By 1980, Genting had become the richest and most profitable single casino in the world, while at the same time becoming the most important institution for funding Malaysia's ruling political party. The cycle of contribution and political influence helped Lim to enter more ventures. In addition to Genting, Lim came to control ten shipping companies, the largest of which was Singapore-based Star Cruises, which accounted for 500,000 cruise bookings annually. He also developed Malaysia's largest paper mill complex, had a 40 percent stake in the country's most prominent independent power company, and through a subsidiary called Asiatic Development Berhad, owned lucrative sugar and rubber plantations in both China and the Philippines. In the 1980s, Lim expanded his business to the United States, buying a hotel in Los Angeles and then in 1988 buying a 20 percent stake in publicly traded Cooper Tires. When Cooper's shares skyrocketed during a period of consolidation and merger in the tire and rubber industry, so did Lim's fortune. Stock in his companies was traded publicly on Asian stock markets under the name Genting Berhad Corporation, and in 1989, Lim spun off a separate, new corporate entity, Resorts World, to handle his burgeoning international gambling and hotel operations. In 1990, Resorts World had an after-tax profit of some $75 million. The following year it earned $167 million on revenues of $386 million, according to its annual reports.

Some of Lim's most lucrative businesses were casinos he had opened in Australia and the Bahamas. He owned the Burswood casino in Perth, had a management contract with the Adelaide Casino in South Australia, and owned the Lucayan Beach Resort and Casino in the Bahamas. None of these ventures would have been possible without the involvement of his American casino consultant, Mickey Brown. "I went there as a kind of pre-opening chief executive to get the project organized, hired people to run it, supervised the pre-opening construction, and then got it open and operational," Brown once told the *Providence Journal*. Despite his tremendous success, Lim's dream was to gain a foothold in either Las Vegas or Atlantic City and play on the U.S. stage with gambling entrepreneurs Donald Trump and Stephen Wynn. Lim believed he'd found a formula in Genting Highlands, which if it could be transported to the States, would simply blow the nonthemed, boring Atlantic City casinos away. But he just couldn't pry open the regulatory door. Several times, Lim explored the possibility of building or buying a casino in Las Vegas.

But state regulators, and U.S. law, made it extremely difficult for a foreign owner to control an American casino.

Lim's foreign investments were a tricky matter for him politically. The Malaysian government, on whom Genting depended for its quarterly license renewal, did not look kindly on a leading Malaysian company investing overseas substantial amounts of capital generated within the country. The rulers preferred that he continue to invest in Malaysia and Singapore, where many of his cruise ships were headquartered. But Lim would not be stopped, and in 1989, when Tom Tureen and his companions first began to think about the idea of a full-fledged casino in Connecticut, Lim was involved in one of the biggest international merger-and-acquisitions deals of his life. He planned to buy the London-based Lonrho Corporation from billionaire British businessman Tiny Rowland, who was nearing seventy-five and anxious to dispose of his industrial empire. Lonrho was a huge British conglomerate that had attracted U.S. government attention a few years earlier when it sold a one-third stake in its Metropole Hotels Group to the Libyan Arab Finance Company, the main investment vehicle of dictator Muammar Gaddafi. Lim had built up a 7.3 percent stake in the Lonrho, and hoped to acquire the rest with his casino cash.

Lonrho's dealings were closely watched by both the U.S. Treasury Department and the State Department. The Treasury Department's Office of Foreign Assets Control was so concerned that it threatened to put Lonrho on its list of "banned companies" if Libya acquired any additional "influence" in the running of a Lonrho company. Such a move would have had dire consequences for the thousands of Americans who invested in a popular mutual fund company called Fidelity Management and Research Corporation, the second-largest U.S. shareholder in Lonrho.

The U.S. government's position on Lonrho lowered its stock value by taking potential American investors out of the picture. Lim felt that shares in Lonrho were a great bargain, and his patron, Malaysian Prime Minister Mohammed Mahathir, personally gave him the go-ahead for the purchase; but the one thing Lim needed most was more cash to sweeten his Lonrho offer. Nothing would create cash as quickly as a new casino, preferably in the United States. But with Las Vegas and Atlantic City closed off, it would take something unexpected to get him into the game. What could have been more unexpected than the sudden appearance, literally out of nowhere, of a tiny Indian tribe, in a forgotten swamp, headed by a remote descendent of someone who arrived on the *Mayflower* and his growing family of African-American "Indians?"

It didn't take Mickey Brown long at all to realize that his airplane meeting with Rob Gips and his conversations with Tureen and Margolin represented a lucky confluence of events for both the Pequots and his clients in Malaysia. Seeing the huge opportunity in Foxwoods, Brown proposed the creation of a three-member Tribal Gaming Commission that would set the rules for the casino. Brown gave Hayward a two-year commitment as chairman of this commission, and he immediately began creating a regulatory scheme for the casino modeled on the rules in place in New Jersey that he had helped to write.

In October 1990, several months after being hired by the Pequots, Brown arranged to introduce Barry Margolin to Lim, his son K. T. Lim, and their business advisor, Colin Au, at the Golden Dragon restaurant in New York City's Chinatown. Brown briefed Lim and his Harvard-educated son on the Pequot situation, telling Lim that his dream of running an American casino was finally within reach. Lim was so charged by his conversation with Brown that he canceled plans to fly to London the next day so that he could drive to the reservation with Brown.

Knowing that Lim wanted in, Brown let Hayward in on the news. Skip was working in the tribe's construction trailer the next morning when Brown called him from a phone in the World Trade Center in New York to say that Mr. Lim was on his way. "I've got a hot one," Brown told Skip. The following morning, the Lims arrived at the reservation. They then spent three days listening to Skip tell the story of his tribe's renaissance. The more Lim heard from Hayward about the culture of New England, the Pequot tribe, and the reaction to the casino project from the bankers, the more the tale resonated with the Malaysian patriarch. When Lim Goh Tong had first decided to build a casino in his heavily Muslim, adopted nation, skeptics had warned that it would never make money. Just as Skip had been told that New Englanders would never visit the casino as customers, Lim had been warned that native Malaysians would never come to Genting Highlands. But it didn't matter, he told Skip. Foxwoods would be built for out-of-towners and large "whales," billionaire baccarat and crap players like Australian businessman Kerry Packer or American publisher Larry Flynt. The target audience was not the economically depressed population of Norwich, New London, and Groton. If that were the case, he told Hayward, the casino would in fact be doomed before it started.

If there was one thing Lim had learned from his years in the casino business, it was that there would never be a shortage of players. Next to the desire for sexual gratification, Lim had discovered, the adrenaline rush produced by the idea of gambling was one of the strongest compulsions he had ever witnessed. Once a gambler had it in his or her mind to play, the number of miles to the nearest casino was of no consequence. He scoffed at the concerns that the reservation was in too remote an area to attract customers. At remote Genting Highlands, people arrived by rickety buses and cable cars, although the high rollers were often whisked to their penthouse suites from a state-of-the-art helicopter pad.

During his three-day visit, Lim became absolutely convinced that the same kind of giant casino theme park that thrived outside of Kuala Lumpur could exist in southeastern Connecticut. The casino would be the financial engine driving the project, Lim told Hayward. But ultimately, Foxwoods could be much more. Lim pictured the casino attracting thousands of tourists, whose families could enjoy theme parks and amusements built on land the tribe could purchase for virtually nothing. Lim was a man of vision, Skip concluded quickly. What really impressed him was that Lim wanted to build a different kind of casino than the model endorsed by American casino operators. Vision was something that Skip had come to associate with Indian wisdom and spiritual tradition. Lim had that same long-term view that Skip associated with his "Indian side," and Skip was totally enamored of him from their first meeting.

Lim quickly decided that he wanted to own the casino or at least go in as a fifty-fifty partner. Barry Margolin had to give a labored explanation of why federal law made this impossible. Outsiders could not have an ownership interest in any property on the reservation land, which was owned by the United States government. Nor could any of the land be used as collateral. The best the Lims could do was have some stake in the profits, but even that would have to be approved by the Bureau of Indian Affairs.

Three days after his arrival at Ledyard, Lim's limousine arrived to take him to the airport to embark on his delayed trip to London. Lim was troubled about the issues of ownership. These were certainly complicating factors, but he felt they would not be insurmountable. As Lim bent down to get into his limousine to return to New York, he turned to Skip. "We're going to find a way," he said with confidence. When Lim returned to New York, he authorized his corporate attorneys at the white shoe New York firm of Cleary, Gottlieb, Steen & Hamilton to begin negotiations with Margolin and Hayward.

On February 25, 1991, just a month after Weicker had attained the governorship and two months before the lobbying battle over the charity gaming laws had even begun, Hayward reached a loan agreement with Lim's real estate arm, Kien Huat Realty Company. But the development was hardly headlined in the local newspapers, nor were the details even disseminated among the tribal members. For nearly a decade, the terms of the agreement have remained secret. For public relations reasons, Hayward would only state that the Malaysians had given the tribe the loan. Not even Hayward's lobbyists in Hartford, such as Charles Duffy, were privy to the terms of the agreement. Nor were the Pequots themselves aware of Mickey Brown's relationship with the Lims, even as Brown advised the Pequot Tribal Gaming Commission in negotiating aspects of the casino loan with his old friends and clients. Under the terms of the compact between the Pequots and the State of Connecticut, the state had the right to investigate all employees and officials of the casino to make sure that they had no ties to organized crime. Though questioned on the subject, Brown never revealed to the state his business ties with Lim's Genting Berhad.

But according to sources who have seen the secret agreement, and confirmed by Brown, Lim had given the Pequots a $60-million loan with which to build the casino. In return, Lim, in addition to interest on the loan, would receive 9.99 percent of the net profit from the entire casino operation until the year 2018. To make sure that the tribe didn't short the Malaysians, Lim reserved the right to have all the casino receipts deposited daily into a special Kien Huat Realty Company bank account. The agreement stated that in the event the tribe defaulted on its loan obligations, it would be required to allow Lim to operate the casino under a management contract. It would also allow the Lims to name the management team that would run the casino and require the appointment of a receiver to handle casino revenues. Hayward granted the Lims a clause in which the tribe agreed to waive its sovereign immunity and consented to the jurisdiction of the Connecticut courts in the case of a dispute between the two parties.

In addition to the $60-million loan, Lim and the Pequots formed a business partnership called Two Trees Partnership, which allowed the tribe and the Malaysians to co-own a hotel on a 30-acre tract of land at the corner of Route 2 and Lantern Hill Road, just a few hundred yards down the hill from the casino. Lim could buy the property for very little, and it was land he could actually own, since it was not part of the federal settlement area. Federal law forbade foreign entities from owning any business on the reservation itself, but the hotel was so close to the reservation that few people realized it was not actually on it.

WITH THE FINANCING for Foxwoods in place, Hayward's new casino team took over. Hayward's point man on the operational side of the casino project was Al Luciani. A veteran of Atlantic City casinos who had run Merv Griffin's Resorts Casino Hotel for a while, Luciani was from the old school. That meant that he wanted to build a casino with no windows, no clocks, and traditionally seductive casino colors— all the gimmicks that Atlantic City casinos had been using for years to separate people from their money. But all these tricks seemed silly to Skip. He wasn't about to build a $60-million casino in the lush forest of Mashantucket and not put in windows. Repeatedly, he fretted to Luciani that the venture would be too risky. He wondered what would happen if during one player's hot night at the crap or baccarat table, the tribe lost all its money.

Luciani talked to Hayward as if he were a child, explaining that the house advantage would overcome any short-term fluctuation in odds. "It's just like running an insurance company," Luciani said. "This is a simple business based upon statistical advantage." It simply didn't matter if gamblers won lots of money or not, he explained. Each game had a statistical mathematical edge for the house, and profits for the casino over the long term were guaranteed. Roulette, for example, the most profitable of all casino games, had a 5.26 percent edge for the house. In other words, if a gambler made 100 consecutive bets on the roulette wheel, betting $100 on each spin, by the end of the day he should lose $526. Hayward looked at Luciani a little glazed. What if the casino had a streak of bad luck? Couldn't they lose? In the short term, this was possible, Luciani explained. But over thousands of spins, the mathematical probabilities would kick in, just as the insurance company depended on actuarial tables. Over the long haul, the casino could not lose and the player could not win. That is the reason why most casinos give players free rooms, comp cards, even massages and hot towels to keep them at the tables. Even if a player has a streak of luck, the casino manager knows that if he or she stays around long enough the casino will win its percentage. Craps was the most difficult to explain of all the games, played on a long hollowed-out table covered with an obscure layout and a language peppered with such terms as "come," "don't come," "pass," "don't pass," "on," "off," "hard ways," "horn," "field," and "32 hopping." It could seem pretty confusing to people who had never played the game before. But the core of the game is the "pass line," where chips are placed at the very first "come out" roll. The idea from that point on is to roll a number and then roll it again before the shooter rolls a seven and "sevens-out." If the shooter rolls lots of numbers before a seven comes up, that is considered a "hot roll" by the crap player and all players. But in its essence, craps can be reduced to a simple proposition: Player puts hard-earned money on table. Casino takes it. Repeat process. So if people weren't going to travel to Ledyard to play craps, what were they going to do? Luciani and Hayward hoped that the answer was blackjack. The card game, known to some people as 21, would have to be the one to carry the load. In this game, players are dealt two cards faceup, and the dealer gets two cards, one up and one down. The object is to see whose cards get closest to a total of 21 without going over. Its popularity in the United States had grown, largely because of systems that led a great number of people to believe the game could actually be beaten. In reality, it can't, of course. If it could, casinos wouldn't offer it. And Atlantic City reserved the right, upheld by the courts, to arbitrarily exclude card counters—players who could beat the house odds—from playing. For most people, blackjack has a smaller house advantage than roulette and is much slower than craps. So it takes money, but at a slower and often more excruciating rate.

If Hayward didn't understand the actual business of gambling, he was starting to understand the overarching principle of the casino—sucker bets money, casino owner takes money. It was really that simple.

Shortly after the loan with Lim was signed, Hayward made the first of what would be many trips to Malaysia to meet with his newfound benefactor. In many ways, it was an inspiring journey that mirrored his first visit to the Seminole reservation in Hollywood, Florida. Here was a casino built above the cloud line, blending with nature, just the way Skip envisioned Foxwoods disappearing into the woodsy rolling terrain of southeastern Connecticut. Hayward was enthralled with the non-casino elements of Lim's Genting Highlands—the water slide, the gondolas, and the virtual-reality rides. Lim had no trouble convincing Skip that it was possible to transport all of these things across the ocean. Hayward began to grasp the financial ramifications of a casino, realizing, even if he didn't yet understand all the math, exactly how much money a place like Foxwoods, midway between Boston and New York, might make. He listened with rapt attention as Lim and his family members described how Genting Highlands had taken down some of the highest rollers in Asia. One was the scion of a distinguished Singapore family, a straight-A student and a graduate of the University of Singapore who had gone into trading in stocks. After losing nearly $500,000 in the stock market, he had gone to Genting Highlands to "recoup" his losses. Instead, he had ended up doubling them.

At one point during Hayward's visit, Lim revealed to him that not everyone was happy about his investing Malaysian capital in America.

Just as Skip had his skeptics, Lim said, "So do I have skeptics." The idea of Lim's getting involved in an American Indian casino had become a source of amusement in the business clubs of Kuala Lumpur, and one corporate executive in his country had openly said of Lim's American adventure, "They [the Lims] have been very good on their own home territory, but I doubt their ability to mix it with the big boys overseas." Lim was as determined to prove his critics mistaken as Hayward was to show his skeptics that he could run a casino his own way. Despite the newfound partnership, Connecticut residents, state officials, even the press had trouble coming up with any significant information about the Malaysian connection. When Connecticut's state capital newspaper, the *Hartford Courant,* covered the financing issues involving the casino on January 12, 1992, the journal reflected the state of knowledge of the moment that the Lims were "virtually unknown not only to officials of Connecticut but also to those of the United States." The family was, according to the *Courant,* "one of the richest and most secretive business houses in the world." The paper further noted that "not one of the state agencies responsible for regulating the Pequot casino, including the governor's office, the attorney general, the secretary of state, the division of special revenue, the chief state attorney and the state police, had any information about Genting Berhad or the Lim Family." Only after the *Courant* began inquiring about it did the State Police Bureau of Special Investigations become aware of the Genting connection. State officials told the paper that they were too busy to worry about where the money was coming from because they had to perform backround checks on 2,000 casino employees before the scheduled official opening on February 8, 1992.

But nobody in the state was going to give the Pequots a hard time. Governor Weicker by this point had lost his taste for battle with the Pequots and was determined to cooperate with them. He took the position that the loan between the Pequots and Lim was a private transaction between a sovereign nation and a private business. The compact between the tribe and the state had not included any requirement that the details of the casino's financing be disclosed to the public. That would have impinged on Hayward's sovereignty.

In Asia, where the Lims were as well known as the Rockefellers, their financial activities were followed much more closely. Media outlets in Asia were not as much in the dark about the Lims as those in the United States. In early 1991, a stock brokerage in Singapore, TA Securities, advised its clients that the Lims' involvement with the Indians might provide an investment opportunity. Now the Lims would have the biggest bank of all, with virtually no regulation at all. They would be intimately involved in the only casino in the world that would be totally free of governmental scrutiny, the only casino that would never even be required to issue a statement of ownership to the Securities and Exchange Commission or the U.S. Treasury. Lim's Asian casinos were not only subject to taxes, but the Malaysian government in 1990 had actually raised its gaming tax from 5 percent to 7 percent, making Genting the single largest corporate taxpayer in Malaysia. In contrast, Hayward's Foxwoods Casino would be totally free of federal, state, and even sales taxes. The supreme irony of the situation was that while taxation from U.S. governmental entities was nonexistent, the Lims would in effect be taxing the Indians, in light of their insistence on taking 9.9 percent of earnings on top of regular interest in exchange for their loan, leadership, and expertise in developing the casino. Instead of Lim's taking capital out of Malaysia and investing it in the United States, as Malaysian officials constantly fretted, Lim would actually be taking money out of the United States and bringing it home. Lim hoped to take much of the profits from the Connecticut casino and pour it into new international gambling complexes at Subic Bay in the Philippines or even in China. There was little downside to his deal with the little tribe of Pequots. When word leaked out in Asia of Lim's American adventure, stock in Lim's Resorts World surged on the Malaysian stock market, creating even more wealth for the biggest shareholders, including Lim, his children, and the Malaysian politicians and political parties who were his biggest investors. It was, Lim told the prime minister with a smile, "a very good deal."

In early 1991, with the casino coming to fruition, the purchase of Lonrho began to seem troublesome and unnecessary. Lim gave up his acquisition attempts, and Lonrho was instead sold to a German businessman, Dieter Bock. Resorts World and Genting Berhad investors, always skeptical that the target was simply too big, were relieved. As one securities analyst observed, Genting had always been a highly profitable but conservative company. The Lonrho deal, he asserted, represented a case of "an ultra blue-chip company suddenly becoming aggressive," which had investors worried.

AS FOXWOODS WENT UP in Connecticut, concern among local residents continued to grow. The link to the Asian investors had caught most people by surprise, and the construction of the Two Trees Inn had set local tongues wagging. After all, if there was one mindset that permeated the New England psyche, it was xenophobia. Not knowing much about the Lims, Ledyard residents imagined they had all sorts of sinister connections, and there were rumors of their involvement in drugs and white slavery. One local businessman told friends that he worried about "the tentacles of the terrorist group Shining Path" creeping from Peru through the Connecticut woods to Ledyard. An engineer complained to a local newspaper that the deal threatened the town with "a cycle of terror."

In May of 1991, three months after nailing down the financing, Al Luciani and Mickey Brown began building a 40,000-square-foot complex that would have about a hundred tables for card games, as well as room for roulette, dice tables, and video games. Though state law prohibited slot machines, Luciani figured they were such a draw, he bought several hundred anyway and lined them up along the inside perimeter of the casino, where people could play for nothing and win nothing. Margolin had a theory that Foxwoods could actually use the slots. He believed that their prohibition was regulatory rather than criminal and urged the casino to challenge the state by turning them on. He tried to convince Connecticut attorney general Richard Blumenthal not to oppose them if slots were included, but Blumenthal promised the state would definitely fight them in court if the slot machines were turned on. Although Margolin was confident he could get a judge to approve the slots, the decision was made not to push the issue. The Pequots didn't want to start their new era with a raid on the casino by state police. So the slots became a rare betting opportunity in the casino. No matter how long a person played, they would break even.

In the winter of 1992, as opening day for the spanking new Foxwoods High Stakes Bingo and Casino approached, neighbors continued to express varying degrees of concern about what was to happen. "I'm not looking for it to be a big problem," said Oliver Searchfield, who lived a mile and a half east of the casino. "A man will go there with his twenty dollars, play, win or lose, and be gone." Oliver was not a gambler. "Once the novelty wears off," he predicted, "traffic will be no worse than it is during beach season." On his 300-acre dairy farm one and a half miles west of the casino, Cliff Allyn, Jr., mixed feed for his dairy cows and said he worried about the changes that might come to the largely rural area. He was already having to wait for forty or fifty cars to pass before he could pull out of his driveway onto Route 2 after the bingo games ended. Allyn had a feeling that the casino would make the situation worse and the traffic jams more steady. Yolande Schick, who lived about 2 miles east of the new casino structure, also had apprehensions. "Bingo players are usually retired people. Bingo is one thing. A casino might be a different ball game. We just have to wait and see."

Influential *New York Times* columnist William Safire decried the approaching opening of the casino as an attraction to "suckers who are addicted to roulette, craps, blackjack and off-track betting." Safire predicted that it wouldn't be long at all before quiet rural southeastern Connecticut was filled with great accumulations of cash, money-laundering of drug wealth, prostitution, mob influence, and political corruption. Safire's picture of the future of Connecticut couldn't have been bleaker. "Gambling feeds the get-rich-quick illusion that debilitates society; because gambling causes individual ruin, despair and suicide, and corrupts a state that seeks a piece of the action," he wrote.

Safire also wondered how many of the members of Hayward's tribe, many of whom would have key roles in the management of the casino and access to the counting room, would actually even have been allowed to work in a casino in a state like New Jersey, where personnel have to pass extensive background checks. Safire had a point. Oddly, though employees of the tribe had to be approved by the state police, sovereign members of the tribe themselves, even those who had extensive criminal records, were subject to no such check.

But no one was wracked with more doubt and uncertainty about the opening of Foxwoods than Skip Hayward himself. On the Thursday night before the casino opened, he could not sleep. Across the woods from his house on Elizabeth George Drive, a beautiful wide residential street built with federal aid, Hawyard could hear the hammering and the opening and closing of the delivery truck doors in the still morning air as if they were unloading it in his own driveway. He poured himself a drink and wandered through the reservation until the sun was nearly up. He was following a piece of advice that he had posted in his office in the trailer: "When the stress gets to be too much, go out and take a walk."

Before the opening on Saturday, February 15, 1992, a medicine man named Slow Turtle pronounced a benediction over the new building as Skip and Mickey stood in 10-degree weather outside the building. Slow Turtle was not a Pequot. There had been no Pequot medicine men for several centuries. Slow Turtle was actually a rent-an-Indian from Cape Cod whose real name was John Peters. A sort of itinerant spiritual figure, Peters handled Indian baby-namings, opened powwows, and presided at tribal funerals. He had once gone to Japan to say prayers to the Indian spirits for the victims of Hiroshima and Nagasaki. Now he prayed for the gamblers who would soon stampede through Foxwoods' gates.

As at the opening of a mall on the day after Thanksgiving, a crowd had gathered impatiently outside the building. When the doors opened, there was an audible whoop, with many making Indian noises, flapping their hands over their mouths, and dashing madly for the gaming tables. Almost crushed in the rush were slinky Pocahontas-like waitresses, scantily costumed in one-feather headdresses, one-inch high heels, and teal-colored squaw outfits. The dealers stood nervously at their tables. Many of them had never dealt craps or blackjack before and had stayed up all night practicing. Foxwoods was a gambler's dream. It opened as the only casino on the East Coast to offer poker, which was banned in Atlantic City at the time. In addition to the forty-five poker tables, there was blackjack, roulette, craps, a big-six money wheel, baccarat, acey-deucy, and chuck-a-luck. Near one of the side entrances was a sports bar with twelve television screens equipped to handle off-track betting on horse races around the country. Pari-mutuel horse-race wagering was also not allowed in Atlantic City. In New Jersey, casinos had to close each night at 2 A.M. on weekdays and 4 A.M. on weekends, but at Fox-woods there were no such requirements. State police estimates that the casino would attract from 500 to 1,000 people on opening day were quickly proven to be on the conservative side. By 6 P.M., 10,000 people were crowded into the casino and there were reports that with the workweek ending and President's Day weekend coming, roughly an-other 10,000 were clogging the interstates from Boston, New York, and Providence. This figure didn't include charter bus operators, who hadn't planned to start their service until Saturday. By 12:15 P.M., the 1,730-space parking lot was full, and by 3 P.M. the police began to tow dozens of cars simply abandoned by eager gamblers along the two-lane Shewville Road, which ran from Ledyard to Mystic.

Opening day was an unqualified success. Eighteen years after he had heeded his grandmother's call to come home to the reservation, Skip Hayward, the former pipe fitter, had hit it big. His accomplishment may not have put him in league with other shipyard legends like Poland's Lech Walesa; but for New England, a revolution was at hand.

8

THE BELLS BEGIN RINGING

WITHIN WEEKS OF the opening of Foxwoods Casino, the most innovative and successful casino executive in the world drove to McCarran International Airport in Las Vegas, boarded his private jet, and asked his pilot to fly to Connecticut. Stephen Wynn was heading home.

Wynn was born in New Haven, Connecticut, on January 27, 1942, but had grown up in Utica, New York, surrounded by loan sharks, bookies, crapshooters, poker players, and bingo callers. His father, Michael Wynn, had begun a life of serious gambling at the age of seventeen in Revere, Massachusetts, and by the time he was twenty, Michael owned three illegal bingo parlors in the northeast, moving after the war from Connecticut to Utica. Steve Wynn was born to take bets, and in 1963 he married Elaine Pascal, the daughter of one of his father's pinochle buddies. Their first date was to a jai alai fronton.

Mike Wynn's dream was that of most people who gamble heavily. He longed to win his way out of the sticks and hit the big time. For Michael Wynn the businessman, that meant expanding his operations to one untouchable place—Las Vegas. In 1952, Mike Wynn took his family to Vegas and applied for a permit to operate a bingo parlor in Nevada. A hearing was held and for reasons that have never been entirely clear, the permit was denied. Mike Wynn was crushed and humiliated by the rejection. For Steve, seeing his Dad's dream dashed was a devastating experience. The Wynns returned east and eventually moved to eastern Maryland, settling in Waysons Corner, a town just east of wild, gambling-crazed Prince George's County. But two years after moving to Maryland, Mike Wynn died after open heart surgery at forty-six. Steve returned home from the University of Pennsylvania to run the family business. Wynn was determined to get revenge for the perceived injustice that had been perpetrated on his father. Mike Wynn may not have been able to get a gambling license from the State of Nevada, but Steve vowed that he would live his father's dream. In 1967, a little more than three years after Mike's death, Steve scraped together a $35,000 grubstake and moved his family to Las Vegas, where he took a job as slot and keno manager at the old mob-run Frontier Hotel. When six of the Frontier's top executives were indicted for skimming profits for the benefit of mobsters back in Chicago, billionaire industrialist Howard Hughes, who had moved to Las Vegas and was buying up properties there, moved in and bought the Frontier. Hughes, in fact, had arrived in Las Vegas only a year before Wynn, taking a train ride there from Boston in November 1966. Owner of the Hughes Tool Company, Hughes Aircraft, and broadcaster RKO, he was generally regarded as the world's richest man. An eccentric who was becoming increasingly neurotic about his health, Hughes had come west thinking that the clear desert air would be beneficial to him. With his entourage he took up two floors of the Desert Inn Hotel, and when Moe Dalitz, the owner, complained that nobody in his group gambled despite taking up more than a dozen rooms, Hughes bought the hotel. The Frontier was his second purchase.

Wynn was the highest-ranking employee who hadn't been involved in the skimming, and Hughes's financial adviser, Parry Thomas, asked Wynn to take the lead in running the hotel until the new ownership was in place. Wynn was eager to do so and became the protégé of Thomas, a Mormon elder who was president of Las Vegas's most powerful financial institution, Valley Bank. After Hughes's control of the Frontier was solidified, Wynn was fired, but Thomas liked Wynn and felt bad enough for him that he offered to set him up in a liquor distribution business in 1968. Wynn took the job, selling popular brands of Scotch to casinos. Wynn was instructed to keep his eyes and ears open, as Thomas understood the value in business of having good information about which casinos were in financial trouble. Sixty percent of his bank's loans were made to casinos, and he frequently acted as a conduit between casino executives and the Teamsters Union's Central States Pension Fund, which had major investments in Las Vegas. Thomas's connection to the pension fund was not something for which he was apologetic. "I've got to see that this community stays healthy. I'll take dollars from the devil himself if it's legal—and I don't mean anything disparaging toward the Teamsters by that," he said.

Wynn performed his snoop function to a tee, schmoozing with the casino executives, then reporting what he had learned to Thomas on a regular basis. He became what he himself described as Thomas's "sixth child," attending Thomas family picnics, learning to ski with him in Utah, and regularly having dinner with him. The one casino in which Thomas was most interested was the downtown Golden Nugget, the most popular and best known of the casinos located in Las Vegas's most dense urban area. He believed that the Nugget, which netted only $1 million per year, could be turned into the equivalent of a Las Vegas strip casino and that under his direction its earnings would skyrocket. In September 1969, Thomas reached an agreement to buy the Golden Nugget, and Wynn participated by buying 14,000 shares of the company himself. But in October, the Securities and Exchange Commission opened an investigation of the purchase and later concluded that Thomas had made "false and misleading" proxy statements. Thomas decided that if he couldn't buy the Golden Nugget, Steve Wynn should. But before that could happen, Steve needed to make some real money himself.

Thomas knew about a strip of land owned by Howard Hughes that was adjacent to Caesar's Palace. Hughes had refused to sell the property over the years and Caesar's was desperate to get it, if for no other reason than to keep a competitor from buying and building a competing casino virtually right in their backyard. It would have been a prime location. Caesar's Palace was always crowded and a rival that close could soak up a lot of overflow. As long as Hughes was in Las Vegas, Wynn's chances of getting the land were virtually nil. Hughes simply didn't sell property; he only bought. But one year after the SEC had successfully blocked Thomas's purchase of the Golden Nugget, the reclusive and mysterious billionaire left his suite of rooms in the Las Vegas Desert Inn and moved to the Bahamas. With Hughes physically removed from the scene, Thomas persuaded Hughes's operatives in town to sell the Caesar's strip to Wynn for $1.1 million. He knew that Caesar's would have paid much more, but representatives of Caesar's didn't realize that Hughes was now willing to part with the land. Eleven months after buying the 10-acre tract, Wynn sold it to Caesar's for $2.2 million. Wynn took the profits and bought a 5 percent stake in the Golden Nugget.

Wynn told the company's board of directors that his share was strictly an investment and that his only operational role might be as a bingo consultant. But within weeks, Wynn began interfering in the casino, acting on tips he had received while delivering J&B Scotch to the Golden Nugget. He had amassed a dossier on misdeeds at the Golden Nugget and went to the majority owner of the casino, Gilbert Blaine, and threatened to reveal what he knew if Blaine didn't step down as CEO. "We can do it the easy way or we can do it the hard way," he told Blaine. Blaine agreed to step down after eliciting a promise that Wynn would pay each of Blaine's employees, whom Wynn intended to fire, $30,000 severance. Although his methods for attaining success may seem ruthless, even in a tough town like Las Vegas, there was no question that he knew how to run a room. Thomas's suspicions that Blaine's ownership wasn't taking full financial advantage of the property turned out to be exactly right. In his first year at the helm, Wynn boosted profits at the Golden Nugget by four times and he imagined turning the Nugget into the first luxury hotel in downtown Vegas, one that would rival the giant themed resorts on the Las Vegas Strip.

But in May 1978, Wynn's plans changed when he went to Atlantic City for the opening of Resorts, the first legal casino on the Atlantic City Boardwalk since New Jersey had decided to legalize gambling. When he saw the throngs gathered as Resorts opened its doors, Wynn was energized. When he learned from friends in the business just how much money Resorts was making per slot machine, Wynn became frantic to get in on the Atlantic City bonanza. Ten days later, he returned to Atlantic City and purchased the Strand, a small hotel at the opposite end of the strip from Resorts. All he needed now was money to tear it down and build a new hotel in its place. But when Wynn asked Parry Thomas to help him with financing, Thomas turned him down, explaining that he would be lynched in Las Vegas if he were seen investing in a New Jersey casino. Wynn then placed a call to a Hilton executive whom he had gotten to know from his liquor-selling days. "Get your ass on a plane and meet me in Los Angeles," the executive told Wynn. "I will introduce you to the only guy who can do this." When Wynn arrived in Los Angeles, he was introduced to the executive's young cousin, a skinny thirty-two-year-old who had already lost his hair and sported a bad toupee. His name was Michael Milken.

Milken explained that he was in the bond department of a New York investment firm called Drexel Burnham Lambert and that he was looking for projects in which to invest. Wynn told Milken how much money he was looking for, and the investment banker quickly upped the ante. "You don't need a hundred million, you need a hundred twenty-five million," he said. "I don't like people to be underfinanced. I'm going to do your deal."

Milken eventually raised the money for the loan from a group of Mormon bankers in Salt Lake City, who were eventually paid off handsomely in high-interest "junk bonds," which were fashionable financial instruments of the time—and which eventually led to Milken's imprisonment for fraud some years later.

Milken and Wynn began construction of the $153-million, 506-room Atlantic City Golden Nugget in July of 1979, and it opened in December 1980. Just like the Nugget in Vegas, it was a sure money-maker, one of the most popular and best-run casinos on the Boardwalk. The poster boy in Wynn's advertising was Frank Sinatra, and eastern television stations were flooded with ads of Frank and Steve strolling the corridors of the hotel, with Wynn promising to make sure Sinatra got enough towels. FCC rules at the time did not allow a casino to advertise its gambling over the airwaves, so Wynn touted his bathroom accessories. By 1982, *Fortune* magazine had declared the Golden Nugget "Atlantic City's biggest winner," and the stock price skyrocketed from $5 to $44 per share. If there was any one glitch in his Atlantic City arrival, it was the difficulty Wynn had with the New Jersey Casino Control Commission in winning a license. Wynn's associations were called into question before the agency's director, Mickey Brown, finally gave the go-ahead for Wynn to operate.

In Atlantic City, Wynn competed head-to-head with New York real estate tycoon Donald Trump, who owned two New Jersey casinos, the Castle and the Plaza. Trump hoped to expand his casino empire by buying Bally's Corporation in a hostile takeover. This purchase would have given Trump three Boardwalk hotels, the maximum number New Jersey law allowed any one person or corporation to own. In 1986, to fend off the hostile takeover, Bally's bought the Atlantic City Golden Nugget from Wynn for $440 million. The thinking of Bally's attorneys was that with two casinos already, Trump could not buy the company because it would give him a total of four, which was one over the legal limit. If Trump had to sell one off, he would lose a fortune since any potential buyer would know he had no bargaining leverage.

After just six years in New Jersey, Wynn was delighted to help Bally's. The glitter of that first day at Resorts was a distant memory to him. By 1986, Atlantic City was a horrible pit of grime, corruption, dishonest labor unions, and nasty employees. Even worse, its casino operators were burdened by a nest of state regulations that tied their hands and made life inconvenient for players. What games one could play was severely restricted compared to the rules set in Nevada. New Jersey law seemed to delight in prohibiting anything that was actually fun. Unlike Las Vegas, Atlantic City allowed no betting on sports, not even horse racing. There was no poker or keno, the big bingolike board game that a person could play for $1 while eating and still win a fortune. Most inane, the New Jersey casinos were required by law to close every night at precisely those predawn hours when most serious gamblers are just getting revved up for action. Telescoping the gambling day by four to six hours made the casinos more crowded than necessary, and on weekends in Atlantic City it was impossible at most places to even find blackjack action for less than $15 a hand. Craps had mostly $10 minimums and many tables had $25 minimums. At this steep a price, there was no place for newcomers to learn the games.

Table games had to fight for floor space in Atlantic City with slots, and it didn't take a very long walk down the Boardwalk to realize that this was a slot town. Everything in Atlantic City was geared toward high volume and quick turnover. Packed buses from New York City rumbled constantly back and forth on the Garden State Turnpike, and most visitors didn't even spend the night, for good reason. Gamblers could usually rent a room in Las Vegas for as little as $19.99. In Atlantic City, weekend rates ranged from $120 to $180 a night, money that could much better be spent on several rolls of the dice. The big buffets that were a staple of the Las Vegas scene were nowhere to be found in Atlantic City. Eating was an expensive chore and the overpriced, poor-quality casino restaurants drove many wonderful old Atlantic City restaurants like Orsatti's and the Knife and Fork out of business. Happy to count his millions and to get out of Atlantic City, Wynn vowed never to come back until all the nitpicking state regulations were gone. He did not leave penniless: in his six years he had made $330 million. Wynn had also made a lifelong enemy. His involvement in the scheme to deprive Donald Trump of Bally's was something Trump would never forgive.

Back in Las Vegas, Wynn used his profits to build the casino that would become his showplace, the Mirage. The name of the hotel would give its name eventually to his New York Stock Exchange listed company, the Mirage Corporation. The Mirage opened in 1989, equipped with a giant exploding volcano, 10,000 trees brought in from North Carolina, a 320-acre golf course, the magic team of Siegfried & Roy and their white tigers, and a lush, tropically themed casino floor that was instantly recognized as a classic in the business. Wynn had gotten out of New Jersey just in time.

WHEN FOXWOODS OPENED to enthusiastic crowds on February 15, 1992, the impact on Atlantic City was felt immediately. One of the reasons Atlantic City had always been so indifferent to its customers was that it had no competition. Las Vegas had Reno. Atlantic City had an East Coast monopoly, and casino operators acted with total disregard for customers. When competition suddenly arrived, Atlantic City was primed for a quick fall. Gambling trade publications estimated that within weeks of opening, Foxwoods was taking in $2 million a day, much of which was coming right out of the pockets of Atlantic City casino owners. Even Atlantic City's dealers, prohibited by yet another picayune law from playing at casinos in their own town, were driving up in vans to gamble at Foxwoods. Gamblers from New York were finding that Foxwoods, 124 miles to the east, was just as accessible as Atlantic City, and there were no tolls. The only thing that was saving Donald Trump and the other Atlantic City operators was that Connecticut had not allowed slots. If slots were legalized in Connecticut, the only logical rationalization for gambling in Atlantic City would evaporate.

Foxwoods' cannibalization of Atlantic City had no negative impact on Las Vegas. If anything, it enhanced its allure. Foxwoods was introducing casino-style gambling to a whole new clientele, and once a person became confident at a casino, making a pilgrimage to Las Vegas was just a matter of time.

Steve Wynn had become the king of Las Vegas in the twenty years he operated there. The white-and-gold-trimmed downtown Golden Nugget, his original property, was cheap, had great food, and was a lively casino that opened up onto the nightly carnival and light show that took place outside on Fremont Street. While the Nugget remained everything a casino should be, the spectacular Mirage transformed the image of Las Vegas from a hedonistic Gomorrah into a mecca for families, making the gambling experience seem as wholesome and refreshing as the big dolphin pool he had built in the back lot. It was not a vision of Las Vegas that everyone appreciated. One of Wynn's Nevada competitors, Bob Stupak, owner of the old-style Vegas World complained: "What this town needs is that scent of vice, a little sin, to stir that desire to come to Las Vegas." But becoming the master of the strip by turning Vegas into a family outing did not fulfill all of Wynn's ambitions. In his heart of hearts, he longed to destroy his hated enemy, Donald Trump. He had always expected that he would return to Atlantic City, when the time was right and circumstances had changed. If the state would only get out of his way, he could show Trump and his Boardwalk friends how a real casino operated. But with the opening up of Foxwoods in

Connecticut, Wynn was struck with a better idea. Why mess with New Jersey if he could decimate Trump in his own native state of Connecticut? Wynn pondered that delicious prospect as his plane circled the Connecticut state capital.

He arrived in Hartford with a sense of excitement and purpose. On the afternoon after his arrival, March 11, 1992, Wynn attended a meeting with key Connecticut legislators who had the power to legalize slot machines for non-Indian operators and thus to pave the way for the opening of a Mirage-owned casino in the Northeast. His goal was to convince the legislative committee to allow him to build a huge resort-casino in Hartford that would bring "jobs and hope" to a state that was suffering severe economic downturn. After the opening of the casino in Ledyard, the reality of how poorly the governor and the legislature had played their cards was just beginning to sink in. There had been a time, during the negotiation of the compact, when to speed things along, Hayward and Margolin might have gladly signed a deal that included giving some percentage of gross casino revenue to the state. But Weicker and his predecessor, William O'Neill, were so adamantly and overconfidently opposed to the Pequots that neither of their two administrations ever came forward with a proposal that would have made the state a partner in the winnings. If the state government had had more foresight, they could have done what Lim did, which was to give the Pequots the money to build the casino and become their partner. Lim was taking nearly 10 percent, and Hayward probably would have given the state even more, just to get the enterprise moving when its success and financing were in doubt. Now neither the state nor the federal government made a penny from the casino. Its profits were constitutionally exempt from taxation by any state or local governmental entity, and it would have taken a special act of Congress to make them subject to federal taxes.

Repeated weekends of heavy traffic and crazed casino crowds had alerted the Connecticut legislators to just how profitable this casino was going to be, and just how little they were going to get out of it. Foxwoods had never closed for even a moment since its splashy opening. The depth of the state's folly was immediately apparent, and many lawmakers were searching for a way to pull the state out of the hole they had dug for it. Now Steve Wynn had arrived in Hartford claiming to be that savior. The state coffers were not going to be enriched by the Pequots, but if the legislature agreed to play ball with him, Wynn explained, the angry taxpayers of Connecticut could be appeased. Wynn's grandiose plan was to build a $350-million convention center, hotel, and grand casino in downtown Hartford. With a videotape featuring stars like Frank Sinatra, Kenny Rogers, and Dolly Parton, Wynn gave legislators a glimpse of his Mirage and Golden Nugget hotel-casinos in Las Vegas. Certainly nothing in Hartford compared with his lavish vision. He declared his verdict on life in Connecticut. "It's boring. There's nothing to do here," Wynn said as only a native could without stirring up resentment. "I don't think that comes as a revelation."

When Wynn paid a courtesy call to Weicker, the two men failed to connect. Weicker told Wynn that he would never sign a bill legalizing slot machines in Connecticut and that he would not be a party to any widespread legalization of gambling. "We are not going to bet on the future," Weicker said. "We are going to invest in it."

But it was difficult to tell if Weicker's view would dominate in the legislature. Lawmakers were dying of envy at the amount of money flowing into Foxwoods and having increasing difficulty explaining to their constituents why Hayward and the Pequots didn't have to pay taxes. Not only was the state not earning any money off of Foxwoods, but it was losing tax revenue from other enterprises that were suffering from the competition. Almost immediately after the opening of Foxwoods, the taxable races at the dog tracks, the legal jai alai games, and even the state lottery immediately began to experience a drop-off in business of up to 22 percent. This was happening at a time when Connecticut was going through its worst economic slump since the Great Depression of the 1930s. Since February 1989, Connecticut's defense industry had eliminated 155,800 jobs. Electric Boat, where Skip had worked after high school, had announced plans to lay off another 15,000 because of continued cutbacks in the submarine-building program. Of course, the state's loss was Foxwoods' gain. It almost seemed that nothing could happen that didn't redound to the Pequots' benefit.

The layoffs were solving what could well have been the casino's biggest problem—a lack of dealers, food service personnel, and hotel maids—workers who could have made better union wages at the boat docks. At the opening of the casino, Chief Executive Officer Al Luciani had asked employees to work seventy-hour weeks until more could be hired, trained, and licensed. But with the defense economy in a free fall, job applicants queued up for hundreds of yards outside the personnel offices. One morning, Luciani counted 30,000 people applying for the 2,300 positions he hoped to fill. Unlike the casinos in New Jersey, Foxwoods did not have to worry about unions. As a separate nation, Hayward's reservation was not only exempt from most Department of Labor regulations, but was also excluded from the entire National Labor Relations Act, which gave worker's rights to collective bargaining.

Wynn admitted in private meetings with legislators that Hayward was having a pretty lucky roll so far. But if there was one thing a good casino operator knew how to do, he said, it was to turn a shooter's luck around. Crap dealers had a whole series of tricks they would use to stop a hot roller in his tracks. They might start an argument with one of the players. More often, they would stop the game to inspect the dice. These tactics slowed a hot roller and often after the dice had "cooled," the shooter would seven out, allowing the casino to win. Wynn was offering himself up to the state, to turn the game around and stop Hayward's hot streak.

Before he could enter into a new partnership with the state, he first cemented his relationship with Hartford state senator William DiBella, the majority leader in the Senate. With polls showing that 59 percent of the state's residents now believed that casino gambling should be legalized, DiBella helped Wynn organize a field trip to the Mirage in Las Vegas.

A "fact-finding" panel of legislators headed to Vegas, where they were met with red-carpet treatment. Wynn was quite a host. He brought them to an extravagant breakfast at a villa apartment that he said was only reserved for his "special, special friends." Over pancakes Oscar and Nova Scotia lox, Wynn was openly bitter with legislators about his experiences in Atlantic City. He referred to the legislators of New Jersey as "those suckers in Trenton" and "dirty rats." The implication was clear. Failure to support Wynn's Connecticut proposal might well make lawmakers in Hartford suckers and rats as well. At a dinner in the casino on Saturday night to honor donors to the University of Nevada at Las Vegas, the visiting legislators were treated to roast loin of veal with shrimp and lobster cordon rouge. The keynote speaker was Elizabeth Dole. Wynn pulled out all the tricks he knew. The waitresses wore name tags with the names of their hometowns on them, and the tag for Janis Jones, one particularly attractive hostess, read HARTFORD. Naturally, this was a big conversation starter. She explained that she had reluctantly left Hartford eight years ago because there was nothing there for her anymore. "Connecticut had better wise up and produce some jobs," she advised the traveling troupe. The legislators bought it hook, line, and sinker, while Wynn's own staff people giggled and joked that she had definitely earned her award as the corporation's next employee of the month.

As the lawmakers prepared to leave, Wynn reminded them what they had to do. Failure to legalize gambling on moral grounds, he told them, would smack of hypocrisy. He argued that compared to Connecticut's handgun, attack submarine, and missile producers, a gambling casino was a pretty benign business. But before they could vote on legalizing Wynn's casino, the legislature would have to vote separately on legalizing slot machines. Without slots, there could be no Hartford casino as Wynn envisioned it, and he had plenty of help pushing that legislation. Wynn's allies in the fight were the leaders of Connecticut's racing and jai alai industries, who had been promised thousands of slot machines at six preexisting gambling sites across Connecticut, including jai alai frontons in Bridgeport, Hartford, and Milford, and the Plainfield Greyhound Park.

At first, it seemed that Wynn's pampering of the legislators had paid off. The senators on the trip returned to Hartford and in April of 1992 voted 24 to 11 to legalize slot machine gambling. But while the Senate reached the two-thirds threshold needed to override a veto by Governor Weicker, enthusiasm in the larger House of Representatives was not as great. Weicker, as adamantly against gambling as ever, declared that gambling posed Connecticut's "single biggest threat," a "near-sighted solution with damaging long-term consequences for the state's quality of life." A debate began in the House of Representatives over whether gambling ultimately lifts people from poverty by providing jobs or grinds them further into misery by stealing their money. "My concern is to get jobs to the people of the city of Hartford," said state senator Frank David Barrows, a Democrat who represented Hartford's North End, a poor, predominantly minority area. Weicker responded that he would fight "with the last breath" in his body to get jobs for poor urban residents. He reminded legislators that no amount of casino glitter could erase poverty, as the ugly decaying city blocks of Atlantic City behind the casinos proved.

"We've got to go ahead now at this very critical moment and define our state," Weicker said. "Is it a gambling state or is it a family state?" state treasurer Francisco Borges, who was considered a voice of conscience for Connecticut's poorest residents, testified that the prospect of full casino gambling in Connecticut was "sickening and unspeakable" because it would rip apart urban families that were already exploited and suffering. "The only shot in the arm a gambling casino would give us is like the ones that the heroin addicts on Hartford's streets depend on for their cheap, quick, dirty, easy and ultimately death-inducing fix," Mr. Borges insisted. Lost in the debate over slots was the welfare of the player. The slots under the Connecticut bill would be among the most parsimonious in the country. Of every dollar bet, 85 cents would be returned to the bettor on average, while 10 cents would go to the operator of the gaming hall, and 5 cents to the state, which would disperse most of the money back to the towns, primarily for property tax relief. The legislature's Office of Fiscal Analysis estimated a total payout of about $89 million a year to local communities once the system was up and running. Throughout the debate, the Mashantucket Pequots' Foxwoods Casino served as a touchstone for both sides. Supporters said the state must find some way to compete with the Indians for the gambling dollar, while opponents said the bill would give the tribe new advantages. Once the machines were legal elsewhere in the state, they would be legal at Ledyard as well. Unlike the owners of the dog tracks and jai alai frontons, for whom the number of machines would be set by state law, Hayward and his Asian partners would be able to install as many machines as they wanted, with any rate of payback and no cut to the state. When the time came for the legislature to adjourn in May, the House of Representatives still had not voted on the slot proposal. The decision would have to wait until the legislature reconvened in 1993. Before the legislators dispersed, they appointed an eighteen-member task force that would issue a full report on the potential financial impact of casino gambling on the state. The results of the study would then be presented to the full reconvened legislature the following January, and DiBella hoped it would then be used to justify passage of the slots legalization bill.

WYNN WAS FAMOUS for spending any amount of money to have what he wanted. Just to get this far he had amassed an estimated $357,879 in lobbying expenses. But the Pequots now had a plan of their own—and the financial means to make it happen. They wanted to have slots legalized—but only at their casino. Their lobbying expenses for the year, according to state records, totaled $363,886, and they knew that when the legislature reconvened the next year, they would have to spend that much and more. But amazingly, they didn't have to. Shortly after the close of the legislative session, at a meeting with state officials held at Foxwoods' bingo hall over what role the state would have in casino oversight, Pequot lobbyist Charles Duffy was approached by a Weicker aide, Robert Werner. Werner told Duffy, "I have no authorization for what I'm about to say," but then added that in spite of this he wanted to make a proposal. Duffy gathered together his team, including Margolin and Hayward, and held an off-the-record meeting with Werner. Werner informed the tribe that Governor Weicker might be interested in making a deal with the Pequots, one that he believed might be "mutually beneficial to all sides."

Werner told the astonished group that despite the governor's public protestations that he would never allow slot machines in Connecticut, Weicker might be willing to let the Pequots have slots in exchange for a generous sum of money that would indicate to the public that the state was getting something out of the casino deal after all and had not simply been had. Duffy and Margolin planned to play hardball in the negotiations and promise the state as little as they could. But when they reconvened for a second meeting, Skip made it clear he had no interest in playing games, promising Werner right away that the tribe would guarantee the state $100 million a year from slot machines. Duffy and Margolin cringed. They had hoped to negotiate for a while before reaching a figure. The big round number sounded great to Werner, since Wynn's proposed Hartford casino was estimated to guarantee the state only $80 million in tax revenue.

Weicker continued to keep quiet about his office's secret dealings with the tribe. But he was determined to make something happen before the scheduled task force report on gambling was delivered to the legislature on January 5, 1993. Weicker had no illusions about the objectivity of the blue ribbon panel and he was sure that it would recommend that Connecticut legalize slot machines and casino gambling in Hartford. He decided to accept Skip's $100-million guarantee.

Weicker's negotiations with the Pequots were kept so secret that in late September, when Weicker suddenly announced that he had unilaterally reached an agreement with the Pequot nation to allow them to install slot machines, the reaction in Hartford was one of utter shock. High-ranking legislators branded Weicker's executive stroke unconstitutional. The Republican leader in the House of Representatives, Edward C. Krawiecki, Jr., asked Attorney General Richard Blumenthal for an opinion as to whether Mr. Weicker had violated the state constitution. Krawiecki said it appeared to him that the governor had set state policy in allowing slot machines at the reservation, despite the fact that setting policy is the province of the legislative branch, not the chief executive. But Weicker's move was described by state newspapers and pundits as a deft political stroke, one "that knocked the wind from the sails of the pro-gaming forces."

Under the terms of the deal, the Pequots agreed to pay $30 million for the time remaining in 1992. In the fiscal year beginning July 1, 1993, the tribe would pay at least $100 million, or 25 percent of the gross revenues from the slots, whichever was greater. Thereafter, the cut would be 25 percent, unless it fell short of $100 million in revenue. But in a community that had been primed by lotteries and charity nights for big-time gambling, this would never happen.

There was nothing in Weicker's secret agreement that made it unlawful for the legislature to go ahead and cut their own deal with Wynn. Yet as the 1993 session of the legislature geared up, what had appeared to be a tilt in favor of legalizing casinos seemed wiped away by Weicker's bold stroke. State editorialists lauded Weicker as a leader with "a genius for changing the rules in the middle of the game." The state attorney general issued a ruling saying that Weicker was within his authority under the Indian Gaming Regulatory Act to make the deal unilaterally. A flummoxed Steve Wynn claimed he could top the $100-million revenue hurdle. But the Senate Finance Committee staff analysis couldn't envision his casino proposal bringing in more than $80 million. After all the criticism the lawmakers had received, they weren't about to now risk trading a guaranteed $100-million payoff in exchange for the hope of $80 million. Under the terms of the state's slot deal with the tribe, if Connecticut legalized slot machines and allowed Wynn into Hartford, the deal with the Pequots would be voided and the tribe could keep all its slot revenue for itself. By cutting the deal he did, Weicker had made Connecticut the most expensive state in the country in which to build a private casino, since beating the Pequots' revenue promise stood as the standard for casino legalization. Wynn was beginning to think that going against Donald Trump in Atlantic City might not be such a bad idea after all. A few months later, he put up a billboard on the highway to Atlantic City promising the future construction of a Mirage Hotel-Casino in Atlantic City. Seven years later Wynn sold his entire company to MGM Grand and bought a new Las Vegas casino, the same Desert Inn where Howard Hughs once lived.

In exchange for their promised monopoly, the Pequots would be paying one of the highest effective tax rates in the country, but Margolin and Mickey Brown were satisfied that it was worth the cost to keep out competition and retain their exclusivity. They rightly believed that Foxwoods had so many advantages—freedom from labor laws, immunity from lawsuits, and no taxes, to name a few—that no one could possibly compete with them.

As soon as the deal was in effect, Mickey Brown called the company that manufactured slot machines, International Game Technology, and excitedly told them to "turn the trucks around." The slots that had rested against the walls were not fancy enough for real play, and as new machines came in, they were removed. On January 15, 1993, slot machines began ringing in Ledyard. One hundred machines were operating by the end of the first weekend, with hundreds more to arrive in the coming weeks. Brown created 29,000 square feet of new casino space by moving the management offices, including his and Hayward's, into ten temporary office trailers. Brown set the machines to pay back 92 to 93 percent of every dollar bet, far better than the 85 percent contemplated by the highway robbers in the legislature.

Just a year after the February 15, 1992, opening, Foxwoods was well on its way to becoming the most profitable casino in the history of the United States. Through a series of events, many of which had been thrust upon them or ordained by outside forces, the Pequots had stumbled into a gold mine. All of Skip's promises of riches that he had used to lead the tribe to gambling were about to be fulfilled. The question now was whether his grandiose dreams of building a cohesive nation out of remote Pequot ancestors could come true. It was one thing to have Utopian ideas about resurrecting a long-lost Indian tribe. It was another thing to keep this tribe intact. In almost every battle they had joined, Skip and his very smart lawyers had prevailed. They had conquered the federal government, outsmarted Connecticut's governor, and sent the fearsome genius Steve Wynn scurrying back to Las Vegas. This was an amazing series of political and financial victories. More challenges lay ahead, though. The suddenly wealthy tribe would have to learn how to handle such good fortune. Dealing with relatives, neighbors, and his own success would be Skip's toughest challenges.

IV

CASHING IN

Kenneth Reels speaking at a Foxwoods forum

9

GRAND PLANS AND GROWING PAINS

FOXWOODS' FAST-GROWING treasury was certain to provoke envy and resentment from neighbors who were not accustomed to seeing rich upstarts in their neighborhood. That was to be expected. But Skip's most dogged opposition came not from outside critics but from within the tribe itself, and not surprisingly, considering Pequot history, the challenge involved elements of rivalry and betrayal between Pequots and Narragansetts.

In 1987, a man named Kenneth Reels moved to Mashantucket from Peace Dale, Rhode Island, as part of a vanguard of Rhode Island Narragansett Indians able to piggyback a distant Pequot relative into a job and ultimately a membership at the increasingly affluent Mashantucket Reservation. Bureau of Indian Affairs policy allowed each Native American Indian tribe the authority to choose its own members. This power was part and parcel of the "sovereignty" that each tribe was guaranteed. The only caveat from the BIA was that no person could be a member of two tribes at once. But given a choice, after the opening of the busy bingo hall, any Narragansett with a possible claim to Pequot ancestry—and many Pequots had been taken in by the Narragansetts after the seventeenth-century war—would have been foolish not to consider making the 30-mile move from the impoverished Narragansett communities in Peace Dale, Charlestown, and South Kingston.

Kenneth Reels's father was a Narragansett Indian, and his mother, Juanita, was three-quarters Narragansett. The other quarter she could trace back to Annie Sebastian, one of the seven sisters of Elizabeth

George. Sebastian had numerous children, and one of them, a registered Narragansett tribe member named Mabel Perry, had twelve children of her own. One of these was her daughter Juanita, who then brought seventeen children into the world herself. Of all her large brood, Ken was the apple of her eye: serious, hardworking, extremely athletic, and talented. At South Kingston High School in Rhode Island, he especially excelled in baseball and tennis. Coaches at his high school marveled that Reels literally picked up a racquet and within months was good enough to be a seeded player on the high school tennis team. Reels worked after class or tennis practice in a variety of odd jobs that ranged from delivering newspapers to pumping gas. In 1978, when the other star members of his class packed off for college, Reels joined the United States Army and was assigned to the 82nd Airborne Division at Fort Bragg, North Carolina, where he served as a supply sergeant. When he came back to Peace Dale in 1981, Reels settled down as the manager of Frisella's Auto Salvage, where he took parts off junked cars. To make ends meet, he took a second job at the Point Judith Fishermen's Cooperative, cleaning cod. So when his mother called in 1987 and said that her cousin, Skip Hayward, might be able to find him a job at the new bingo hall in Ledyard, Reels didn't have to think twice. He got a job buying bingo supplies and soon thereafter moved to Mashantucket. One job was never enough for him, however, and he soon took over management of the tribe's sand and gravel pit as well.

By the time the casino opened in February 1992, Reels had worked himself into a position of influence at the reservation, especially among the growing faction of Narragansetts, which included his numerous brothers, sisters, and cousins, all descended from Annie Sebastian. Like Kenny, virtually all of them had renounced their Narragansett membership and used their mother's tribal link to become enrolled members of the Pequot nation. For many of them, Pequot identification offered hope for a future unimaginable to them in Rhode Island. One person drawn to the opportunities at Mashantucket was Reels's first cousin Michael Thomas. Shortly after Reels moved to Mashantucket in 1987, Thomas, still living at home in Rhode Island, was cited for driving an unregistered car without a license. While the state trooper waited for the tow truck, he noticed thirteen bags of cocaine in the back seat, ranging in size from one to three grams. Thomas was arrested, tried, convicted, and sent to prison. In 1991, released from jail after serving three years, Thomas decided it was time to turn his life around and to join his cousin Kenny Reels at Mashantucket, where they became close friends and confidantes. In 1992, Reels obtained another ally when his cousin Antonio Beltran arrived at the reservation from California under similar circumstances. Beltran's arrival attracted more attention than those of most of the immigrants to Mashantucket. In 1980, when Beltran was seventeen years old, living outside of Los Angeles and just off juvenile probation, he announced to a car full of friends that he wanted to "kill a white boy." The conversation was more than teenage bluster. Beltran and his friends found a victim who met their color target walking alone in the early morning darkness, and Beltran jumped out of his vehicle and stabbed him in the back. The victim did not die, but was left paralyzed. Instead of being tried for murder, Beltran was convicted of aggravated assault and was sentenced to just seven years in the California State Penitentiary in San Quentin. While being led from the courthouse after the sentencing, he gestured toward his victim. "You may be smiling," he said, "but I'm walking." After four years of incarceration, Beltran was paroled, and like his cousin Michael Thomas, he was no sooner out of jail than he drove across country to Mashantucket to join the Pequots. In an interview with a New England paper after his arrival, Beltran spoke of the difficult period of his life that had just ended and why he had come to the reservation: "I wasn't sure where I was going but I was damn sure it was better than where I was leaving."

At Mashantucket, Reels gave Beltran a job in the tribe's sand and gravel department. Beltran was happy to have a place to start life over again, and he, Reels, and Michael Thomas swiftly became a fearsome clique. All three were anxious to move ahead, to put their past miseries behind them, and to enjoy the tangible rewards that the new casino promised to provide. They chafed at Skip's leadership and influence and plotted among themselves about how they might get a bigger share of the responsibility, decision-making, and naturally, the casino money. In the first six months the casino was open, the envy of Reels and his friends was more of a nuisance to Skip than anything else. It was actually the casino's chief operating officer, Al Luciani, who more often felt the brunt of their ambition and resentment at not being on the inside of the business. Reels had assumed that once the casino opened, he and his former Narragansett relatives would hold key positions in the enterprise. After all, they had been instrumental in running the bingo game for four years. But the Lims had let Skip know in no uncertain terms that the casino would have to be run professionally. Mickey Brown had been waiting a long time to run a sophisticated American casino, and he wasn't about to turn the operation over to amateurs. In the months before the opening, Luciani hired as many qualified dealers, stick men, and pit bosses as he could lure away from Atlantic City. Nearly all of the supervisory personnel were people that he had known in New Jersey, men—and a few women—who knew their way around a casino floor or had worked on casino regulation for the State of New Jersey. There were few members of the tribe among their ranks, and those that were tended to be more closely related to Skip than to Reels and Thomas.

If Luciani and Brown were particularly sensitive about not allowing rookies onto the casino floor, it was because they knew how gamblers would try to take advantage of a new casino with inexperienced dealers. Blackjack and crap players will look for any edge they can find, and many unscrupulous types flock to a new casino just to gain a slight advantage from dealer mistakes or even through deliberate intimidation of rookie dealers. Luciani was also naturally distrustful of dealers and pit bosses who had no experience in a casino. Most successful cheating scams, as he knew, involved collusion on the dealers' part, and in the first week the casino had been open, they had caught one dealer stuffing black $100 chips into his cheeks before break. But having so many people working at the casino who seemed close and loyal to Luciani, and who had no loyalty to the tribe, fostered increasing suspicion and frustration among Reels and his friends. Their outspoken dislike of the "Atlantic City crowd" resonated with those who felt left out of the process and resentful of Skip's globe-trotting and sudden connections. Jobs that Reels's cousins were offered seemed to be menial, and Kenny was determined not to have a situation where the darker-skinned Narragansetts were relegated to kitchen, security, and housecleaning jobs. Reels wanted his people to be out front in vital, important, and visible positions.

At a tribal council meeting in March 1992, Reels, supported by his allies, demanded that if tribal members couldn't be guaranteed management positions at the casino, then each supervisory employee should be assigned a "shadow," a tribal member who shared the position and title and who would learn the job until he or she knew it well enough to take it over. When the bingo hall originally opened, it had been run by the Penobscots. Over time, the Pequots had learned what they needed to operate on their own and bought out the Maine tribe's management contract. This was precisely what Reels envisioned happening with the casino. His comments made it clear to Luciani that he did not have the slightest notion of the difficulty of running a casino, of how much money was at stake, and of how much more sophisticated the players and clientele would be. Luciani and Brown convinced Skip that the shadow concept was a useless idea at an operation as large and as sophisticated as Foxwoods and they resisted the concept. But in an attempt to appease the Reels faction, Luciani agreed to establish the Pequot Academy at an old school building in Westerly, Rhode Island. Here, he promised, the casino would train tribal members in the various executive jobs that a casino provides. Hayward did his best to help the situation, explaining to Reels that the casino was just the engine that was going to drive a huge billion-dollar resort and theme park, and he promised to keep Reels in the loop on these projects.

In partnership with the Lims, Hayward had already signed off on a grand plan to build a giant theme park across the road from the casino. Just as the Lims used monorails to get people from Kuala Lumpur to Genting Highlands, Hayward envisioned a regional monorail system that would link the theme park and casino with the popular Mystic Aquarium to the south and the city of Norwich to the west. In an effort to make Reels feel a part of the process, in June 1992, Hayward asked him to go to China and evaluate a deal to establish a "Great Wall of China" theme park at the reservation. Reels readily agreed and organized a trip that included many of the "tribal elders," a group that included many of his large number of aunts and uncles, who spent their time exploring Tivoli-style gardens, Asian restaurants, Chinese cultural exhibits, and the Beijing zoo. The group was treated to a red-carpet tour, compliments of the Lims, of Hong Kong, Singapore, and Malaysia. Lim was a charming host, and Reels returned awed by the theme park concept and, as Hayward hoped, pleased with the attention that had been lavished upon him. Skip soon went back to China to further nego-tiate the China theme park, this at a time when relations were still chilly between the United States and Chinese governments as a result of the June 1989 massacre at Tiananmen Square. Chinese government officials reciprocated by making an official state visit to the sovereign Pequot na-tion that summer. At this summit meeting, Hayward and Reels partici-pated in the signing of a "memorandum of understanding" with the Chinese. Reels spoke at the ceremony, telling tribal members that the deal was to "honor" the ethnically Chinese Malaysians who had loaned the tribe the original $60 million. He predicted the agreement would provide a better understanding between Native Americans and Chinese. The "Great Wall of Ledyard" would be 30 feet high and 20 feet wide, and Reels himself suggested that it be put on the highest possible vista, surrounded by Malaysian fountains, so, as he said, "it can be seen for miles." It would contain a piece of the real Great Wall of China, and was planned to be one of only three places in the country where an authen-tic piece of the wall would be on display in the United States, the others being at the United Nations and at the Richard Nixon Presidential Li-brary in California.

But even getting Reels on board for some of the tribe's important projects didn't eliminate the internal conflict. One family of tribe mem-bers held their own equivalent of a freedom march, walking through the casino at peak hours demanding special seating in the restaurants. Their intent, as one tribe member would explain, was "to let the Atlantic City crowd know who was boss." One tribal member, Margery Pinson, an aunt of Reels, caused a scene when she was asked to give up a seat in the restaurant to casino patrons. "We're tribal members," she said loudly. When a cadre of white executives came in to try to defuse the situation, she began screaming loudly of racism. Other members of the tribe would come into the restaurants to eat, then refuse to pay. "Whoever heard of paying for your food when you own the place?" one tribe member protested to one of Luciani's supervisors. These chafing incidents led many of the black tribal members to openly long for the day when Hayward's clique would be voted out of power.

The disgruntled tribe members got their first chance to strike in September of 1992, just seven months after the opening of the casino. Luciani had come to suspect that someone who worked in the casino gift shop was stealing from the store, and he installed a hidden camera to find out who it was. When the evidence revealed that the culprit was the tribal member who ran the gift shop, Luciani fired her as a casino employee. She complained to the tribal council, and almost instantly Luciani was called in for questioning. Hayward felt powerless to intervene on his behalf lest he be accused of siding against a member of his own family. Luciani was informed that he had never been given the authority to install the hidden camera and therefore had no choice but to give the tribal member her job back. Burning with anger, Luciani assured the tribal council that such behavior on his part wouldn't happen again. He had suffered his last indignity at the hands of the Reels faction. He packed his suitcase and moved back to New Jersey, leaving the casino without a chief executive officer at the most formidable moment of its development.

Skip asked Mickey Brown to replace Luciani as the CEO of the casino, and Brown agreed. He was determined not to let the obvious rifts between tribal factions break the enterprise apart, especially since this was the very moment the tribe was in negotiations with the state for permission to operate slot machines. Brown didn't need any bad publicity, and he successfully convinced Luciani to tell the press that the departure was merely the result of a difference in view as to how the casino should be run.

As Brown hoped, Luciani's departure did not foil the slot machine negotiations, and when that piece of business concluded in September, Hayward and the Lims began a second phase of construction at Foxwoods. In late 1992, in a second loan agreement with terms similar to the first, the Malaysians contracted to finance a $142-million expansion that included a 302-room hotel, a five-story underground parking garage, additional casino space, three new theaters, and a two-level shopping concourse complete with holograms, robots, and live performers. On an architect's drawing board for Phase Three was an 800-room hotel, a 70,000-square-foot convention center, and a heliport that would link Foxwoods with Hartford's Bradley International Airport as well as with Kennedy Airport in New York City. Also envisioned was a lake and waterway for paddle boats, two new golf courses, a new hotel off the reservation, an amusement park, a bowling alley, an ice-skating rink, and the crowning item—a Swiss-crafted high-speed monorail that would link all the separate elements of what was now being talked about by Hayward as an "Epcot-like destination resort." The drawings of the monorail showed that it would initially loop from the employee parking lot off Route 2 to Foxwoods, back to the tribe's planned history museum, across Route 214 to the planned 280-room New England Inn—also to be built by the tribe—and across Route 2 to the site where the tribe wanted to build the two giant golf courses. Brown hired Bon Roll of Switzerland to build the monorail, the same company that had built similar monorails at Hershey Park in Pennsylvania and at the Vancouver World's Fair. An internal trolley system would be used to carry customers over a 1,500-foot pathway from the expansion area to the existing casino. With the planning costs for Phase Three included, the total amount of the Lims' loan to the Pequots quickly escalated to $250 million. For the moment, at least, Hayward seemed to have mollified the critics within the tribe. But for his grand dreams to become reality, he and the Lims would need land, and plenty of it. Three hundred and fifty-seven years after the Pequots were thought to have been extinguished, in a strange reversal of history, this tribe of Indians developed a plan to drive the white settlers from their land—in part, so they could build their railroad.

10

TURNABOUT IS UNFAIR PLAY

AT THE END OF 1992, Hayward and his ever-growing band of lawyers and Asian advisors had begun spending many of their afternoon hours hunched over large topographical maps of southeastern Connecticut. As Barry Margolin was aware, but few who weren't so knowledgeable about the law didn't realize, the Indian Reorganization Act of 1934 made it possible for federally recognized Indians tribes to purchase land adjacent to their reservations and to incorporate that property into their tax-free reservation. Like most of the federal legislation involving Indian affairs, the act was passed with western tribes and vast open spaces in mind. It had come about at the urging of John Collier, who had become commissioner of Indian affairs in the Interior Department in 1933. An appointee of Democratic president Franklin Roosevelt, Collier was opposed to the policy of termination, which was intended to effect the total assimilation of Indian cultures into mainstream American life. The loss of Indian culture and identity, Collier believed, would be a tragedy, and his bill sought to strengthen Indian reservations and to repair the disappearing fabric of Native American life and culture.

The provision on the annexation of land was intended to remedy a situation particularly severe with the Navajo and Pueblos out west, where the sales of reservation land at various times had resulted in a checkerboard effect. Reservations were not contiguous and often had private land and developments in the middle of their historic reservations. Collier's law, after it was passed by the New Deal Congress, allowed tribes, with Interior Department permission, to buy back their land and to restore the compactness of a reservation. It addition, the act attempted to stop the shrinkage of reservations by not allowing any Indian lands to be sold to any entity except the tribe itself. Although Collier had the best of intentions, the passage of the bill was due largely to total congressional confidence that Indian tribes would never again be rich or powerful enough to annex land in populated areas. The 1934 law had a firewall, anyway. Any annexation plan had to have the approval of the Bureau of Indian Affairs and thus indirectly the approval of the president. But now, some sixty years later, those caveats were of little concern to Mickey Brown, Barry Margolin, or Rob Gips, the Tureen-trained lawyer who would be playing an increasingly large role in tribal affairs since Tureen himself had moved on to other projects as the head of Tribal Assets Management. The tribe had a master plan in place that made them confident that they would have not only the law on their side but the support of the secretary of the interior as well.

Looking at the map of the reservation pinned to the wall of his temporary office trailer (the tribe's $30-million permanent city hall–type offices were not yet finished), it was clear to Hayward that the most likely spot for the Great Wall of China theme park and his other visions was just across the highway from Foxwoods on the north side of Route 2. Slowly but surely, lawyers for the tribe, led by the veteran real estate lawyer Jackson King, who now worked full-time for the Pequots, began purchasing land and taking options on the property across the road. One 1,200-acre parcel, known as the Lake of Isles Scout Reservation, included a boat ramp and the promise of luxury lakefront homes to be built in the near future. The tribe quietly purchased the property and bought an additional 247 acres that spread across three municipal boundary lines in Ledyard, Preston, and North Stonington. Hayward's attorneys then filed a petition with the Bureau of Indian Affairs asking that those 247 acres of land be annexed and taken into trust by the reservation, in accordance with the 1934 law allowing the addition of adjacent tribe-owned land to the untaxed, sovereign reservation property.

These transactions were handled with such discretion, and the law on annexation was so obscure, that few of the Yankee residents from the towns of Ledyard or North Stonington or Preston knew that anything unusual was taking place. Those who did know of the sales were un-concerned. After all, the wording of the original annexation bill had specifically stated that the act settled all the tribe's land claims and that they therefore could not claim any additional property as part of the reservation. It had never occurred to anyone that the tribe could pur-chase land outside of the bounds of the original 2,000-acre reservation and then add to it. But on a Saturday morning in July 1993, the *Hartford Courant* broke the story that the tribe was not only seeking approval from the federal government to annex 247 acres, but had offered $15 million to the three town governments in exchange for the promise that they would not oppose annexation requests for an additional 9,000 acres. These tracts of land included some 800 occupied dwellings.

The breadth and audacity of the proposal set telephones ringing over all three towns. Several emotional meetings were held in kitchens throughout the towns that night. Residents brainstormed about what they could do to stop the land purchases and the proposed annexation, which would have the dual negative effect of bringing unwanted devel-opment to the area while at the same time taking hundreds of acres off the tax rolls. For accountant Sharon Wadecki, who had lived just a few miles from the edge of the reservation for nearly twenty years, the shock was severe. Wadecki lived in the beautiful two-story New England–style home where she had raised her children and played with them in the large driveway and grassy yard. Her entire tree-lined street, Fanning Road, was included in the land being purchased. The Pequots had a special reason for claiming Fanning Road. Right behind Wadecki's house was the ancestral graveyard of the Pequots, containing the burial plots of Cyrus George, Elizabeth George, and nearly a hundred other mostly unmarked graves. Skip's brother Rodney, who had been killed in the motorcycle-police-chase accident back in 1984, was also buried there. From the second-story windows of their home, the Wadeckis could hear the construction of the new Foxwoods hotel and see it climbing higher and higher through the cedars. The day of the *Hartford Courant* story, Sharon was so upset that she finally went upstairs and pulled the shades shut.

The residents of the towns, stereotypical New Englanders in some respects, banded together in the kitchen at Madeline Jeffery's house. The Jefferys had moved to North Stonington from New York City in 1969, buying an old farmhouse—their lifelong dream—for $48,000. In the twenty-five years they had lived in southeastern Connecticut, they had passed the reservation countless times but had never met anyone who lived there. Like most of the local residents, they simply hadn't paid all that much attention to developments at Mashantucket. For a long time, their sole relationship with the Pequots had been one of distant sympathy. People like the Jefferys had come to the area out of commitment and idealism, 1960s refugees of big-city life and the oppression and corruption it represented. Anything that helped right such a gross historic injustice as had been dealt to Native Americans was something they were inclined to support. Soon after these early kitchen meetings, a town meeting was held at Ledyard High School at which Ada Deer, President Clinton's new head of the Bureau of Indian Affairs and herself a member of the Menominee tribe from Wisconsin, was the special guest. The session, in September 1993, attracted 900 angry residents. Deer was surprisingly blunt, saying that while she would listen to their complaints, she had no basis to stop a tribe from buying and annexing property as long as it was done within the provisions of the 1934 law. It was clear that the "firewall" of BIA approval was not going to get between the Pequots and their annexation efforts.

Disturbed by the lack of response from Deer, Madeline Jeffery decided to take a train down to Washington to meet with her congressman, Sam Gejdenson, as well as other top Interior Department officials. But when she made the rounds on Capital Hill, she wasn't very satisfied with the reception she received. Curiously, the residents of North Stonington just weren't getting much sympathy. Most odd was the chilly reaction from Congressman Gejdenson, who inadvertently referred to Mrs. Jeffery and her friends as "the settlers." Jeffery found the reference a little pointed. Gejdenson was clearly sympathetic to the Pequots, and he expressed pride to Jeffery at the role he had played a decade earlier in helping them win their federal recognition. The one gesture Gejdenson had made was an offer to serve as "helpful mediator" in the dispute, an offer neither Jeffery nor other North Stonington residents were anxious to accept. Gejdenson did not reveal at the time that he had accepted thousands of dollars in campaign contributions from the Pequots and their non-Indian employees, including Michael Brown, Al Luciani, and Jackson King.

Torn between a potentially limitless fountain of campaign contributions and voter anger from the non-Indian residents, most of Connecticut's elected politicians, like Gejdenson, refused to take the residents' side on the issue. When Senator Christopher Dodd was asked about his feelings during an editorial board meeting at the *Norwich Bulletin,* his response could not have been more equivocal. "It's a very complicated set of questions," he said. "The implications of this go far beyond the state of Connecticut. Obviously this is a hot issue and there are people who want to put people in one camp or the other. Some of us don't feel comfortable with that." Dodd's ambivalence was to be expected. The Pequots had not only contributed to his campaign as well, they had made plans to build a new minor league baseball stadium in Norwich and name it after his father, former Connecticut senator Thomas Dodd. The only politician decisively sympathetic to the North Stonington residents was Connecticut's other senator, Joseph Lieberman. Appearing at a town meeting at the Ledyard Library, Lieberman said he was prepared to do anything he could in Washington to defend them. "Annexation is wrong here," Lieberman declared. "The Indian Reorganization Act was intended to help tribes economically, but this tribe is no longer in economic need," he added. At the time Lieberman made these remarks, his staff had scheduled a campaign fund-raiser for him at the Sands Hotel in Las Vegas, where non-Indian casino operators like Stephen Wynn were looking for someone to take on the Indians.

But unfortunately for the North Stonington residents, it was Dodd, not the conscientious Lieberman, who held most of the influence with the administration and especially with Interior Secretary Bruce Babbitt. Dodd was not only close to the president; he was in charge of fund-raising for the Democratic National Committee. Feeling that they were getting nowhere with their elected officials, Jeffery, Wadecki, and other allies decided to fight the annexation proposal at the ballot box. They turned their kitchen talk into an organized assault on annexation, stuffing mailboxes, writing letters, and covering the landscape with signs that cried out: NO ANNEXATION—NOT ONE ACRE. With no shortage of enthusiasm for their task, they gathered signatures that successfully placed a referendum on the November ballot that would forbid the North Stonington town council from even negotiating annexation with tribe lawyers. The referendum passed in November 1993, with 73 percent of the vote, 4,034 to 1,020. Wadecki and Jeffery had spent the morning at the polling place draped in blankets in below-freezing weather. But they were thrilled with the result.

However, the referendum failed to quell homeowner panic in the targeted area. Although the question of whether the land would be annexed and taken off the tax rolls remained unanswered, the tribe still could not be stopped from buying up nonreservation lands. On the Wadeckis' street, every homeowner but them sold out to the tribe. Sharon Wadecki watched countless real estate agents swarm the neighborhood from behind the blinds of her house. The Pequots went on a buying spree. Along Shewville Road at the eastern boundary of the reservation, the tribe purchased twenty beautiful brick homes at an average price of $200,000 each. These homeowners, who had lived in Ledyard all their lives, saw no option but to sell. No one wanted to be the last property owner remaining.

Slowly but surely, the residents of long standing were replaced by nouveau-riche tribal members. Typical of the newcomers were couples like Patricia Fletcher and her husband, Leo, who had just moved to Mashantucket from Brooklyn. Patricia had been attending a family wedding when her aunt Olive informed her that a relative of theirs was a Hayward cousin. She suggested that Fletcher call Skip and see if she could join the tribe. "Go claim it," Aunt Olive told her. After raising five children in a rough section of Brooklyn, Patricia thought Mashantucket was worth checking out. She took a cab all the way to Ledyard and literally ran into the enrollment office to stake her claim to membership. When she explained that her father was descended from one of the original George sisters, she was notified of her acceptance into the tribe called the Pequots, of which she had never heard until it was mentioned by her aunt.

It was two years later, in 1992, that Fletcher decided to give up on Brooklyn. From a life of poverty, she moved into a brick colonial that the tribe had purchased on Coachman's Pike, a connecting street off Fanning Road. The Fletchers' new 3,500-square-foot house had two fireplaces, a sauna, a Jacuzzi in the master suite, two staircases, an upstairs music room, and a wooded yard surrounding a fancy outdoor pool. The Fletchers "purchased" the home from the tribe for $1,500 down and a nominal monthly "mortgage" payment. Under the agreement with the tribe, Fletcher would be refunded the money she put into the house when she left. She was also informed that she was eligible for free driving lessons and tuition-free classes at the local community college. Her son's $2,650 tuition to North Stonington Christian Academy was paid for by the tribe, as were tutors. Medical services were free, as well as day care and health-club memberships. In addition to her $45,000 annual salary for the job she had gotten running a vocational training program for tribe members, Fletcher received a $50,000 annual dividend check as her share of casino profits. Her high-school-aged son also received a $50,000 annual check, which went into an escrow fund that he would be able to cash when he turned twenty-one.

North Stonington wasn't the only land that the tribe was buying. Lantern Hill, the 315-acre, high, stony outcrop where Skip believed his ancestors had once showed the first settlers how to kill rattlesnakes, became Hayward's for a mere one weekend's casino revenue, $3 million. This cliff had been used for several decades as a silica mine, but Skip drew up plans to plant new trees at the mined-out site and to add bicycle trails. Along Route 2, where he hoped the amusement park and two golf courses might one day stand, Hayward purchased twelve additional parcels that encompassed over 500 acres of highway frontage.

Residents beseeched the Interior Department to oppose the petition to incorporate these purchases into the reservation, but Ada Deer and Interior Secretary Bruce Babbitt supported allowing the tribe to put all this land in trust and make it tax-exempt. The argument that extensive development would change the nature of the region did not move Deer, and she issued a statement saying that none of the Pequot projects "affect the quality of the human environment." In the face of political obstinacy, Wadecki, Jeffery, and the others finally hired an attorney and waited over what would be an eighteen-month process while the Interior Department continued to consider the annexation proposal and take public comment about it.

How the tribe had managed to become so popular in Washington was a direct result of what Skip had learned from his savvy mentor, Lim Goh Tong. Lim's success had come from spreading money around, by giving generously to politicians and political parties. In early 1992, shortly after his casino began producing cash, Hayward had begun sending contributions to Bill Clinton, the up-and-coming Democratic presidential candidate from Arkansas. Eventually, the preelection contributions would total $100,000. These contributions were solicited by Kevin Gover, a full-blooded Pawnee Indian who had been raised in Oklahoma and "discovered" by a federal volunteer working with an antipoverty program known as VISTA—Volunteers in Service to America. The volunteer helped him win admission to the prestigious St. Paul's prep school in Concord, New Hampshire. Gover then went on to Princeton University and the University of New Mexico Law School. After opening his own law firm in Albuquerque, Gover got involved in national politics, and in 1992 he organized Native Americans for Clinton/Gore.

After the election of Bill Clinton as president, Gover was recognized by Clinton as having almost singlehandedly put the traditionally Republican state of Montana into the Clinton column after an extraordinarily high voter turnout on seven Montana reservations made the margin of difference for the Democrats. Hayward's contribution to the Clinton campaign was warmly rewarded. Shortly after the election, but before the January 1993 inauguration, Gover arranged for Hayward to be invited down to Little Rock to meet with Clinton and to attend policy meetings chaired by Vernon Jordan, the chairman of the Clinton transition team. In his talks with Jordan, Hayward stressed the need for the federal government to support Native American gambling operations and to oppose a move supported largely by Republican legislators to impose federal taxes on gambling profits. A 1993 Democratic National Committee briefing paper listed Hayward as one of the ten most important supporters of the president.

IN THE EARLY FALL of 1993, Skip drove down to Noank, near the very spot where in 1651 Governor Winthrop had given the Pequots 500 acres at their most popular crabbing and shelling grounds. For Skip, Noank had become hallowed ground. For sixteen years before the rattlesnake-infested Mashantucket reservation lands were granted to the Pequots in 1667, Noank had been the first American Indian reservation in the New World. There the Pequots who had survived their encounter with Captain Mason's forces had scraped out an existence at the sea's edge until encroachment and threats from English settlers had moved the Pequots off those lands. As Skip drove through Noank in his taupe Lincoln Continental, he felt his heartbeat accelerate. Maybe twenty-five years ago, when he first started visiting his grandmother, he was his seafaring father's son. But now he felt within him his mother and grandmother and the generations of Pequots all the way back to Scattup that had preceded him. The years living on the reservation had changed him. Skip was a New England businessman in a suit and his skin was white. But deep inside of him, he had become Pequot.

During that 1993 drive, Skip approached the owner of a large slate gray Cape Cod–style house on the western side of an exclusive point in Noank. "I'm going to buy this house," Skip told his wife, Carol, whom he had married in 1988. Money, naturally, was no object. On November 13, 1993, Hayward promised the owners $200,000 in cash and took a $520,000 mortgage on the rest. In purchasing this house, Skip had triumphantly returned to the site of America's first reservation. It was a stunningly gorgeous home jutting into Long Island Sound at a place where the ferries from New London passed by every day on their way to Orient Point. The site was the perfect melding of the two worlds from which Skip had been created. Skip's new home was idyllic, but his move off the Mashantucket Reservation unleashed a torrent of whispers from his tribal family members, many of whom were just moving onto a reservation and resented that it no longer seemed good enough for Skip. But Kenneth Reels, who himself would later move off the reservation to a bigger house in New London, saw the move as a chance to take advantage of Skip's physical remoteness from the tribe. Skip's leaving the reservation symbolized the chief's increasing isolation from his extended family and was a reminder of the friendships he had developed with Mickey Brown and the Atlantic City crowd, most of whom lived in Groton–Long Point or Mystic, not far from Skip's new house. Even before Skip moved, in late 1993, he had spent much of the year away, traveling to China, Malaysia, even joining the sultan of Brunei, the world's richest man, on a cruise near his home in the Indonesian archipelago.

Anxious to take advantage of Skip's absences, Reels worked hard to add more members of his Narragansett family to the tribal role. He knew that if he could bring more of his family into the tribe, eventually he could throw Skip out and take the $1.5-million-a-year tribal chairmanship for himself. On November 7, 1993, the tribe held a stormy fourteen-hour annual meeting and admitted 100 new members, almost all of them from the large Narragansett branch of Reels's family. The white tribal members argued that they were in danger of diluting the Pequot faction and that the larger the tribe, the smaller the individual pie. But Reels countered with accusations of racism. Each of the proposed new members was as entitled to membership as he himself, Michael Thomas, and Tony Beltran, he argued. These three men were formidable, and in the end the Hayward faction yielded to their demands. Skip assured his six sisters and one brother that ultimately there would be enough money for everyone. Overnight, the Pequot tribe grew from 275 to 375. But even with the additional members, the Narragansetts complained that the leadership and the casino management were too white. Reels urged the establishment of a Peacemakers Grievance Council to hear complaints over the distribution of jobs, housing benefits, and the incentive payments. Phyllis Monroe, Reels's aunt and one of the most outspoken anti-Hayward members of the tribe, was named chairwoman. Reels also won a fight to increase the tribal council from five members to seven, which would give the Reels family members a majority of the board over the Hayward family members.

For Skip, these lost battles were unpleasant diversions from the main task at hand. In another week, the casino would be hosting its greatest visitor yet, and Skip had no time to brood over lost power.

11

THE BATTLE OF OLD BLUE EYES

ON NOVEMBER 19, 1993, a week after the papers were signed for the house at Noank, a very special guest arrived at Ledyard for the grand opening of the new Fox Theater. Fifty years earlier, almost to the day, Frank Sinatra, then a skinny matinee idol, had arrived in Norwich to play the opening of Loew's Theater. Now the silver-haired crooner, who had attained the status of an entertainment god, was coming to southeastern Connecticut as the star of a sold-out, five-night, $1,000-for-the-cheapest-seat gig to celebrate the grand opening of the Pequots' 1,500-seat theater and hotel complex.

In casino-land, having your facility opened by Frank meant instant credibility, and Skip and Mickey Brown had made a personal visit to the Sands in Atlantic City to assure Sinatra's presence. The new hotel, concourse, restaurants, and shops that the Lims' money had built was worthy of their illustrious guest. In obvious homage to Steve Wynn's giant volcano that erupted every fifteen minutes out on Las Vegas Boulevard, Hayward had commissioned a huge sculpture of the Rainmaker, a kneeling, loincloth-clad figure with a bow and arrow pointing toward a skylight and the heavens. Every hour, thunder rumbled through the hallways. Clouds of light rushed across the 3,100 slot machines that surrounded the statue and a taped narrator repeatedly told the story of the original Pequots. Mickey Brown, who had seen a lot of casinos in his life, watched the spectacle in honest amazement. "By the year 2000," he predicted, "Foxwoods will be to the state of Connecticut what Disney World is to the state of Florida."

Even hard-to-impress casino officials from Las Vegas and California were awed by the additions. Saul Leonard, president of a prestigious Los Angeles consulting group commented, "This puts the tribe in the big leagues, and it opens them up to people who didn't know if Foxwoods was a summer camp or what." The Sinatra gig had created great international publicity for the tribe and the casino, but it had also created further conflict for the tribe. For one, it angered Reels and Thomas, who felt left out of all aspects of the event. But they weren't the only people who were steamed over Sinatra's appearance at Foxwoods. Three thousand miles away in Las Vegas, it was more than the volcano outside the Mirage that was exploding that November.

Stephen Wynn may have been rebuffed by the Connecticut legislature, but neither he, nor his archenemy Donald Trump, was about to walk quietly into the night. Wynn's plan for a casino in Hartford may have failed, but the sight of Frank Sinatra at Foxwoods made him more determined than ever to have the last word in regaining a casino foothold in his home state. Wynn was not about to forget that when he had opened the Golden Nugget in Atlantic City, Sinatra had been *his* spokesman in a well-known series of television ads. If Wynn merely disliked the Pequots, Trump was absolutely fulminating over their success and the negative effect that Foxwoods was having on his Atlantic City properties. Foxwoods had almost immediately cut the take at Trump's Castle by 10 to 15 percent, and the idea that he could be bested by an organization that paid no taxes, had no fear of lawsuits, and initially couldn't even have capitalized a New Jersey casino was simply more than Trump could take. Throughout 1993, even before the Sinatra opening in November, Trump was becoming more and more irked by Indian casinos in general and by Foxwoods in particular.

On June 18, 1993, Trump appeared as a guest on shock-jock Don Imus's live radio show in New York City. The topic of conversation was a possible copycat Indian casino that a small tribe of New Jersey Indians was suggesting be built in Wildwood, New Jersey. When Imus asked Trump about Foxwoods, Trump was unequivocally skeptical. "I think if you've ever been up there, you would truly say that these are not Indians," Trump said. "I think I might have more Indian blood than a lot of the so-called Indians that are trying to open up the reservations."

"A couple of these Indians up in Connecticut look like Michael Jordan, frankly," Imus responded.

Trump grunted his agreement, adding, "They call it the sovereign nation, this great sovereign nation, that sovereign nation," said Trump. "All of a sudden, it's nations. Before gambling, it wasn't a nation." But Trump, like Wynn, was aware of the difficulty of fighting the tribe either in Congress or in the courts. "General George Custer was against it also and look what happened to him," he observed.

American Indian leaders were outraged at Trump's comments and quickly attempted to discredit their foe. They hoped to use Trump's intemperate observation to undercut a movement in the United States Senate to alter the provisions of the Indian Gaming Regulatory Act that forced states to negotiate with federally recognized tribes. Following that broadcast of Imus, the National Indian Gaming Association, a nationwide organization of tribes that own gambling parlors, filed a formal complaint with the Federal Communications Commission. They demanded an apology for remarks that were "blatantly racist, sexist and thoroughly offensive," and a spokesman for the association compared Imus's reference to Michael Jordan to the 1986 incident in which CBS sports analyst Jimmy "the Greek" Snyder was fired by his network for making racist remarks concerning black athletes. "The American people have made it clear that they will not tolerate this kind of racism over the airwaves," said Myron Ellis, a spokesman for the Minnesota chapter of the Indian Gaming Association. "Racial slurs and insults are no more acceptable coming from Donald Trump and Don Imus than they were from Jimmy the Greek." Ellis added, "It's tragic that Donald Trump is using his billions to inflame tensions and stir up hatred between people. His words and those of Don Imus are an insult not only to American Indians, but to all Americans who believe in social justice and the fair treatment of minorities."

The tribes did not really expect Donald Trump to back down, but they did hope to embarrass Trump pal Robert Torricelli, the newly elected senator from New Jersey who at the time was supporting major changes in the Indian Gaming Act that would make it more difficult for tribes to obtain casino licenses from the Bureau of Indian Affairs. But neither man seemed to be intimidated. On October 5, 1993, Trump and Torricelli went together to a congressional hearing on Capital Hill to testify about the problems created by Indian gaming. In the process, they renewed the old argument that the mafia would run rampant over little Indian tribes like the Pequots. "That an Indian chief is going to tell Joe Killer to please get off his reservation is almost unbelievable to me," said Trump. "I think it's obvious that organized crime is rampant—and I don't mean a little bit—on Indian reservations. People have got paper bags over their faces and nobody's looking," he protested. "At the Taj Mahal I spent more money on security and security systems than most Indians spend building their entire casino and I will tell you there is no way the Indians are going to protect themselves from the mob." Trump's tirade enraged the chairman of the House Interior Committee, George Miller, who claimed he had never heard more irresponsible testimony. But Trump kept on. "This will be the biggest crime problem in the nation's history," Trump declared. "I believe you folks have created a monster. How is it a sovereign nation? It's only a sovereign nation in that Indians don't have to pay tax." Trump reserved his most pointed criticisms for the Pequots: "They don't look like Indians to me and they don't look like Indians to Indians," he sputtered.

Following Trump's congressional testimony, Hayward got a statement of support from Arizona senator John McCain, who had been one of the tribe's most loyal supporters during the original debate over IGRA: "Mr. Trump's statements reflect the kind of misinformation and misunderstanding that has plagued the controversial issue of Indian gaming. Some of it is also probably derived from a concern about economic competition. But it is clear that misinformation and uncertainty undermine the environment of reason and good will that is necessary to resolve issues such as those involved in Indian gaming," McCain said.

Supporters of Indians painted a picture of Native American life that was far from the existence currently being celebrated at Mashantucket. Richard Hill, then the top lobbyist for the Indian Gaming Association, told the committee, "This may be hard for you, but try to picture living

in one of America's poorest communities without adequate health clin-
ics, clean drinking water, safe roads, sturdy housing or permanent
schools, without self-sufficient local economies. That's where most of us
live, Mr. Trump. No yachts. No jets. No Palm Beach mansions or Fifth
Avenue penthouses. But we have our identity, our heritage and culture,
our pride in what it means to be First Americans and that's no joke, sir."
Hill's description of humble reservation life may have been accurate for
those impoverished tribes that constituted the vast majority of Indians.
But whether the description was accurate or not with respect to a few
extraordinarily wealthy tribes, Congress was not about to jump into the
controversy again. Trump's hopes of putting Foxwoods on equal legal
turf were slowly dashed by congressional lassitude—to say nothing of
Skip's campaign-season largess. If Trump and Wynn were going to get
back in the action in Connecticut, they couldn't count on Congress to
help them. Neither man was without resources, and both stubbornly
clung to the belief that ultimately, one day, they would get the better of
the dreamy welder from Ledyard.

BY EARLY 1993, the City of Bridgeport was in total economic chaos
and had declared bankruptcy. The economic base of urban Connecticut,
centered on defense contractors like Pratt & Whitney and Sikorsky He-
licopters, was in shambles. Bridgeport had eliminated its street sweepers,
closed its snowplowing operations, fired its lifeguards, and slashed ex-
penditures for recreation, libraries, and senior citizen services. Some 15
percent of the population was on welfare. And even with all the cuts, the
Bridgeport City Council still couldn't balance its $308-million budget.

Of all the cities in Connecticut that had suffered from the recession,
Bridgeport's problems were the most acute. The city had gone belly-up
and was surviving only by a series of high-interest revenue bonds that
the state had authorized. Bridgeport had put the state legislature in a
bind. They could either burden Connecticut's taxpayers to bail out the
city, or they could consider what the local elected officials were already
thinking about—a casino that would jump-start the local economy. For
Steve Wynn, Bridgeport's poverty was a rich opportunity, the most

likely place where the legislature might legalize a non-Indian casino in Connecticut. A gambling operation that close to New York City would deal a double blow—one to the Pequots, another one to Trump. On December 17, 1993, just three weeks after Sinatra opened the new Fox Theater some ninety miles away, Wynn sponsored a Christmas party at the Dolphin Cove Marina restaurant in Bridgeport, entertaining more than two hundred local supporters and politicos. It was the ceremonial kickoff for his renewed effort to win state approval to open up a casino and the celebration of the opening of a Bridgeport office from which his reinvigorated lobbying and political effort would be launched. Wynn, however, had made a major adjustment in his negotiating position for his second attempt at challenging Foxwoods. In his losing attempt to win the right to open a casino the year before, Weicker had outflanked him by approving the slot deal with the Pequots. He had then used the argument that the state dare not risk the $100-million minimum it was going to get from Foxwoods with a partner that couldn't promise a definite reward. A year earlier, Wynn had wanted slot machines legalized before he opened his casino. This time he decided not to challenge the state on slots. Instead, he would try to get state permission to open a casino with or without slots. He figured that once the casino was up and running, he could work on pressuring the state to legalize slots. Among the powerful state politicians in Wynn's camp was Mary Fritz, the chairwoman of the Connecticut House of Representatives Public Safety Committee. She had drafted the bill that would legalize construction of a Wynn casino. The legislation was cleverly designed to get union and minority support by requiring that Wynn guarantee Connecticut contractors 75 percent of all the construction work and that 20 percent of the employees on the project be hired from state welfare rolls. None of this, however, did anything to soften Weicker's bitter opposition to letting a Steve Wynn casino into the state of Connecticut under any circumstances.

Initially, Mickey Brown also reacted to the renewed Wynn effort with total opposition, reiterating the tribe's position that it would consider any state deal with Wynn or Trump as an abrogation of the slot deal with Governor Weicker. But at the same time, Brown and Hayward began secretly talking to Governor Weicker about a proposal that would allow the neighboring Mohegan Indian tribe, which had also won federal recognition, to open a casino. Brown was skeptical about supporting a new casino in the area since the key concept for him, when it came to Foxwoods, had always been exclusivity. But Skip was determined to do something to show his goodwill, as an Indian, toward his brother Indians.

Skip had been stung in recent days by comments from various Native American quarters that Foxwoods was disrespectful of Indian culture and that the tribe itself was of dubious Indian ancestry. Most importantly, many Native American leaders, who were hoping to get their own gambling parlors, worried that the high profile the Pequots had provoked by asking for so much so soon in their annexation request might spark a political backlash. They were also concerned about increased public support for a Republican-sponsored proposal in Congress that would force Indian casinos to pay federal income taxes as high as 35 percent of their profits. Although state governments could not tax the tribes, the unique federal relationship between Indians and the United States government might have allowed the federal tax proposal to withstand whatever court challenges tribes' lawyers would have been likely to mount.

No figure in the American Indian orbit was more resentful of the Pequots' lifestyle than Moonface Bear, chief of the self-proclaimed Golden Hill Paugussetts in the coastal town of Trumbull, Connecticut. Moonface Bear was one of six children of the Paugussett chief Big Eagle and had grown up outside of Bridgeport on the one-quarter-acre remnant that his family claimed as their reservation. Like other New England reservations, the Paugussetts were not federally recognized and the one-quarter acre that had been passed on to Moonface Bear, whose legal name was Kenneth Piper, Jr., was the smallest "Indian reservation" in the United States. Moonface Bear had no luck getting Congress to consider a federal recognition bill, and he convinced himself that this was because Hayward was white and he was not. The BIA had conducted an extensive investigation of the Piper family and determined that there was no conclusive evidence that either Moonface Bear or Big Eagle was an actual descendant of the authentic Paugussetts who had lost most of their reservation in 1802. The BIA rejection, when virtually every other New England tribe was winning federal recognition, drove Moonface Bear to desperation. At first, he attempted to file suit in federal court, claiming 80 acres of downtown Bridgeport as belonging to him. When that failed, he proclaimed himself "war chief" and in 1993 opened a tax-free cigarette store on his tiny reservation. State authorities served notice that he had no legal right to sell cigarettes and ordered him to desist. Moonface Bear refused, claiming that Indian sovereignty was innate and supreme and could not be "given" by the state. His argument drew support from radical Indian activists, who helped him create an armed camp that included a makeshift lookout tower filled with armed guards. For thirteen weeks, the thirty-five-year-old chief confronted Connecticut state troopers, but the episode eventually ended with his surrender and arrest. He was put on trial and convicted of unlawfully selling cigarettes and interfering with police business. First in jail and later in the hospital with Lyme's disease, which claimed his life on May 24, 1996, Moonface Bear had watched bitterly as the Pequots grew rich, and he died convinced that had his face been as white as Skip's, he would have been the millionaire.

Moonface Bear's criticisms might have been written off as pure jealousy, but the feeling was shared by others in the Indian world. Philip Martin, the full-blooded chief of the Choctaws in Philadelphia, Mississippi, had spent years developing a plan to revive the economic fortunes of his 8,000-member tribe. A casino was part of his plan, but he had also signed deals with General Motors to build wire harnesses for car parts in a giant industrial park he had created on his 25,500-acre reservation. Overall, his Choctaw Industrial Park was a model of tribal industrial development, and he had no intention of allowing fast, easy money to affect the work ethic he had instilled on the reservation. Privately, Martin expressed worries that the Pequot experience would stir up negative feelings in Indians across America: if the idea gained credence that all a tribe had to do was open a casino and become instantly, fabulously rich without working, the hard nine-to-five labor might be viewed by the Choctaws as a raw deal.

Martin was reluctant to go public with his feelings, but others were not so reticent. In an article in a Lakota Sioux newspaper, *Indian Country Today,* Tim Giago, the weekly's publisher, accused the Pequots of seeking federal recognition only "because that is where the money was to be found." Giago charged that the Pequots' compact with the state "set a bad precedent for the older, more established tribes of America." He complained that cocktail waitresses at the Foxwoods Casino "cavort about in thigh-length, fake buckskin minidresses and wear headbands with chicken feathers protruding from the backs of their heads—an obvious insult to all the tribes who hold the eagle feather sacred—and traditional tribal leaders say nothing. It is as if they are afraid to speak out for fear of antagonizing such a wealthy tribe." Giago also criticized the Pequot practice of enlisting friends and relatives, "many of them non-Indians," as tribal members to help them get in on the casino riches.

As Giago's article noted, Skip had initially fought Native American hostility with what had worked in the past—millions of dollars in giveaways to Indian causes. After all, cash was the one commodity the tribe had in excess. In early 1994, Skip gave away hundreds of thousands of dollars to the American Indian College Fund and the Native American Rights Fund, the latter the same organization that had once helped finance his early legal actions against the State of Connecticut. When small tribes requested it, Hayward authorized his nation's equivalent of foreign aid, paying over $1 million to less fortunate tribes in the Midwest. He also pledged $10 million to the Smithsonian Institution's new American Indian Museum, after being personally buttonholed on the issue by Daniel Inouye of Hawaii, ranking Democrat on the Senate Indian Affairs Committee. Skip dared not anger the powerful senator from Hawaii, particularly at a time when the Smithsonian's museum needed $60 million in private donations to get matching federal funds. The $10 million pledged by the Pequots made national headlines as the single largest gift for any Smithsonian project. It was the most difficult check Skip had ever had to sign. As he later said of the experience, "I was kind of numb." But it made him and the tribe heroes of sorts, and since it dramatized their commitment to traditional American Indians, he figured the investment was worth it.

Skip's charity did not stop with Native American causes. From 1992 to 1996, he spread an additional $30 million in political and charitable contributions, including $2 million to the Special Olympics, $500,000 to the Hartford Ballet, $70,000 for a fireworks display on the Thames River, $50,000 to the Old Mystic Baptist Church, where his mother had belonged until her death, and $15,000 to the Ledyard Mavericks girl's softball team. One of his more stunning contributions was a gift of $5 million to the Mystic Aquarium, which was designated to finance a new collection of Beluga whales. Oddly enough, at the same time they were giving all this money away, the tribe was still a major recipient of federal aid. The tribe was building houses on the reservation with a $1.4-million grant from the U.S. Department of Housing and Urban Development. In 1994, they received another $419,000 from the Bureau of Indian Affairs for scholarships, road projects, law enforcement, and other projects, and approximately $20,000 more to help administer those programs. The U.S. aid received in 1994 was more than they had been allotted in either of the previous two years, when the casino was making less money but was not as politically generous. BIA officials explained that just because the tribe had hit the slot jackpot was no reason for them to be deprived of federal assistance. "Think of it like someone hitting the lottery and suddenly getting forty million dollars," said BIA spokeswoman Alicia Sandoval. "They would still be entitled to Social Security."

Skip's political largess was working, and he made no apology for taking U.S. government money, telling the tribal council that it was a matter of pride to receive "foreign aid" from the U.S. government and a symbolic act that "maintains our status as a government."

BUT THE TRIBE ITSELF remained its own number-one charity. They established their own police, fire, health, and ambulance services; developed their own court system for civil cases; continued to build and buy homes that were free to tribal members; and launched extensive archeological investigations. The tribal council decreed that any Pequot who was admitted to college would be guaranteed a full, tribally financed scholarship. Eventually, they bailed out a failing private school in the town of Stonington called Pine Point, which was in danger of going bankrupt, and in return were permitted to place several tribal members on its board of directors. Pine Point then became the prep school of choice for tribal children, with the casino footing the $11,000-per-year tuition bill for every student. Any adult who wanted additional education or training could get it, compliments of the tribe. In addition to the $17-million "city hall," where Skip had his offices, the Pequots built a child-care center and a separate $9.2-million community development center. The Pequots, who had barely 50 members enrolled in the 1960s—more than a few of them on loan from the Narragansetts—had, by 1994, placed 165 of its first 250 members in modern, nicely landscaped reservation homes.

With this overwhelming prosperity, there even came a time in 1994 when the Pequots came incredibly close to landing their own professional football team. In late 1994, James Orthwein, the owner of the New England Patriots, decided to sell his team. Although the team, once known as the Boston Patriots, had always played its games in Massachusetts, Governor Weicker felt it would be a coup if he could entice the Patriots to become Connecticut's team. When Weicker surveyed possible owners who might be interested in buying the team and moving it to Connecticut, he suddenly realized that the one person who had the money and the land on which to build a stadium was Skip Hayward. Weicker talked to Hayward and Brown and found they were willing to try anything. Brown still had visions of a regional sports and entertainment complex that would turn Mashantucket into the biggest, most important tourist destination in all of New England. There was probably nothing they could do that would bring as much publicity and attention as buying an NFL franchise. But in the early stages of their inquiry, they were stymied. NFL commissioner Paul Tagliabue informed Weicker and Hayward right up front that the league did not want a team so closely connected to gambling. He would never allow a gambling tribe to own the team. Brown and Hayward then changed course. Instead of pursuing a bid on their own, Hayward offered to become partners with popular fiction writer Tom Clancy and Walter Payton, the former Chicago

Bears Hall of Fame running back. Clancy, who had made millions on his books and movies, would be the principal owner of the team, but the Pequots would agree to finance and build a stadium in Hartford, where Clancy would present his Patriot games. The deal fell apart when Orthwein decided instead to sell the team to Boston businessman Robert Kraft. The setback hardly dampened Skip's determination to see the Patriots move to Ledyard. When he read that the new owner had expressed dissatisfaction with the Patriots' stadium in Foxboro, Massachusetts, Hayward offered to build Kraft a stadium on 250 acres of tribal land that had been purchased near Interstate 95 in North Stonington near the Rhode Island border. Like Clancy before him, Kraft came down and discussed the project with enthusiasm. But Tagliabue stepped in again. Not only would he not allow the tribe to own a team, he didn't want games played next to a casino. With that word from the commissioner, Kraft decided to stay in Massachusetts.

Despite all this attention and all the additions he had made to Foxwoods, Hayward still felt besieged by distrustful chiefs, jealous cousins, angry competitors, and restive neighbors. He continued to believe that economic development and the creation of even more wealth would ultimately solve most of those problems. If Skip was going to achieve harmony within his tribe, he could not ignore the threat posed by Steve Wynn.

12

THE PEQUOTS LOSE A BET

SKIP REALIZED THAT if Steve Wynn was going to be defeated, a new alliance would have to be forged with one of the Pequots' ancient rivals: the Mohegans. The Mohegans were one of New England's oldest, largest, and most venerable Indian tribes. With a tribal roll 1,000 members strong and a firm history tracing their lineage back to Uncas and his descendants, they were led by a seventy-five-year-old marble sculptor, Ralph Sturges. Aided by Tureen, after he finished with the Pequots' application, they had no problem also winning federal recognition. There was division within the tribe about whether to go into gambling or not, and the Mohegans' initial indecision had given the Pequots a huge head start. Now the Mohegans were determined to catch up, and they pursued a gambling compact with the state that was modeled almost to the word on the one that had been negotiated with the Pequots. But since the Pequots had been granted an exclusive license to have slot machines, Weicker needed Skip's permission to grant the Mohegans the same privileges.

For seven weeks in early 1994, Skip and his representatives negotiated with Weicker over the terms of a Mohegan casino. The key element of the three-way negotiations between the Mohegans, the Pequots, and Governor Weicker was that the Mohegans would guarantee the state a minimum of $80 million a year in annual gambling revenue. In return, they would receive the same promise from Weicker that the Pequots had: that if a non-Indian casino were allowed to open, the slot payments would no longer be required. In his proposal to the state legislature,

Wynn had counted on surpassing the Pequots' $100-million guarantee, but the deal with the Mohegans made the hill he would have to climb to achieve this all that much higher, since the Mohegans' guarantee would now be added to the equation. Although Mickey Brown was at first adamantly opposed to the yielding of the exclusive franchise that the Pequots had won, Skip was determined to show his critics in Indian Country that he would never stand in the way of another Indian tribe's progress. Weicker was pushing the deal for a different reason, one that also made sense to Skip and Mickey. Weicker had never abandoned his resolve to keep Steve Wynn out of Connecticut, and the Mohegan casino would make Wynn's proposal to the state legislature harder to fulfill.

On April 25, 1994, the three-way agreement was signed, although it would be two more years before the Mohegans would actually open their casino next to an old nuclear fuel plant on the Thames River, twelve miles to the east of Foxwoods. As Weicker, Chief Sturges, and Chief Hayward signed the document, Skip observed: "The Pequots and the Mohegans have a long history together, and I believe at one time were one people. We wish the Mohegans the best of luck."

ON APRIL 30, 1994, as he awaited the Interior Department's final decision on annexation, and as the North Stonington and Ledyard residents remained frustrated by the lack of sympathy in Washington to their cause, Hayward was invited to the South Lawn of the White House to attend a speech and ceremony at which President Bill Clinton signed a bill allowing Indians to use the feathers of endangered eagles in their religious ceremonies. It remained illegal for anyone else to possess the feathers of the endangered American eagle, as long as they weren't cocktail waitresses in Skip's casino. Some 322 leaders and chiefs of the nation's tribes were there, but it was Hayward who was seated in the front row during Clinton's speech, and it was Hayward who was given the honor of awarding the president a statue of an Indian pointing his hands to the sky, a model of the one that stood in the lobby of Foxwoods. Clinton gave Hayward his favored double handshake and hug, and to the astonishment of many of the other chiefs who were in the group, showed his familiarity by referring to the Pequot leader by his nickname. By now, Clinton was foursquare in support of Indian gaming, opposed to taxation of casinos, and considered Indians an important base of political support and campaign contributions. Clinton announced at the ceremony, "Indian gaming operations give tribes a competitive edge and you've had precious few." In a total turnabout from the position he had taken as governor, Clinton added, "Some of you are now able to invest more in housing, in health care, in child care, in infrastructure, in taking care of your elders. I want tribes to continue to benefit from gaming." Skip also met with Vice President Gore and his wife, Tipper, at a dinner and toasted them as "the people who will someday occupy the White House as First Family." During a prayer, Skip and Tipper held hands.

Although a Republican-led U.S. Senate investigation would later conclude that there was a clear link in the Clinton administration between campaign contributions and Clinton's support for the pet issues of large campaign donors, it did not take such a study for the townspeople of Ledyard to get the message that the Pequots and the U.S. government were on the same side. Bill Clinton had reason to feel comfortable with Skip. Federal Election Commission records revealed that by 1994 the Pequots had become the nation's largest contributors of soft money to the Democratic Party. Eventually, nearly $800,000 was contributed by the tribe to organizations raising money for Clinton's reelection. But showing just how savvy Hayward had become politically, he hedged his bets, giving $50,000 to the Republican National Committee as well. Skip told his fellow members of the tribal council that they needed to give this money to the Republicans as a way of thanking Arizona senator John McCain, who had opposed the Las Vegas interests in the Indian Gaming Regulatory Act debate and who had spoken out so forcefully after the vocal challenge by Donald Trump. Ironically, the $50,000 contribution did more damage with Republicans than good. Incoming Speaker Newt Gingrich said the disparity between the amounts was an insult, and he told Republican leaders that he would support a proposal by House Ways and Means Committee chairman Bill Archer to put a heavy federal tax on Indian casinos. His anger prompted several tribes, mainly Philip Martin's Choctaws, to hire—for $500,000 in one six-month billing period—a well-known Republican lobbyist named Jack Abramoff, whose job it became to convince Gingrich that reservations were an example of free-enterprise zones and could therefore be used by Republicans to demonstrate how economic development could flourish in a low-tax environment. Abramoff's ploy worked, and although he remained dissatisfied with the flow of contributions to Democrats, Gingrich dropped his insistence on taxing Indian casinos.

Skip's visit to the White House had emboldened the tribe in its battle against the antiannexation residents. The Pequots lost interest in appeasing the local landowners and became increasingly frustrated and hostile over their opposition. "You'd think we threatened to grab our guns and tomahawks and burn people out of their homes," said Bruce Kirchner, a senior vice president at the casino. "We're buying the land legally and we're doing everything we're doing totally legally. We're here to stay, and people are going to have to get used to change." Skip came to believe that the antiannexation forces were motivated in part by "jealousy and maybe a smidge of racism." Frustrated by the referendum the residents had won, the favorable press they were getting, and the legal maneuverings they had in store, other tribe members became increasingly vocal and combative. On August 20, 1994, Skip's first cousin Jo-Anne Isaac told the tribal council to back off on its demand for annexation "negotiations." Confident that all the money they had given to Washington politicians could get them whatever they wanted, Isaac then called a press conference in front of an old reservation cabin and declared that all the property in dispute was Indian land to start with. Claiming to be a "tribal historian," Isaac insisted that the Pequots were entitled to "thousands of acres taken by unscrupulous state-appointed overseers." Her comments reflected the increasing distance between the homeowners and the tribal members. "The residents against annexation—you should be ashamed at your ignorance, your greed, at the disruption you cause your neighbors who are gainfully employed, receiving education funds from their employment. If you are unhappy living next to Mashantucket Indians—move," she demanded.

While the Pequots battled their neighbors, both Wynn and Trump took further steps to ingratiate themselves with those who they hoped would soon be their own new neighbors. Several days after Isaac's outburst, Trump purchased several downtown warehouses on the Bridgeport waterfront and announced the development of a $350-million theme park for the impoverished city. Trump innocently claimed that his development had nothing whatever to do with gambling, at least for the moment, and that his project would include a waterfront terminal for cruise ships and high-speed ferries to Long Island. The seaport park would include specialty shops, restaurants, and entertainment. "This has nothing to do with the casinos," he told the press in Bridgeport. "This is a separate plan. If casinos should happen in Connecticut, we'd be involved, but not here."

By early 1995, the Pequots' strategy with regard to the Bridgeport projects was one of staunch opposition. But one major player in the casino drama was off the scene by this time. Governor Weicker had left office and been replaced by Republican John Rowland. Rowland had been elected as a supporter of the Bridgeport casino rescue effort and thus was not initially viewed favorably by the Pequots' top lobbyist in Hartford, Charles Duffy. Duffy advised Brown and Hayward to keep an open mind, while he worked on gaining support from the new governor. Before the legislature could act on legalizing a non-Indian casino in Bridgeport, it had to await the results of a referendum in the city that would be held on March 28. Required by law, the decision by the voters of Bridgeport would be the first step in the process of putting a casino in the bankrupt city. With all the public officials in the city supporting one casino plan or another, a favorable vote seemed a foregone conclusion, especially since Wynn had agreed to spend $100,000 on procasino billboards and advertising, and was bankrolling the local organizations who were on his side. Opponents posted only one billboard, spending just $5,000.

But if there was not much of an anti-Wynn movement from the community of Bridgeport, there came from Mashantucket a steady stream of ominous warnings. If a casino opened in Bridgeport, the tribe would be exempt from its $100-million-plus payments to the state; and so would the Mohegans once they opened. Their public intransigence on the issue was beginning to rile up anti-Pequot sentiment not just in surrounding towns but across the state. One legislator seriously proposed the setting up of tollbooths on roads that led to Mashantucket. "Roadblocks, tollbooths, repaving projects, bus safety checks, just about anything you can think of, we could do," one state official told the *Hartford Courant*.

Because of the deal they had made with Weicker and the Mohegans, the Pequots were publicly committed to opposing the casino bill in the state capital. But behind the scenes, Mickey Brown began pursuing a different course, which involved sharing the expertise on Indian gambling regulations that he had obtained with other tribes. Brown's attorneys had even created a new corporate entity for the purpose called Foxwoods Management Company. The tribe owned some 75 percent of the company and Brown and the Lims shared the other 25 percent. Foxwoods had become a magnet for tribal leaders who came to inspect the physical plant and to see how they could transport its success to their reservations in Michigan, Wisconsin, Kansas, and Iowa. Once they were at the casino, Brown would then sell Foxwoods Management to them as the consulting company that would build and operate their casino for as much as 35 percent of the gross revenue. Brown had successfully negotiated a management deal with the Kickapoo tribe in northeastern Kansas. If the Pequots were going to be in the casino business, and if Bridgeport was going to grant a license for one public, state-authorized casino to be built, Brown didn't see why Foxwoods couldn't get a piece of the action.

Governor Rowland was thinking exactly the same thing. Rowland had inherited many of the same doubts about Wynn that Weicker had harbored. Skip certainly seemed to be a more dependable person with whom to do business, and by now he was a known quantity in the state capital, well liked by politicians on account of his willingness to write checks for campaign contributions when asked. Foxwoods was certainly better run than many of Trump's Atlantic City properties, and Wynn's involvement with felons such as imprisoned financier Michael Milken made Rowland wary. Rowland slipped the word to Mickey that the Pequots should seriously consider submitting their own proposal to operate in Bridgeport.

While Brown contemplated his next move, the U.S. Department of the Interior in May finally reached their decision on the Pequots' application to annex the 247 controversial acres of land. Interior Secretary Bruce Babbitt announced that the annexation was permissible, but called on the tribe to make "annual payments in lieu of taxes" to the towns and to pledge not to develop the property without environmental approval from the Bureau of Indian Affairs. The BIA officials, notably Ada Deer, had not wanted the exceptions, but they were the result of direct intervention with Babbitt by Connecticut senator Joseph Lieberman, the member of Connecticut's congressional delegation least swayed by the tribe's case. Although the "concession" that they would have to file environmental impact statements seemed major at first, Babbitt, who would later face (and be cleared by) a special prosecutor's investigation for allegedly allowing campaign contributions to affect his Indian gaming policies, announced two days later that the tribe would only have to submit an environmental "assessment," a far less burdensome requirement than what would be required by the Environmental Protection Agency. Shortly thereafter, Ada Deer declared that the tribe's plan to build a visitors center, parking garages, golf courses, and a hotel on the site would have "no significant environmental impact." So much for the impact statement.

Though they had little success in the political arena, the residents of North Stonington, Ledyard, and Preston had better luck in the courts, the one branch of government difficult to influence with money. They quickly hired a prominent Washington attorney and filed suit in federal court to block the BIA-approved annexation. Almost immediately, federal judge Robert Chatigny dismissed the annexation application with regard to 85 of the 247 acres, ruling that it had actually been bought not with casino money but with federal funds not designated for that purpose. The annexation was thrown into further legal turmoil the following December when a federal appeals court in South Dakota struck down the annexation portion of the 1934 Indian Reorganization Act as unconstitutional because it was too broad, had too few guidelines, and represented "an abandonment of congressional authority" to the Bureau of Indian Affairs.

Following the passage of the nonbinding Bridgeport referendum, the legislature had set up a bidding system to determine which company would operate and manage the Bridgeport casino. Virtually everyone assumed that Wynn's Mirage Corporation would be selected, particularly since Trump, who was having some financial problems, had decided not even to submit a bid. Rowland and his aides, particularly John Meskill, the state's director of special revenue, grew increasingly concerned about losing the Pequots' and the Mohegans' millions. Duffy had made it unmistakably clear to the legislature and the press that as soon as the deal with Wynn was made, the Pequots would cease their payments to the state. It was unrealistic to think that Wynn would open his casino right away, and a report from Meskill's Connecticut Division of Special Revenue revealed that the legalization of casino gaming in Bridgeport would cost the state over $150 million in the interim. Even if the new casino was taxed at a 20-percent rate, twice what Wynn was lobbying for, the state would still have trouble making up for losses incurred by a cutoff of the Pequots' slot revenue.

Rowland set a mid-September deadline by which the casino bids had to be made, and Mickey Brown went to work. A study of the clientele at Foxwoods had revealed that 80 percent of its business came from Boston and Providence. New York City was viewed as an area of growth for Foxwoods, and the Phase Three plans for the casino included a new seventeen-story hotel that presumably would be filled with overnight visitors from New York. If the Pequots could open the Bridgeport casino, they wouldn't need the new hotel. Foxwoods could continue to serve its current market and Bridgeport could handle all the New York traffic. On September 13, 1995, Brown, Gips, and Wynn met before the commission in Hartford. Wynn spoke first and announced his plan for the HarbourTowne Resort, which would include a a resort hotel, a waterfront amphitheater, night clubs, and a fancy movie and shopping complex. He claimed HarborTowne would generate 10,500 new jobs and create $240 million annually in new taxes for the city and the state. Politically, the most important aspect of his proposal was that he would not oppose allowing 6,200 slot machines in existing pari-mutuels throughout the state, such as jai alai frontons, dog tracks, and off-track betting parlors. In exchange for that guarantee, Wynn's bid had the support of the racing and jai alai industries.

Brown's presentation emphasized the speed with which he could get a casino up and running and reminded the commission of how successful the Pequots had been in Ledyard. He promised to pay 16 percent of all casino revenues to the state and to donate 10 percent of revenues to a Bridgeport Economic Development Fund. Foxwoods would put a temporary casino in an existing building while the first phase of the permanent casino was under construction. But he would not yield on allowing additional slots at any non-Indian facility in the state. He promised, however, that the Ledyard casino would continue to pay its 25 percent fee for the use of slots.

A month later, on October 2, Rowland announced his decision. He would ask the legislature to approve a casino in Bridgeport, a casino built by the Pequots. He called for a special session of the legislature on October 25 to ratify the deal he would make with Skip and Mickey and thus to rescue Bridgeport. But both Rowland and Brown recognized that they faced an uphill battle in convincing the state senate to go along. In an initial canvas of the thirty-six-member Senate, only three had announced their intention to vote for the proposal. But Rowland promised the Pequots that he would expend all his political capital to get the casino deal done. Ironically, the first big political battle waged by Rowland's predecessor was an effort to keep the Pequots from building a casino. Now, four years later, the new governor's first legislative battle would be to make sure that they did build one. Rowland's biggest obstacle in winning passage was that the Pequots' proposal failed to do anything about introducing slot machines at the state's racetracks and jai alai frontons, as Wynn had agreed to do. That was not something that Brown would compromise on and Bridgeport's mayor, Joseph P. Ganim, anticipated that if some compromise wasn't worked out, the casino vote would have no chance. "I don't see a landslide victory without it," he said. "And I see a landslide as one vote." Ganim added that unless the casino bill was passed, residents of his city "might as well turn out the lights."

Brown got Skip's authorization to expend $2.1 million of the tribe's money on the lobbying campaign to win the vote in the legislature. They would eventually spend $1,500,000 on lobbying and lobbying expenses, $292,000 for outside public relations firms, $210,000 for billboards and newspaper advertising, and $188,000 in consulting costs. The stakes were tremendous, almost unprecedented in the American casino business. Nobody had ever built a casino that close to populous New York City. Sitting over drinks one night at the Mystic Hilton, Brown told Skip, "If we win this, we would control more gaming business than any other casino company in the world." Despite the intense and expensive campaign, and the importance Brown now attached to Bridgeport, in fact, the Pequots had managed once again to maneuver themselves into a no-lose situation. If the legislature approved the governor's plan, the Pequots would attain unheard of riches, more than doubling what each family was already making from their enterprise. If the legislature did not approve it, the monopoly that had produced the Pequots' wealth would remain intact since it was now unlikely that either Wynn or Trump would threaten them in the future. Observed state senator William A. Aniskovich, "In many respects, the Pequots, more than any player in this game, win if they win and win if they lose." For the lucky modern-day Pequots, that seemed par for the course.

TWO WEEKS AFTER ROWLAND announced his decision on Bridgeport, the Mohegans unveiled the details of their plan for the casino that Weicker had approved before he left office. They had hired a South African–based management company to run their facility, a choice that did not sit well with Kenneth Reels. He had been vehemently opposed to the arrangement and was miffed that Hayward had made the Mohegan deal with Weicker in contradiction to his views. Like Brown, Reels felt that Hayward was giving away the franchise in allowing the Mohegans to compete with them. When it was made, the agreement had represented what Skip had argued was a convergence of interest for the three principals. But now, events had made many of the original motives for the alliance moot. The Mohegan agreement had been crafted in part to keep a casino out of Bridgeport. Now the Pequots were actually trying to get a casino in Bridgeport. The Mohegans had entered into the agreement assuming that the Pequots would stand with them in opposing competition, but before they could even open—the target for their grand opening was the fall of 1996—the Pequots were planning a new casino that would sop up all the Mohegan Sun's potential customers from New York City.

Neither the Mohegan leadership nor their South African partners were happy with this turn of events, and they secretly began plotting ways to undermine the Pequots' position in the legislature. To start, they hired David Boies, one of the best-known and most-feared antitrust lawyers in the United States. It was Boies who had once defended IBM from a government breakup. And it would be Boies, several years later, who would win a landmark decision from the federal courts that found software giant Microsoft guilty of breaking the federal antitrust laws. Boies, who was such a crap enthusiast that he once kept a table in his law office, was possibly the most-skilled private antitrust lawyer in the United States and was convinced that the Pequots had double-crossed the Mohegans. Boies let it be known that he was prepared to file suit against the State of Connecticut if the Bridgeport casino was authorized by the legislature and approved by the governor. The draft of Boies's suit claimed that such authorization would violate the state's agreement with the Mohegans and excuse the tribe from paying 25 percent of their slot revenue to the state. "It's a very clear agreement," Boies advised Sturges. "The Mohegans make payments if and only if casino gambling is restricted to Indian lands."

Rowland suspected that if he accepted the Mohegans' position, the game in Hartford would be up, as the state simply couldn't afford to lose the $100 million plus that it expected from the Mohegan casino. Further, it was likely that if the Mohegans halted their slot payments, lawyers for the Pequots would later find a way to do so as well. Rowland was firm that the state would fight Boies in court if necessary.

The governor had extolled the virtues of the Pequots in announcing his decision to give them the franchise to run the casino, and Rowland knew that by supporting the Pequots he was guaranteeing a rich source of campaign funds for any future political office he might seek. But for all the good things the Pequots did, and for the all the good publicity their charity generated, occasionally things happened at Mashantucket that made even Rowland wonder just what was going on inside the closed doors of the tribal council.

In the middle of the debate over Bridgeport, internecine tensions inside the reservation hit the boiling point. With the apparent knowledge of Ken Reels and at least three of his allies on the tribal council, the casino's chief of security engineered a break-in at one of Brown's offices where financial documents were kept, apparently looking for material that might implicate Brown with either kickbacks or bribes. Brown found out about the break-in only after an employee noticed a locksmith's report stating that the office had been opened to investigate a "foul odor." As the story later spilled out, the casino's chief of security, Richard E. Sebastian, had notified the state police that he had reports of double payments being made to casino vendors and that incriminating documents were being shredded. Working with two state policemen, Sebastian got the locksmith to break in to the office, where they removed and inspected payment ledgers. When he learned of the break-in—nothing incriminating was found—Brown was outraged that the security head had invaded his staff's space. Hayward was furious as well, but for a different reason. He was astonished that state police had gone onto the reservation without authority, an act he felt was a clear violation of his small nation's sovereignty. Hayward immediately complained to Rowland, who quickly launched an investigation. The two police officers were suspended, Brown fired the security chief, and though he had suspicions that the break-in was prompted by dissidents on the tribal council, he was unable at that time to prove it.

A later state police report on the incident contained affidavits and evidence that Reels and three tribal council allies had approved the break-in. Then the attorney for the two suspended police officers, who successfully fought disciplinary action as the result of Hayward's complaint, claimed that his clients had been victims of a smear campaign designed to cut short a police investigation into organized crime. Those had always been the two words about which Skip was most sensitive. Hayward wrote an angry three-page response to the attorney's charges, calling them "sensationalist, unfair and grossly misleading. We have zero tolerance when it comes to organized crime." Hayward added, "We have permanently banned 25 members of organized criminal groups from even entering the casino as customers. He did not mention that one of those who had not been banned was John Gotti, Jr., the son of the imprisoned "Dapper Don" of New York's Gambino family, who was using the casino to hold private meetings. Gotti's activities on the casino floor had been captured on the overhead security cameras and were at virtually that very moment being subpoenaed by the FBI.

"The sad thing about this whole matter is that if the state police officer now being investigated by his own department wanted information, all he had to do was ask instead of sneaking around in the dark," Hayward said. Ironically, while he could complain and get action taken about state police sneaking around the reservation, there was nothing he could do about Reels's rearguard actions to undercut his authority. When Reels was asked about his knowledge of the break-in, the tribal vice chairman issued a classic nondenial denial, saying he couldn't recall knowing about the double-billing investigation but he might have been aware of it. According to the final state police report, so were Michael Thomas and the tribe's treasurer, Pedro Johnson.

The squabble over the break-in had come at a bad time and did nothing to help the tribe's cause in Hartford. Charles Duffy called the struggle the toughest sell he had ever encountered. He compared it to a parliamentary battle with twenty-seven parties: the pro-Mirage anti-Pequots; the antigambling pro-Pequots; the antigambling anti-Pequots; and the progambling anti-Pequots. Suburban senators lined up against the urban senators. The racing and jai alai lobbies were adamantly opposed. But the final straw was what the Pequots considered the double cross of the Mohegans, and not the first one in the tribes' complicated histories. Granting the Pequots the license to the Bridgeport casino would simply open the door to yet another state legal battle, one for which the legislators had no enthusiasm. In the end, the hurdles were too large to jump. On November 25, 1995, the state senate voted 24 to 10 against the Pequots and Rowland. The defeat was crushing and expensive. The $2.1 million in lobbying expenses, compressed into six months, was the largest single amount ever spent on a piece of legislation in the state of Connecticut and it left Skip vulnerable to charges by Reels that he was throwing away the tribe's money.

The special session had left Skip with a bitter taste in his mouth. He had quite a different interpretation of events than did Ralph Sturges and David Boies. As he and Brown saw it, they had given up their most precious asset, their exclusive gambling franchise, to help out the Mohegans. Now their ancient nemesis had once again stabbed them in the back. Skip and Mickey believed that they were the ones who had been the victims of a double cross, and not the other way around. Yet their anger paled beside that of Governor Rowland, who had humiliatingly lost the first high-profile political battle of his term. He let the Mohegans know that he would not attend their groundbreaking ceremony, and he asked state officials to launch an investigation of Sol Kerzner, the South African casino magnate who would operate the Mohegan Sun. This investigation turned up nothing to stop the Mohegans, and their project went ahead on schedule. John Meskill, the state official who had strongly advocated for the Pequots' bid, did not suffer from the defeat. Several months after the vote, Meskill left his state job and was hired by the Pequots as the chairman of their tribal gaming commission for a salary many times what he was paid by the state.

Though the Pequots had lost a $2.1-million bet, they could make that back in a weekend. In the long term, they still had only the competition from the Mohegans to worry about. Brown ordered his staff to go full bore on the new seventeen-story hotel and to make it lavish and irresistible to the high rollers from New York City that he hoped to attract. They would just have to travel a little farther than the Pequots' had come to hope.

13

HAIL TO THE CHIEF

I T WAS THE WINTER of 1996. Although a thick layer of white snow covered the reservation, along Route 2 a trail of black exhaust marked the path from the casino all the way to the Rhode Island border where the road spilled onto I-95. Just a decade earlier, winter would have brought life in Ledyard almost to a hibernating, chilly halt. But those days were gone, replaced by a constant rumble of buses, the sirens of police and ambulances, and speeding limousines stocked with nervous, anxious gamblers.

In the wake of the Bridgeport fiasco, and with the opening of the Mohegan Sun slated for later that fall, the snowstorm prompted Skip and Mickey to come up with an efficient method of getting high rollers to the casino from New York City. The icy roads were a danger, and Brown himself had already slid off of one once that season, crashing his Cadillac DeVille into a century-old stone wall.

It would be only a matter of months before Sun International, the Mohegans' South African management company, held its grand opening, and it wasn't hard to see that Sun already had two big advantages in the competitive race for New York slot players. Not only was it closer to New York City, but more significantly, it was conveniently located right off an interstate highway. On days like this, when snow was up to the knees, it would be much easier to reach than Foxwoods. Brown was sure that Skip's willingness to give up the guarantee of exclusivity that they had won was a mistake of historic proportion. Indian solidarity aside, Mickey couldn't help but think that Skip's decision to give it away ranked right up there with the sale of Manhattan. The only way the damage would have been mitigated was if the Bridgeport deal had gotten through the legislature, and Brown had no illusions about the competition Foxwoods would soon face. Sol Kerzner and his Sun International were experienced veterans of the casino business. Although the Mohegan Sun would be its first casino in the United States, Sun operated some thirty-seven elaborate casinos throughout the world, of which the most famous was Sun City, a giant entertainment and gambling center in Bophuthatswana, near Johannesburg, South Africa.

With the death of the Bridgeport proposal, Brown had reinstituted the expensive plan to build the seventeen-story Grand Pequot Towers. To make sure the project was managed the way he wanted, Brown rehired Al Luciani, who had overseen the construction of the original casino and had been the operation's first CEO until he was driven off by Reels just six months after the February 15, 1992, grand opening.

In many ways, the winter of 1995–96 was a season of discontent on the Mashantucket Reservation. Although the tribe seemed to be minting money, Skip and Mickey were spending it almost as quickly as the quarters were being poured through the slot machines. The problem of raising money from local banks had long since disappeared. Skip had been placed on the board of directors of one local bank, and large regional institutions like Fleet Bank of Boston were more than happy to have loaned the tribe $500 million to fund construction of the new hotel, as well as Skip's Mashantucket Pequot Museum. But in January of 1996, the tribal council, and Skip himself, was stung by a series of critical articles in the region's largest newspaper, *The Day,* published in New London. The first of these accused the tribe of harboring members of Asian gangs, who allegedly were running rampant through the casino, laundering drug money. Over the next weeks, a string of stories followed about possible corruption at the casino, including a report that the Connecticut State Police had arrested the manager of the Foxwoods theater for taking kickbacks from agents and promoters. Another story reported that a boxing promoter working at Foxwoods had links to organized crime. But what really got the tribe's attention was a series of reports describing how an "unnamed" group on the tribal council was demanding an investigation and audit of alleged bribes and kickbacks by administrators inside the casino. The last time there had been an attempt to uncover a scandal implicating Mickey Brown, the whole thing had backfired. Richard Sebastian, the head of the casino security force, was fired, and Skip was so angry that Brown was rewarded with a three-year, $1.5-million-per-year contract. Reels and his allies had hoped that these new efforts would be somewhat less public than the break-in at the financial office. Having their investigation attempts telegraphed in the area's biggest newspaper was not in keeping with their strategy.

The stories in the New London paper unified the tribal council at least in one respect. Both Reels and Hayward were furious, anxious to demonstrate their innocence to one another by denouncing *The Day* and claiming the paper was making things up. In January, the tribal council voted unanimously to ban *The Day* from the reservation's newsstand and ordered the paper to pull its boxes off the grounds. More significantly, the tribe canceled its advertising in *The Day,* revenue worth $200,000 a year to the paper. Then the tribe bought full-page ads in the *Westerly* (R.I.) *Sun,* the *Norwich Bulletin,* and the *Hartford Courant* describing *The Day* as "trafficking in reputation-ruining statements." But around the newspaper community, even at the rival papers, the feeling was virtually unanimous that the tribal council, which never opened its meetings to the public or cooperated in answering questions about tribe businesses or finances, was engaging in a coercive effort to curb critical stories. By canceling ads in one paper, then buying full pages in the others, the tribe was sending a none-too-subtle message to the press of the region to leave it alone or face a similar cutback in ad revenue. Banning *The Day* was quickly deemed to be a self-defeating exercise. Reels and Hayward realized after a few weeks that there was a reason that they advertised in *The Day* to start with—to attract patrons to the casino and to their shows at the Fox Theater. Besieged with angry calls from people wanting to know how they could find out what was showing, the tribe eventually lifted their ban and the newspaper boxes returned, although they never again distributed free copies of the paper to rooms as they once had. In the sovereign Pequot Nation, freedom of the press was yet another principle that was unrecognized.

The issue of getting people to the reservation continued to be an obsession for Skip. If the Mohegan Sun suddenly began eating into his tribe's revenues, Skip, who had given up the exclusivity concession, would shoulder the blame. The money that had been spent on the Grand Pequot Towers could only be recouped by tapping the critical New York market. There was little room for revenue growth from Boston and Providence, from which Foxwoods received most of its business. It was from the west that new customers had to be attracted, and Skip pondered the problem of moving customers to Foxwoods from New York City in a way that might not involve passing the sign to the Mohegan Sun along the way. During the late winter and early spring, Skip sat on the edge of his yard in Noank, a glass of Scotch resting upon the weather-beaten outdoor table on his lawn. Virtually every day, the New London ferry to and from Orient Point on Long Island blasted its horns as it cruised by his home on the Long Island Sound. It was this ferry that inspired a new idea. As he approached his fiftieth birthday, the old Electric Boat welder decided to become a shipbuilder again.

Working through the Lims' connections (they owned one of the largest cruise-ship lines in the world), Hayward, in May of 1996, signed a licensing agreement with FBM Marine Group of Great Britain, the designer of a high-speed, 330-passenger, three-pontooned catamaran ferry. His contract gave the Pequots the exclusive franchise to manufacture and sell the TriCat in the Western Hemisphere. The TriCat would be capable of traveling at nearly 60 miles per hour, which meant it could transport high rollers from Manhattan to the reservation, 125 miles east, in less than three hours. Skip threw himself into the idea with an excitement that he hadn't felt since the museum's groundbreaking three years earlier. He personally went out and scouted building and docking sites, eventually spending $2.9 million to buy a dock from his old employer, Electric Boat in Groton. He then bought an old steel-company plant in Norwich, and in New London he bought the Pequot River Shipworks on the Thames River. He hired sixty veteran boatbuilders, many of whom he had known from his Electric Boat days and who had been laid off in the recession. Twenty-two years after he had left Electric Boat to move to the reservation, Skip was back in the business as a great entrepreneur. Just as he had saved the tribe from extinction, he now believed that he could resurrect the entire boat-building culture of New London and Groton, which had been devastated by the economic depression that had hit industrial Connecticut. Working at a feverish pace, the Pequot River Shipyard, now a fully owned subsidiary of the tribe, was finished with its first vessel, the *Sassacus,* by May of 1997. It was the fastest, most-expensive, and technically sophisticated ferryboat every built in the United States. Its plush seats were copies of the first-class seating configuration on British Airways jumbo jets.

The Pequots worked out a tentative agreement for an arrival and departure dock at the Chelsea Piers at 12th Avenue and 23rd Street in Manhattan. Brown was as anxious as Skip to throw the *Sassacus* into service, but they were stymied when New York City mayor Rudolph Giuliani ruled that the *Sassacus* was a "gambling boat" and therefore could not operate out of the city. At the time, a number of private gambling boat companies were trying to get their foot in the door of the New York market by offering gambling cruises out of New York City. Hayward argued that there would be no gambling on the boat itself, but Giuliani could not be swayed. The *Sassacus,* unable to get a berthing space in Manhattan, sat idle in New London.

While the *Sassacus* waited to find a home, work continued on a second vessel called the *Tatobam.* Soon, three others were built and sold, one to Argentina, one to a company operating out of Catalina Island in Southern California, and one to the Bahamas. When Hayward sold the tribe-built *Bo Hengy* to Bahamas Fast Ferries of Nassau, it marked the first sale of an American-built passenger boat to a foreign country in fifty years. But the high-speed vessels were not without problems. On October 22, 1997, the tribe scheduled a public demonstration of their incredible new high-speed TriCats. A crowd gathered along the New London marina to watch the *Sassacus* strut its stuff. The vessel sped into the inner harbor at New London at a speed of 20 knots, some 15 knots over the harbor speed limit, jostling private boats, knocking a yachtsman into the water, and causing nearly $50,000 in damage to the marina. After conducting an investigation, the harbormaster contacted the Pequots and cited the operator of the vessel for reckless operation, which carried a $50 fine. Skip agreed to pay for all the damages created by the ferry's huge wake. But he couldn't recoup the bad publicity. Neither the *Sassacus* nor the *Tatobam* would ever carry a passenger from New York City. Instead, Skip tried to run the boats in the summer from New London to Martha's Vineyard, where residents vociferously objected to the wake and the noise of the engines. As a final blow, a highly publicized accident in Maine, involving an older British-made TriCat that collided with a Canadian fishing boat off of Nova Scotia, dampened the buying public's enthusiasm for high-speed catamarans. After selling three vessels, the Pequots could summon up no more buyers and were stuck with two expensive and bumpy TriCats that nobody much wanted to ride on. Skip's great dream of reviving the boat-building economy of yore seemed to have been dashed at sea.

SKIP'S BOAT-BUILDING PLANS may have failed, but this hardly dampened his ambition to become a modern-day Henry Flagler, the visionary Standard Oil millionaire from Florida who in the early 1900s built a rail line from Miami to Key West. Just as Skip had bought the exclusive right to build the TriCat, he now wanted not only to operate a railroad but to build it as well. After working out a deal with HSST of Japan, makers of Tokyo's famous bullet trains, he spent $3 million buying and renovating an old train-repair facility in Groton, not far from the northeast Amtrak line. Skip hoped to use the 250-mph bullet train to connect Foxwoods with the Providence airport and with the new boat docks in Norwich where he still hoped his ferries would arrive one day. At full speed, the train would be able to make the 12-mile trip from Norwich in three minutes and the 44-mile trip from Providence airport in fourteen minutes. Only after sinking millions in the railyards and the planning did Skip realize that his railroad plan was financially unfeasible even for a tribe as rich as his. No bullet trains ever went into production and no rail line ever came closer to Foxwoods than the Amtrak train at New London, where passengers transferred to a rickety old bus that made numerous stops along the way to the casino. The ferry and train debacles were increasingly cited by Skip's critics as examples of his willingness to throw away the tribe's money on projects that could never work out. Skip's experiments with boats and trains had cost the tribe many millions, and neither had made any headway toward solving the problem of filling the new hotel.

The downturn in Skip's luck since the Bridgeport debacle fueled anxiety among the members of the tribe and strengthened the position of Reels, who was increasingly anxious to take over chairmanship of the tribe himself. All that held him back was the belief of his influential aunts and cousins that a takeover of the tribe by the African-American Narragansetts would harden local opposition and weaken political support at a critical moment. His tribal council colleagues Michael Thomas and Antonio Beltran urged him to make his move, but Reels continued to wait. He knew that as long as Brown was around, the tribe would always be in the middle of some new political battle, and as long as Skip was head of the tribal council, the tribe would always be chasing some grand dream. If he wanted the right moment to challenge Skip, he decided, he would have to knock Brown off first.

By the middle of 1997, Reels had filled the tribe and the tribal council with his own Narragansett cousins and friends. For years after its reestablishment, the tribe had always publicly claimed it was a regathering place for anyone with a certain amount of Pequot blood. By 1997, however, the tribe no longer made a pretense of inclusion, and Reels bragged openly that the only way to get in was if his membership committee let you in. Reels claimed that any other method would amount to allowing the outside world to dictate to them who could or could not be a Pequot. He argued that allowing entrance to any resident of the area who might have some claim to Pequot ancestry would weaken and pollute the bloodline. Reels further explained that the modern Mashantucket tribe was not defined as having descended from the Pequots, but from only a specific line, the family of Elizabeth George, Annie Sebastian, and their sisters. With the exception of Skip, who had no children, and his eight siblings, only a handful of residents at Mashantucket had any significant Pequot ancestry at all. But the bloodline had become insignificant to those who had declared themselves Pequots. Skip's sister

Theresa Bell, who had fashioned herself as a tribal historian, was the first to admit that, while she believed herself to be a Pequot, she had no physical proof of Pequot lineage.

Skip's journeys abroad to look at bullet trains were viewed by Reels as opportunities to strengthen his own position against the tribal chairman. On one occasion in early 1997, when Hayward was out of the country, Reels decided he wanted to talk about the annexation holdup with ranking Democrat Daniel Inouye of the Senate Select Committee on Indian Affairs. But when he called to make an appointment with Inouye, Reels was told that the senator's relationship with the tribe was through Skip, and that the senator could not schedule a meeting without the tribal chairman in attendance. Reels was furious and humiliated by the rebuff. As a matter of pride, he decided to go to Washington anyway and determined that his message to Inouye would get through one way or another. Reels, traveling with an entourage of his tribal council allies, stopped by the office of Senator Christopher Dodd, to ask if Dodd would set up the meeting with Inouye. In Dodd's Senate office, Reels clumsily reminded Dodd that the Pequots had contributed lavishly to his campaign and warned him that if he did not call Inouye and set up the meeting, Dodd could forget about any hope for reelection. Dodd turned red with anger, leaped out of his chair, and stormed out of the meeting, warning his aides to keep Reels away from Senator Inouye.

Humiliated by the experience, Reels returned to the reservation more determined than ever to depose the chairman. Although the attempt to link Brown to double billing in 1995 had failed, Reels decided it was time to strike against what he now routinely and derisively referred to as the "Skip and Mickey Show." Reels found time to pour over a state financial disclosure document that Brown, as a tribe employee, was required to file for his state-issued permit to work in the gaming industry. And Reels did find one nugget of information that had promise. The information provided to the state revealed that Brown had owned stock in IWERKS, the company that had built one of the theaters at the casino complex. He also discovered that Luciani, whose return to the reservation was of unceasing aggravation to Reels, had owned stock in a company that had provided keno games at Foxwoods.

Reels was convinced that these disclosure statements provided proof that Brown and Luciani were profiting unduly from their position as Pequot employees. Reels kept the information secret and waited until June 19, 1997, when Skip was called away with Carol to Wisconsin to visit his ill mother-in-law. At about 4 P.M. that afternoon, Brown was about to begin a regularly scheduled afternoon staff meeting with the top members of the casino team when he received a call summoning him to the tribal council chambers. When Brown arrived, he was asked to explain his ownership interest in IWERKS. But before Brown could even get through explaining, Reels announced that Brown and Luciani were fired, and he ordered tribal security officials to move in and lock down the executive suites. When Skip returned from Wisconsin, Brown and Luciani were gone. Skip was on his own.

Brown predicted to Skip that the chief's days as chairman of the tribal council were numbered, and it was impossible for Skip to disagree. Bud Celey, a former Hilton Corporation executive was hired to run the casino. But unlike Brown, Celey would be subservient to Reels, who began taking on more and more of the tribal decision-making and was finally able to implement his idea of putting his family members in casino jobs. After nearly twenty-five years as tribal chairman, Skip was earning $1.5 million a year, making him one of the highest-paid sovereign rulers in the western world. His salary was a good seven times that of the president of the United States. But by the late summer and fall of 1998, the demographics of the tribe had doomed him. The next tribal election for chairman would come in November. Before that, Reels would allow Skip to preside over the opening of the Mashantucket Pequot Museum and Research Center.

Of all Skip's dreams, the museum was the oldest and the one that mattered most to him. For years, he had heard naysayers declare that the Pequots weren't legitimate Indians. Skip's museum was his answer to them. A tour of the museum began with an exhibit about the ice age and went on to a depiction of an 11,000-year-old caribou hunt. Another exhibit recreated the seventeenth-century Pequot fort burned by the English, and eventually one would land at the government-issued trailer in which Skip wrote his first grant. But the museum's *pièce d'résistance* was a 22,000-square-foot reconstruction of a sixteenth-century Pequot village where visitors walked through chestnuts, oaks, and maples and could peer into Pequot wigwams. From one of thirteen theaters, Tom Tureen described his role on videotape. Throughout the process of becoming multimillionaires, Skip and his cousins had benefited by what some jokingly referred to as *Dances With Wolves* syndrome. Sympathy for the plight of the poor red man played at the heart of the legislative struggles that had gone into making the casino a reality. Now the most expensive and grand Indian museum in the country, one that cost only marginally less than the one the Smithsonian planned—to honor *all* Indian tribes—was totally dedicated to Pequot history. It would provide the justification to gamblers for blowing their life savings at the crap, baccarat, and blackjack tables. On August 10, 1998, Skip presided over the grand opening of his greatest monument. Senator Inouye, who had been Skip's closest and, as Reels had learned, most loyal friend in Washington, cut the oversized purple ribbon to open the 308,000-square-foot building. Inouye declared that the museum represented the "triumphant return of the Mashantucket Pequot." Skip's other Washington friend, President Clinton, provided videotaped congratulations. The museum was truly an architectural and technological wonder, grander in many respects than the great public museums on the mall in Washington. But it would be the last expensive project on which Skip could spend the tribe's money. While the museum opening celebrated Pequot history, it marked the end of the Pequot resurrection. As Skip saw his power slipping in August and October of 1998, it was as if Pequot-Narragansett history was repeating itself, and Skip knew there was nothing that could be done about it.

In 1636, it had been the Narragansetts from Rhode Island who had trod the narrow Indian paths along the coast to help the Englishmen find and burn their more successful, bitter enemies, the Pequots. In modern times, the Pequots had again become the regional power, successful and resourceful at every turn—winning the casino and outsmarting their adversaries. The Narragansett tribe in Rhode Island, from which Reels and his family had come, had gotten nowhere. They were growing increasingly bitter at seeing the Pequots thrive, while their own attempts to build a casino were dashed. Rhode Island, unlike Connecticut, had repealed its charity gaming laws rather than allow the Narragansetts a casino. But as they stood on the stage in the new museum, surrounded by a giant amphitheater of windows, looking out on woods and forest—the casino was not visible through the trees—Reels and Hayward hugged and tears rolled down Skip's ruddy cheeks.

On November 2, 1998, the tribal council ousted Skip as chairman and replaced him with Reels. From nowhere did the whoops of victory come louder than from across Interstate 95 in Peace Dale and South Kingston, where Reels had grown up and where every year, even after becoming a Pequot, he attended the Narragansetts' annual meeting dressed in his old tribe's regalia. Reels had little interest in the visionary projects that Skip had championed or in his dream of some sort of socialist Utopia born of his identification with a sixties-era lifestyle. Symbolically, one of Reels's first acts was to announce that he was closing down the shipyards and giving up on the ferries.

In addition, his ascension to the leadership of the tribe represented a marked change from the laid-back accommodationist style that Hayward had championed. Reels was openly hostile toward residents and politicians who wouldn't give him what he wanted. In a public meeting in Washington with Kevin Gover, by now Clinton's director of the Bureau of Indian Affairs, Reels urged Gover to do everything in his power to appeal the court's annexation rulings and to get the tribe's property annexed into the tax-free reservation. "The Pequots are not by nature a peaceful people," he warned.

Among the main issues on which Reels had won support from the tribe was the distribution of the tribe's share of the casino money. For too long, Reels believed, Hayward had directed too much money toward development projects, some of which had not gone well. Reels and his supporters on the tribal council, such as Michael Thomas and Antonio Beltran, were anxious to put more money into the hands of the tribal members and less money into the hands of the New Jersey crowd. Toward that end, the salaries of tribal council members were doubled after Reels's election to $1 million per year. In addition, each councilman, who worked out of offices far more plush than those accorded members of the Connecticut legislature, was given a $10-million office budget. The tribal chairman's salary remained $1.5 million per year.

When the tribal council learned at the end of the year that their share of the casino profits, after expenses, interest, and payments to the Malaysians, would fall short of the previous year by some 20 percent, due to competition from the Mohegan Sun, the tribe went to local bankers and borrowed an additional $100 million to make their dividend payments to tribe members.

ACROSS THE COUNTRY, Foxwoods' success would be emulated but never equaled. In the ten years after the casino's grand opening, some 352 gambling parlors would open across the country, mostly in sparsely populated areas west of the Mississippi River. For years, the Wampanoag tribe in Massachusetts had threatened to build a casino and compete with Foxwoods. But, as with the Narragansett tribe in Rhode Island, the state legislature had blocked any deal. The Pequots had been able to go to court and sue the state to force it into an agreement, but other tribes did not have that option. In March 1996, the United States Supreme Court ruled that the Indian Gaming Regulatory Act had gone too far in stripping states of their ability to control the growth of gambling and casinos. A tribe, it said, could not sue the state to compel it to grant a casino license. The effect of this ruling was to bolster the anticasino position of the Rhode Island and Massachusetts legislatures, and the practical effect was to virtually ensure that no New England competitor of the Pequots and the Mohegans would open a casino in the near future. When the Pequots had gone to court, every federal court decision along the way had bolstered their claim to a casino. Now that they had the most profitable casino in the nation, case law had suddenly been changed to make it harder for competitors to challenge them. It couldn't have been more perfect.

Mickey Brown returned to New Jersey, and most of the Atlantic City executives he had hired went along with him. The Lims asked that their entire loan minus $20 million be paid off, and they withdrew from being actively involved with the casino, though their contract would ensure that they continued to receive 10 percent of the net profits. Over at the Mohegan Sun, business continued to grow, and Sun International prepared to open a thirty-seven-story hotel and casino expansion to accommodate its growing business.

In this little corner of southeastern Connecticut, the unthinkable had taken place. No one called it quiet any more, and there was no doubt that the pace and nature of life had changed, although not as dramatically as it might have. Many of Skip's dreams had never come to fruition: there was no theme park, no NFL team, no monorail, no shipyard, and no amusement park. Still, the remote descendants of the Pequots had exacted from the system more than a small dose of revenge. They had turned a government, which for four centuries had committed brutal acts of oppression and termination, into knots. Using the same legal processes that had been used against American Indians for so long, they had trumped the ruling class and implausibly become the wealthiest Indian tribe in the history of North America. If the American Indian had in some respects been done in by succumbing to alcoholism and other European-introduced diseases, their economic revival had in large part been the result of a turning of the tables, taking advantage of an addiction to gambling that non-Indian Americans couldn't seem to stem. Skeptics could and would argue endlessly about whether the new Pequots were or were not authentic Indians, although no one had questioned their right to declare themselves Pequots when they were poor.

Nonetheless, Tom Tureen and Skip Hayward had accomplished something monumentally different from what they originally intended. Drawn together from disparate worlds, opposite cultures, but with a well-meaning purpose, they had unexpectedly gone beyond the historic resurrection of a proud, all-but-extinct Indian tribe. They had created a new modern-day paradigm that changed the face of the country—not Native American but Casino-American.

Acknowledgments

IN MAY OF 1997, I journeyed to Pimlico Race Course on the evening before the Preakness Stakes and bet on a speedy gray horse with whom I had fallen in love. His name was Silver Charm. When I arrived home that night, I discovered that I had invested nearly $1,000 in tickets on the wrong horse. After a sleepless night, I drove back to Baltimore the next morning to change my tickets, arriving in the press parking lot before the sun went up.

Eventually, I was able to change the tickets, and Silver Charm won the race in a thrilling three-horse photo finish. Exultantly, and with my pockets bulging with cash, I returned to my green 1996 Mazda only to find that when I had parked in the early morning light I hadn't noticed my lights were on. The battery was dead.

I was forced to use a portion of my winnings to buy some jumper cables, and I then began searching for a good Samaritan who would help me give my battery a boost. Sitting atop their car, waiting for the traffic to subside, were Pete Fornatale and Frank Scatoni. While my battery revved up, Frank and I began talking. I learned that he was a young editor at Simon & Schuster. He learned that for some time I had wanted to write a book about the political and legal machinations that had led to the establishment of Foxwoods Casino in Connecticut.

While a number of agents and other editors had been skeptical of such a project, Frank jumped at the opportunity to get involved, and our chance meeting in the Pimlico parking lot led to an agreement to write this book. Unfortunately, Frank left Simon & Schuster before the book could be completed. But before leaving, Frank put the project in the capable hands of Marysue Rucci and Nicole Graev. Nicole became more than my editor on this project; she became a partner as well. Whenever it seemed a digression might be leading the book down a dark path, Nicole stepped in and kept the project on the rails. I couldn't have finished it without her.

I would also like to thank my two best friends in Connecticut, Dick Bartley and Jim Heym, who took care of me on my many trips to the area. I am also indebted to "Poker" Dick Cook, who drove me up to Foxwoods for the New England Poker Classic, where I finished fourth among 370 in a Texas Hold 'Em Tournament. The prize money helped me avoid the pitfall of blowing my funds before I got out of the casino on my first reporting day. In addition, I am grateful for the help of Jack Abramoff, Kenneth Adams, Edward Nelson, Edward Klein, Chuck Conconi, Ken DeCell, Jack Limpert, Joel Chineson, and my parents, Meigh and Bert Eisler.

One of the main sources of inspiration for this project was my brother-in-law, Peter R. Sarasohn, who was convinced there was a story to be told, even when the agents insisted there wasn't. Sadly, Peter did not live to see the book completed, but I dedicate it to his memory.

Finally, I am most indebted to my wife, Judy, and my daughter, Sara. Several times I was on the verge of throwing away the notes I had collected on the topic only to be told by Judy that I should hold on to them, this story was simply too good to be ignored forever. Thanks to Judy, I kept them long enough to run into Frank Scatoni.

Source Note and Bibliography

As NATIONAL EDITOR of *Washingtonian* magazine, I have been writing about the gaming industry for nearly two decades and have written lengthy stories about Foxwoods, Steve Wynn, and Indian gambling, as well as the Las Vegas and Atlantic City scenes, for numerous magazines. In addition to using my own background in the field to report this book, I relied on the following written sources to supplement the history of Native American casinos. Besides consulting published sources, court cases, and congressional committee reports, I conducted extensive interviews with the key players at various stages of the casino's development. These interviews included sessions with presidential attorney David Kendall; tribal attorneys Tom Tureen, Jackson King, and Robert Gips; tribal lobbyist Charles Duffy; anticasino activists Larry Greene, Sharon Wadecki, Madeline Jeffery, and Joan Simonds; former Foxwoods executives Al Luciani, Robert Winter, and especially G. Michael Brown; former Connecticut attorney general Clarine Riddle; Washington lobbyist Jack Abramoff; and former national Indian gaming czar Tony Hope. I also spent time with and confirmed many details of the book with Skip Hayward during a meeting at the National Building Museum in Washington in mid-1999.

BOOKS

Ambrose, Stephen E. *Crazy Horse and Custer.* Doubleday, 1975.

Avery, John. *History of the Town of Ledyard.* Ledyard Historical Society, 1986.

Bell, Janice Wightman, and Carolyn Smith. *Historic Ledyard.* Ledyard Historic District Commission, 1976.

Bernstein, Alison. *American Indians and World War II.* University of Oklahoma Press, 1991.

Brodeur, Paul. *Restitution: The Land Claims of the Mashpee, Passamaquoddy, and Penobscot Indians of New England.* University of Nebraska Press, 1985.

Brown, Barbara. *Black Roots in Southeastern Connecticut.* Gale Research Co., 1980.

Brown, Dee. *Bury My Heart at Wounded Knee.* Holt, Rinehart & Winston, 1970.

Calloway, Colin G. *After King Philip's War.* University Press of New England, 1997.

Church, Thomas. *The History of the Great Indian War of 1675 and 1676, Commonly Called Philip's War.* Silas Andrus & Son, 1854.

De Forest, John W. *History of the Indians of Connecticut from the Earliest Known Period to 1850.* Connecticut Historical Society, 1852.

Earley, Pete. *Super Casino: Inside the New Las Vegas.* Bantam Books, 2000.

Eisler, Kim I. *A Justice for All: William J. Brennan and the Decisions that Transformed America.* Simon & Schuster, 1993.

Ferrara, Peter J. *The Choctaw Revolution.* Americans for Tax Reform Foundation, 1998.

Gardiner, Lion. *Gardiner's Relation of the Pequot Wars.* Massachusetts Historical Society, 1660.

Goodman, Robert. *The Luck Business: The Devastating Consequences and Broken Promises of America's Gambling Explosion.* Free Press, 1995.

Greenhouse, Melanie. *Point of Land: A Dive Beneath the Surface of Noank.* N.p., 1997.

Gridley, Marion E. *American Indian Tribes.* Dodd, Mead & Co., 1974.

Hauptman, Lawrence, and James Wherry. *The Pequots in Southern New England.* University of Oklahoma Press, 1990.

Lane, Ambrose. *Return of the Buffalo: The Story Behind America's Indian Gaming Explosion.* Bergen & Garvey, 1995.

Mason, John. *A Brief History of the Pequot War.* Kneeland & Green, 1736.

O'Brien, Timothy L. *Bad Bet: The Inside Story of the Glamour, Glitz, and Danger of America's Gambling Industry.* Random House, 1998.

Olson, James C. *Red Cloud and the Sioux Problem.* University of Nebraska Press, 1965.

Perkins, Mary. *Chronicles of a Connecticut Farm, 1769–1905.* Privately printed, 1905.

Starkey, Armstrong. *European and Native American Warfare, 1675–1815.* University of Oklahoma Press, 1998.

White, Robert H. *Tribal Assets.* Henry Holt & Co., 1990.

ARTICLES AND PUBLIC DOCUMENTS

Abbott, Elizabeth. "Pequots Oust Longtime Chairman: Kenneth M. Reels, the Tribe's Second-in-Command Since 1991, Who Grew Up in South Kingston, Will Take Over Jan. 1." *Providence Journal,* November 3, 1998.

Adams, James Ring. "Clintonism in One State." *American Spectator,* November 1993.

Azano, Harry J. "Making Security a Sure Bet at Foxwoods Casino and Resort." *Security Management,* November 1994.

Bailey, Douglas. "Two Tribes in Maine Parlay a Settlement into Economic Power." *New England Business,* June 17, 1985.

Baker, Amy Brooke. "Shays May Amend Federal Law That Requires Pequot Casino in Ledyard." *States News Service,* May 7, 1991.

Baker, Wayne. "Seminole Speaks to Sovereign Immunity and Ex Parte Young." *St. Johns University Law Review,* Fall 1997.

Barker, Emily. "Mapping New Territory for Native Americans." *American Lawyer,* November, 1991.

Bass, Carolyn. "Chiefs in Charge." *Connecticut Law Tribune,* May 9, 1994.

Baumgold, Julie. "Frank and the Fox Pack." *Esquire,* December 1993.

Bessette, Claire. "Traffic Accidents, Injuries Rising Sharply in Norwich." *The Day* (New London), November 13, 1997.

Bird, Kathleen. "Indian Tribe Turns to New Jersey Lawyers for Casino Help." *New Jersey Law Journal,* June 13, 1991.

Blechman, Andrew. "Annexation: Fighting Word; Townspeople Vote to Make 'Not One Acre' Stand." *Norwich Bulletin,* November 24, 1993.

———. "Numbers Show Casino Turning Traffic to Tide." *Norwich Bulletin,* February 8, 1994.

Blumfeld, Michael. "Bingo Spells Happiness for Many: The Game Has Become a Multimillion-Dollar Business." *Orlando Sentinel,* June 21, 1992.

Boon, Tan Ooi. "$280 Million Project to Turn Genting into a Family Attraction." *Straits Times,* May 31, 1993.

Borg, Linda. "Ferry Leaves Damage in Its Wake: Pequots Agree to Pay for Damage." *Providence Journal,* November 24, 1997.

Burgard, Matt. "3 Kids Left in Car at Casino." *The Day,* May 19, 1994.

———. "Two Officials Quit as Tribe Probes Taping." *The Day,* November 23, 1996.

———. "Woman's Casino Losses May Have Led to Suicide." *The Day* (New London), March 7, 1996.

Chia, William. "Genting, Metroplex in Subic Bay Tie-Up." *Business Times,* February 24, 1993.

Chira, Susan. "Pequot Indians Prevail in Battle Begun in 1637." *New York Times,* October 20, 1983.

Clines, Francis X. "Casino Minds Image of Integrity in Hiring Executives." *New York Times,* January 31, 1993.

Collins, David. "Billing Scam Suspected in Casino Probe." *The Day,* March 13, 1996.

———. "Foxwoods Pay Scale Not Up to Par." *The Day,* September 27, 1994.

———. "High-Speed Trains from Foxwoods Proposed: Tribe Eyes Magnetic Rail to Link Casino with Norwich, R.I. Airport." *The Day,* June, 12, 1997.

———. "Pequots Add $500,000 to Democratic Coffers." *The Day,* August 24, 1994.

———. "Regulators Probe Foxwoods' Vendors Link to Asian Gangs." *The Day,* January 31, 1996.

————. "Thomas Elected to Tribal Council While on Probation for Drug Charges." *The Day* (New London), January 12, 1996.

————. "Tribe to Buy Hilton for $18 Million." *The Day,* December 14, 1996.

Cooke, Kieran, and Roland Rudd. "Genting Takes an Overseas Gamble." *Financial Times,* September 9, 1992.

Coopersmith, Jarred. "Bingo Game." *Rocky Mountain News,* July 24, 1994.

Crombie, Noelle. "Tribal Member Wants More Land." *The Day* (New London), August 21, 1994.

Daly, Matthew, and Christopher Keating. "Pequots Selected for Bridgeport Casino." *Hartford Courant,* October 3, 1995.

————. "Tribe Challenges Pequots' Proposal for Bridgeport." *Hartford Courant,* November 1, 1995.

Davis, Paul. "Future of Mashantucket Pequots' Leader Is Uncertain." *Providence Journal,* October 31, 1999.

Davis, William. "A Gamble in the Woods: Tribal Casinos Have Transformed a Once Quiet Corner of Connecticut." *Boston Globe,* January 17, 1999.

Edgecombe, Kathleen. "Mashantucket Charged in Rape Claims State Has No Jurisdiction." *The Day* (New London), December 12, 1997.

Edwards, Marc. "More Casinos in Connecticut?" *International Gaming and Wagering Business,* May 1, 1995.

Eisler, Kim I. "Family Man." *M Inc.,* October 1990.

————. "Revenge of the Indians." *Washingtonian,* August 1993.

Ferrell, David. "One Tribe's Triumph: Indians Have Found a Bonanza in the Casino Business." *Los Angeles Times,* December 14, 1998.

Fitzgibbons, Patrick M. "S&P Rates Connecticut Casino Debt: Agency's First American Indian Issue." *Bond Buyer,* September 13, 1995.

Flower, Charles. "New England Tribe's New Chairman Stresses Gaming, Sovereignty Issues." *Indian Country Today,* June 14, 1999.

————. "Newspaper Series Smears Seminoles." *Ethnic Newswatch,* January 23, 1988.

Fromson, Brett. "The Pequot Uprising." *Washington Post,* June 21, 1998.

Gaines, Judith. "New England's Invisible Natives." *Boston Globe,* April 17, 1989.

Garber, Greg. "Tribe Commits to Stadium Project: Clancy Group Completes Work on Bid." *Hartford Courant,* January 15, 1994.

Gattuso, Greg. "What's Ahead for Charity Gambling? Industry Overview." *Fund Raising Management,* September 1993.

Giago, Tim. "Indian Sovereignty in Question." *Indian Country Today,* August 13, 1995.

Goldstein, Brad, and Jeff Testerman. "In Seminole Gambling, a Few Are Big Winners." *St. Petersburg Times,* December 19, 1997.

————. "Seminole Gambling, a Trail of Millions." *St. Petersburg Times,* December 20, 1997.

Gorman, Stephen J. "Mob Said to Control Indian Bingo on 12 Reservations." *UPI*, February 9, 1989.

Greene, Larry. "Sovereignty: Indians Find Recognition of Tribes a Racist Idea." *The Day* (New London), October 10, 1997.

Harris, Art. "Appreciation: Edward Lowe, the Bingo Baron." *Washington Post*, February 26, 1986.

Haygood, Wil. "Tribe's Riches Create Divisions Among Some: Not All Feel They Are Treated Fairly." *Boston Globe*, August 19, 1995.

Hays, Constance. "Manager of Indian Tribe's Casino Quits." *New York Times*, October 21, 1992.

Hayward, Richard. "Annexation Editorials Remiss." *Norwich Bulletin*, October 26, 1998.

Hileman, Maria. "Senator Questions Pequots' Donations." *The Day* (New London), November 11, 1997.

Hill, John. "Mohegans: Casino to Open in a Year Ten Miles from Foxwoods." *Providence Journal*, November 7, 1995.

Hodges, Sam. "How Bingo Got Going: A New York Businessman." *Orlando Sentinel*, March 19, 1991.

Jacklin, Michele. "Weicker Leaves Office as He Governed: On His Own Terms." *Hartford Courant*, January 1, 1995.

Jansen, Donald. "Golden Nugget Wins Its License as Casino in a Unanimous Vote." *New York Times*, October 14, 1981.

Johnson, Kirk. "Town's Anger at Rich Tribe Is Measured by the Acre." *New York Times*, May 4, 1995.

———. "Weicker to Veto Any Expansion of Gambling." *New York Times*, February 28, 1992.

Jones, Daniel. "Indians, Laws, and Land: Tribes Put Nation's Promises on Trial." *Hartford Courant*, May 23, 1994.

Kaplan, Karen. "Tribe Asserts Rt. 2 Lot Part of Reservation." *The Day* (New London), June 28, 1994.

Katz, Ian. "The Tribe That Found a Fortune." *Manchester Guardian*, October 8, 1995.

Kemper, Steve. "This Land Is Whose Land." *Yankee Magazine*, September 1998.

Libby, Sam. "Tribe Sees a Future in Passenger Boats." *New York Times*, July 11, 1999.

———. "Who Is an Indian and Who Decides." *New York Times*, January 14, 1996.

Liberman, Ellen. "Pequots Admit 100 New Members, Enlarge Tribal Council." *The Day* (New London), November 9 1993.

Lightman, David. "Pequot's Prosperity Hasn't Stopped Flow of Federal Aid." *Hartford Courant*, January 15, 1995.

———. "Report: Pequots Bought Access; Tribe Rejects Criticism of Political Donations." *Hartford Courant*, February 11, 1998.

Lopez, Leslie. "KL Companies Expect a Rush of China Deals." *Business Times,* June 8, 1993.

Lynch, James P. "A Report on the Lineage Ancestry of the Eastern and Pawcatuck Eastern Pequot Indians." Prepared on Behalf of the Towns of Ledyard, North Stonington, and Preston, Connecticut, December 1988.

Malinowski, W. Zachary, and Mike Stanton. "Patriarca Returns to a Downsized but Still Potent Mob." *Providence Journal-Bulletin,* December 13, 1998.

Miller, Julie. "When All Busy Roads Lead to the Casino." *New York Times,* March 14, 1993.

Mollard, Beth. "B-I-N-G-O Spells Cash for Nonprofit Organizations." *Business First of Columbus* (Ohio), October 29, 1990.

Montford, Richard. "Pequots Wrong in Dispute with Newspaper." *Norwich Bulletin,* March 3, 1966.

Moore, John W. "A Winning Hand." *National Journal,* July 17, 1993.

Nesbitt, Jim. "A Well-Seasoned Independent: Weicker Barrels Through Tough Times in Connecticut." *Minneapolis Star Tribune,* July 23, 1993.

Neuffer, Elizabeth, and Kevin Cullen. "Region's Mafia Awaits Leadership After Arrest Sweep." *Boston Globe,* March 28, 1990.

O'Toole, Francis, and Thomas Tureen. "State Power and the Passamaquoddy Tribe: A Gross National Hypocrisy." *Maine Law Review,* 1971.

Overton, Penelope. "Casino Execs Contributed to Gejdenson." *The Day* (New London), August 8, 1993.

————. "Interior Grants Mashantucket 247 More Acres." *The Day,* May 1, 1995.

————. "Tribe Closes Deal for Lantern Hill." *The Day,* August 17, 1994.

Owens, Patricia. "Maine Lawyer, Passenger Hurt in Plane Crash." *Boston Globe,* February 2, 1989.

Painton, Priscilla. "The Great Casino Salesman (Steve Wynn)." *Time,* May 3, 1993.

Peters, Jennifer. "Tribe Spent $2.1 Million Lobbying for Bridgeport." *The Day* (New London), January 23, 1966.

Pfeifer, Ellen. "Pavarotti Will Work the Crowd at Foxwoods." *Boston Herald,* August 25, 1994.

Primack, Philip. "Tagliabue May Discuss Pequots' Role in Pat's Sale." *Boston Herald,* January 5, 1996.

Rabinowitz, Jonathan. "Head of Foxwoods Casino Quits Suddenly." *New York Times,* June 21, 1997.

————. "Race for Bridgeport Casino Is Down to 2 Big Operators." *New York Times,* September 6, 1995.

Richard, Randall, and Peter Phipps. "The Deal That Built Foxwoods." *Providence Journal-Bulletin,* September 19, 1999.

Richardson, Michael. "Some Odds-On Favorites in the Malaysian Market." *International Herald Tribune,* December 15, 1992.

Rivera, David. "Ex-Officials Sue Tribe Over Eavesdropping." *Norwich Bulletin,* February 6, 1997.

Roberts, Jim. "Mirage Resorts Hope Odds Are in Its Favor to Win Legislators' Support." *Fairfield County Business Journal,* January 3, 1994.

Rosenbaum, Ron. "Mohegan Power: No Wampum for Big Chief Trump." *New York Observer,* November 16, 1998.

Rowe, Sean. "Big Chief Moneybags." *Miami New Times,* March 26, 1998.

Scheffey, Thomas. "Weicker's Slots Deal Trumps Pro-Gambling Forces—For Now." *Connecticut Law Tribune,* February 1, 1993.

Schuerman, Matt. "Luck Runs Out for Local Bingo Crowd: Sacred Heart Game; A Groton Tradition Folds After 41 Years." *The Day* (New London), April 17, 1996.

Seligman, Dan. "The Winning Hand." *Forbes,* July 26, 1999.

Stone, Peter. "Upping the Ante." *National Journal,* June 6, 1998.

Straits Times Staff. "Economic Crime Rings Have Penetrated Government Agencies." *Straits Times Press,* September 9, 1992.

Sulong, Wong. "Genting Drops Casino Venture." *Financial Times,* March 23, 1983.

Tat, Ho Kay. "Malaysia's Lim to Develop Casino at Subic Bay." *Reuters Asia-Pacific Business Report,* February 24, 1993.

Tesoriero, Kerry. "Mirage Casino Preview Party a Hit." *New Haven Register,* September 25, 1995.

Tomasson, Robert. "May Is a Dangerous Month." *New York Times,* April 4, 1982.

Tyerman, Robert. "Bock Deals into Tiny's School." *Sunday Telegraph,* December 13, 1992.

U.S. General Accounting Office. "Casino Gaming Regulation." GAO, May 1998.

U.S. Senate, Committee on Indian Affairs. "Authorizing Funds for the Settlement of Indian Claims in the Town of Ledyard, Conn." *Government Printing Office,* September 14, 1983.

———. "Gambling on Indian Reservations and Lands." *Government Printing Office,* June 26, 1985.

———. "Veto Message on the Mashantucket Pequot Claims Settlement." *Government Printing Office,* April 5, 1983.

U.S. Senate, Committee on Interior and Insular Affairs. "Hearings to Examine Implementation of the Indian Gaming Regulatory Act, Public Law 100-497. *Government Printing Office,* February 4, 1992.

———. "Mashantucket Pequot Indian Claims Settlement Act." *Government Printing Office,* October 18, 1983.

Waldman, Hilary. "Expanding Westward, Pequots Win Casino Business in Kansas." *Hartford Courant,* August 1, 1993.

———. "Maine Parable: Two Tribes Discover $80 Million Won't Buy Independence." *Hartford Courant,* May 27, 1994.

———. "A New Life for a Forgotten People." *Hartford Courant,* May 22, 1994.

———. "Pequots Hope Friction Won't Chill Casino Success." *Hartford Courant,* December 31, 1992.

Waldron, Martin. "4 are Convicted of Running Criminal Syndicate in Jersey." *New York Times,* June 21, 1980.

Weiner, Lisabeth. "Assets Manager Helps Make Deals for Indian Tribes." *American Banker,* August 23, 1985.

Willcock, John, and Dan Atkinson. "Malaysian Group May Take 10 Percent Stake in Lonrho." *Guardian,* August 20, 1992.

Winton, Ben. "The Pequot Museum." *Native Peoples,* Fall 1998.

Yoshihashi, Pauline. "The Gambling Industry Rakes It In as Casinos Spread Across America." *Wall Street Journal,* October 22, 1993.

Index